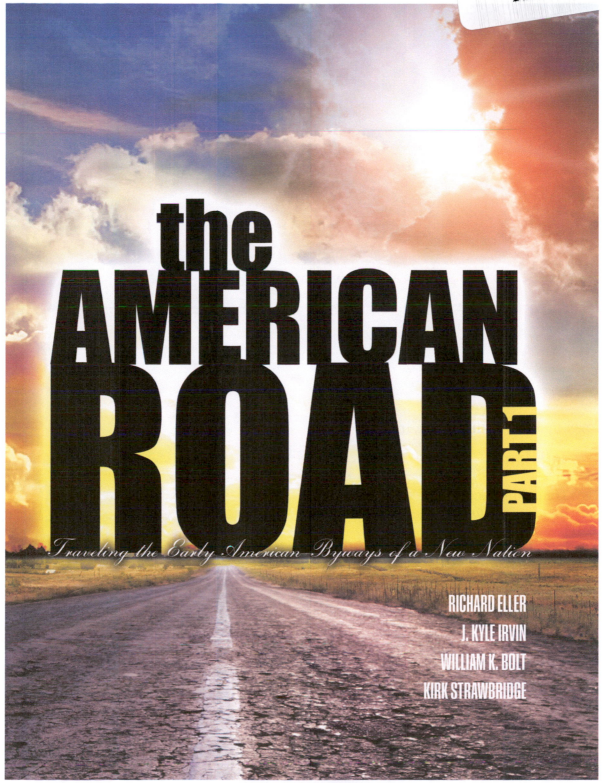

the AMERICAN ROAD PART1

Traveling the Early American Byways of a New Nation

RICHARD ELLER

J. KYLE IRVIN

WILLIAM K. BOLT

KIRK STRAWBRIDGE

Kendall Hunt
publishing company

CONTENTS

TEXTBOOK INTRODUCTION

Roads connect us. Not only do they carry us to work and play, but they also bind us with each other. They reveal our wishes, strengthen our ties, and offer us our next adventure. It's been that way since humans first stepped onto this hemisphere. While technology has yet to make time travel possible, *The American Road* nonetheless takes you on an exciting journey through our nation's past. The story of America is a fascinating one, and to understand where we might be going we must have a sense of where we have been. The great southern writer William Faulkner once stated, "History isn't dead, it's not even past." When events occur they never literally repeat, but the spirit and atmosphere in which they happen continue to resonate now and in the future.

On July 4, 1776, the country's leading statesmen signed the Declaration of Independence. This document proved revolutionary because of its justification for independence and what it articulated about humanity. In the preamble, Thomas Jefferson states, "We hold these truths to be self-evident, that all men are created equal, that they are endowed by their Creator with certain unalienable Rights, that among these are Life, Liberty and the pursuit of Happiness." We are hard pressed to find more powerful words written in the English language. However, as revolutionary and eloquent as they are, Jefferson's vision was only partially realized after a civil war, and later a civil rights movement. America has traveled from a nation with slavery as part of its heritage to a land that witnessed the election of its first African-American president in 2008. The pathway of a nation that is, "indivisible, with liberty and justice for all" is a work in progress, but Jefferson's vision was never dead, nor is it past.

The issue of racial justice and equality is only one of many pathways that *The American Road* examines. Others concern the broad subject of war and peace. In his famous "Farwell Address" in 1796, George Washington stated that the "great rule of conduct for us regarding foreign nations is in extending our commercial relations, to have with them as little political connection as possible. So far as we have already formed engagements, let them be fulfilled with perfect good faith. Here let us stop." While the exact meaning of Washington's words remains controversial, it is clear that he was concerned about America's proper role in the world. At the turn of the eighteenth century, the United States was hesitant to involve itself internationally. However, it shed its conservatism beginning with Matthew Perry's 1853 naval expedition to Japan. In the following decades, America engaged in diplomatic and military matters all over the globe. These policy choices often connected to each other and led to more complex future events. By the end of the first half of the twentieth century, the United States had fought victoriously in two world wars, and in the process, became a global superpower. However, that new position would come with a high price.

In 1965, the United States entered a war in Vietnam which eventually cost tens of thousands of American lives. While the number of military personnel lost was less than experienced in World War I, World War II, or the Civil War, Vietnam was and continues to be one of our most controversial conflicts. Questions have abounded during the post-Vietnam War years: Why did our government feel the need to involve its citizens in an area of the world that is over 8,500 miles away from its shores? Was communism a real threat to America, and if so how so? Was it in our national interest to allocate numerous human and material resources to this conflict? The questions of when, where, how, and why America involves itself in overseas matters are ones we have faced before and will continue to confront in the future. The road to safety, security, and living up to our ideals is a challenging one, but it will likely face even greater obstacles if our past is not part of our conversation now and in the future.

As a superpower, America faced many global challenges with energy and a sense of purpose. On July 20, 1969, Apollo 11 made humanity's first landing on the moon. Not only did it swell the nation with pride, but it led to numerous scientific and technological advancements such as Landsat, the longest-running program for the acquisition of satellite imagery. The millions of images collected by this program have provided valuable data used in agriculture, government, agriculture, business, with numerous other applications.

There are many beliefs, events, ideas, people, and places that make up our nation's history. *The American Road* addresses what we think are the most vital aspects of these issues. By reading and learning about our past, we find connections to who we are today. The trip is not always smooth. Along the way, there are many bumps, turns, potholes, and yes, dead ends. But, the journey is worth the effort. Indeed, it is only by traversing our past that we can learn how to build a better road to the future for all who call America home.

WEBSITE INTRODUCTION

History begins with an **experience,** quickly moving to the written word to be chronicled and interpreted. But the highway between the two **travels** in both directions. We all need to see, feel and listen to the past to appreciate its **value**. Hearing and watching Jimi Hendrix is much different than reading about him as a unique guitarist. The same goes for anything of relevance that occurred before our time. We need the written word to begin our journey into the past of this nation, but to really **comprehend** it, to turn it back into something **real**, we need a sensory connection to it as well.

The website that accompanies this book offers an important element to understanding history, the ability to make an influential/emotional/meaningful **connection** to the past, as well as an intellectual one. In many ways the website can give you an experience in historical study that is absolutely **vital** to grasping why all this happened the way it did and why it matters.

Get ready to watch the authors of "The American Road" **unravel** the events that turned the United States into the nation we know today. **View** the images that have come down to us from those years, depictions that illustrate the passions of many from an earlier time. As you click these items, you will **enliven** your understanding by bringing the process full circle, back to an experience to which you can **relate** and from which you can **grow**.

CHAPTER ONE

Beginnings

Chapter 1: Key Concepts

- What key characteristics stand out most from early Native American civilizations?

- What do you feel were the main motivations behind European exploration efforts?

- What is your evaluation of the positive and negative long-term impacts of European exploration efforts?

Introduction

Long before Europeans set foot in North America, native peoples had carved out their cultures. Initially pursuing big game, they adapted to a changing climate and combined hunting with farming that allowed a more sedentary lifestyle. Their populations gradually increased, and complex social structure followed. By the 1400s, European navigational knowledge and technology had developed to the point that they were able to extend their reach across the Atlantic Ocean. While Columbus was not the first European to set foot in North America, he did initiate an avalanche of explorers eager to explore and exploit this "undiscovered" continent. However, once here, Europeans from the Spanish to the English wasted little time and resources exploring and settling. While many had certain expectations upon arriving, they often had to adapt to their surroundings. It was clear though that once Europeans began arriving they were here to stay.

Native Americans: From Hunters and Gatherers to Planters

Human beings emerged as a distinct species over millions of years, gradually spread worldwide, but finally arrived in the Western Hemisphere less than 30,000 years ago. While there are contending theories on how the first Americans arrived on the North American continent, it is likely that the earliest migrants crossed over via an exposed area of land that today is the Bering Strait, the body of water separating Alaska from Siberia. It was their descendants, which spread across both North and South Americas over thousands of years that became the first Americans. Today, as many as 95 percent of native peoples throughout the Americas are likely descended from this original migration.

We know little about any Americans of this early period except that they lived largely a hunting and gathering existence. They pursued big game animals, some of which are now extinct, including saber-tooth tigers, wooly mammoths, and mastodons. Their predominant red meat diet was supplemented by wild berries, fruit, and nuts gathered from surrounding forests.

Time passed, and North America's climate warmed. Many of these big game species vanished as a result of either climate change or perhaps over hunting. Smaller animals were now the target, with deer now emerging as the most important meat in the diet. The warmer climate also caused the number of edible plants to increase, and they too became more important. The earliest peoples did not practice agriculture and had no domesticated animals, except maybe for dogs, which likely came with the original Asian migrants.

Over time, climate changes throughout the Americas would support the development of crops such as corn, beans, squash, and potatoes. Early Americans discovered that corn and beans could be planted together; the bean plants climbed the cornstalks. Corn or beans alone lacked certain nutrients, but their combination provided a healthy diet. Both plants required a long growing season and for centuries, and were planted only in tropical or near-tropical areas. Gradually, American farmers developed strains of corn and beans that matured more rapidly, and cultivation of these fast-ripening varieties spread throughout North America, reaching the American Southwest around 2500 BCE and spreading as far north as southern Canada by the year 500.

The development of agriculture had a profound effect upon the American peoples. For most, hunting became less important, and wherever soil and climate encouraged crops, the need to maintain vast, unpopulated areas for wild game declined. At the same time, the cultivation of crops made nomadic life impossible since people had to tend their crops until harvest.

Even with systematic agriculture, it was difficult to remain in one place for good. Corn, unfortunately, rapidly depleted the soil of crucial nutrients. Farmers learned to put fertility back into the soil by burning their fields after each crop. These burned fields also produced an abundance of certain plants, which provided food for deer. After a number of years, however, the soil became so poor that the cornfields had to be abandoned. Native peoples then moved on to clear new parts of the forest for fresh fields. Moreover, inhabitants seasonally migrated to places that provided different food sources such as fish or fruit.

The Effects of Agriculture

With the rise of cultivated crops such as corn, a larger, more readily obtained food supply almost certainly led to an increase in population and societal complexity. One such place was Moundville, a native settlement near Tuscaloosa, Alabama situation on the banks of the Black Warrior River. Moundville was occupied from around the year 1000 to 1450. It was one of the largest centers of Mississippian Indian culture in North America. It is estimated that at its cultural height, Moundville's native population was around 1,000, but thousands more lived in surrounding villages that were economically and socially connected to the larger center.

Mississippian Indian culture was heavily dependent on the cultivation of corn. This nutritious and abundant plant could be easily stored for the winter months and used for spring plantings. The river valleys of the Mississippi provided the proper landscape for the growing of corn. Native societies, such as Moundville, evolved along these rich, alluvial plains and Archeologists, and historians use the term Mississippian to characterize these societies that arose.

Deborah McCague/Shutterstock.com

Mound built by Mississippian Indian culture of North America

Most Mississippian Native societies, including Moundville, were organized in chiefdoms. These were kin-based societies in which people closely associated them, and where one's social status within the community was determined. In these chiefdoms, the ruler typically belongs to a family of notoriety and whose privileges others did not share. A close comparison might be that of a king, but typically he was not as powerful. Chiefs would not, for example, have a full taxing authority or the power to maintain a standing army.

A key characteristic of Moundville, as well as with most other Mississippian cultures, are large earthen, flat-topped mounds. Within Moundville's 300-acre site, there are 26 mounds that enclose a central plaza. They are of varying sizes, which suggest that they were built for different purposes. It is still unclear to the precise purpose of the smaller ones, but the larger ones are thought to have supported noble residences as well as structures for religious ceremonies.

Moundville is a testimony to the fact that America has a rich and diverse past. We dwell in a land that has been inhabited for millennia. The Mississippian culture, of which Moundville was associated, was the only one of many native cultures that had inhabited the land over the stretches of time. Distinctive groups with differing languages, social organization, religious practices, and sources of livelihood gradually evolved.

North American Indians in 1500

While Moundville and other Mississippian civilization centers were substantial in their organization and influence, they did not last. While it is not clear why the Moundville settlement disappeared, but by around 1450, some of the mounds had been abandoned, and a loss of religious importance is noted in others. There was also evidence of a decrease in the importation of goods that had given prestige to the nobility. It is thought that for some reason the Chiefs lost their ability to reciprocate services to the people in exchange for their loyalty. As this mutually beneficial relationship waned, cultural centers such as Moundville fragmented and the population scattered.

By 1500, the American Indians, as Christopher Columbus would so famously misname, thinking that he had found the outer reaches of India and its peoples, had been in this land for thousands of years. They had evolved from nomadic hunters and gatherers to having built and maintained largely settled communities, whose societal complexity was most impressive. Although genetically closely related, the different Indian tribes and villages spoke hundreds of languages and thousands of dialects. Social units were governed by complex rules that recognized the primacy of the family-based clan, yet tribes frequently ignored clan loyalty to split into new ones.

Europeans thought of tribal Chiefs as kings, but typically, like with Moundville, few Chiefs held the absolute power of European monarchs. Although they often inherited their positions, Chiefs could be deposed easily. Chiefs ruled by following the consensus that emerged from tribal councils. Political discussion and negotiation, both within councils and between tribes, included many rituals, and leaders sealed agreements by passing around and smoking a tobacco-filled peace pipe.

Indian cultures showed significant regional variation. In the Northeast, with its long winters and short growing season, corn was less important in the diet than game and fish. The Algonquin and Iroquois built snug wooden houses as long as 90 feet, aptly called long houses by Europeans. Each long house had a series of rooms and housed several nuclear families. These tribes built their houses inside villages walled with wooden palisades to protect themselves against their enemies.

In the Southeast, the warmer climate and longer growing season enabled the Greek and Choctaw to plant two corn crops a year. Plentiful food gave rise to a denser population, larger villages, and more powerful Chiefs. In this region, natives designed housing to let in breezed during the hot summers as well as to protect against the cold winter weather. Families lived one to a dwelling, but housing was relatively close, and villages were usually fenced.

Among the Creek Indians, young men from rival clans took part in a ball game similar to modern lacrosse. In fact, some of the better collegiate lacrosse players today are of Native descent. The original game involved using a stick with a loop at the end to put a ball through a goal. All the men from two clans played at the same time, with hundreds of players crowding the field. As violent as football, the game had no real team strategy. Each warrior-player sought individually to put the ball through the goal. Games sometimes lasted for hours, and severe injuries, even deaths, occurred. Spectators and players placed bets, and a clan might even disband in humiliation after losing several matches in a row.

San Esteban Del Rey Church and Convent in Acoma, New Mexico. This town has been continuously settled since 1075, making it the oldest community in the United States

The plains area, stretching from Texas to South and North Dakota and west to the Rocky Mountains, was sparsely populated by Arapaho and Pawnee buffalo hunters. Having neither horses nor guns, they captured buffalo with cunning. They might frighten the animals into self-destructive stampedes or force them off a cliff. These nomadic Indians lived in teepees, whose buffalo skins and wooden poles could be put up and taken down quickly.

In the dry Southwest, the Pueblo tribes, such as the Hopi and Anansi, built dense villages of adobe houses and grew corn using dry farming techniques, principally mulching to prevent evaporation of water from the soil. The most stationary of the tribes in North America, they developed elaborate rituals, including rain dances and sun worship, which revolved around the desert landscape. They conducted religious rites in underground ceremonial chambers called kivas. One native village, the town of Acoma, New Mexico, was established at or near its present site in the year 900 and has been continuously settled since 1075, making it the oldest community in the United States.

The Europeans Cometh

Around the year 850, people known as the Vikings or Northmen burst from the frigid seas of Northern Europe to rage havoc on many European towns and villages. The Vikings were able to venture far out to sea because of their very seaworthy and highly adaptable vessels known as long ships. These aggressive Europeans used the long ship to make it all the way across the Atlantic, briefly building a settlement in the year 1000 in North America in what is today Newfoundland. However, by the time Christopher Columbus arrived in the Caribbean Islands, this Viking colony had been long forgotten. Despite the exploits of this fearless culture, it was Portuguese sailors and especially the Spanish explorer Christopher Columbus who would touch off a European race to build colonial empires in the Americas. The pope, with the Treaty of Tordesillas in 1494, tried to divide the world between Spain and Portugal, but other countries, particularly France and England, ignored the papal decree and sent out expeditions. The Spanish, however, gained the lead in the early 1500s. Not to be outdone, the French joined the party but focused their energies on the northern mainland. Last but certainly not least were the English. Despite the failures of their early expeditions, seeds were sewn that would later produce much fruit.

A handmade Viking sketch

Fernando Cortes/Shutterstock.com

The Earliest Sailors

While the Vikings are thought to have been the first Europeans to set foot in North America, their settlement did not last long. However, their adventures piqued the interest of other Europeans who were more than ready, able, and willing to seek out their adventures. Europeans had long sailed back and forth across the Mediterranean and along the coastal regions of Europe and northwest Africa. The desire to venture further out into the rough waters of the deep Atlantic required the construction of larger and more seaworthy vessels. These ships had come online by the late fifteenth century as well as better sail rigging to enable ships to sail into the wind. Instruments such as the astrolabe allowed sailors to chart their courses more accurately. The ships were small and boxy, certainly so compare to today. Most were only about 70 feet long and easily buffeted by the high seas and strong winds of oceanic travel. However, sail they did and despite tremendous challenges made progress first sailing along the coast of Africa, and later venturing further out to sea.

In the 1400s, the Portuguese became Europe's premier maritime explorers. They sailed along the African coast, settled the Azores Islands, and eventually passed around Africa's Cape of Good Hope, making contact with India and the Africa–India–Middle East trade. Their advances in maritime sailing would prove decisive as the stage was set for greater oceanic adventurers.

The Spanish Emerge and Beyond

The Spanish, too, were interested in exploration. King Ferdinand and Queen Isabella in 1494 commissioned Christopher Columbus to sail west from Spain in search of a short route to Asia and its spices. On August 3, 1492, Columbus set sail from the southwestern coast of Spain, and on the morning of October 12, 1492, he and his three ships blundered upon what he thought was the outskirts of the Asian continent. Instead, it was an island in the Caribbean Sea, a part of a chain of islands known today as the Bahamas. Columbus, mistaking the islands of the Caribbean for outposts on the Asian mainland, called the area the "Indies" and the native peoples "Indians." Both names stuck although people eventually renamed these islands the West Indies to distinguish them from the East Indies off the southeastern coast of Asia.

Christophorus Columbus

Portrait of Christopher Columbus

Within a generation of Columbus's death in 1506, the first wave of Spanish adventurers had seized possession of most of the coastal lands of Central America and South America. The conquest of the Caribbean basin climaxed in 1513 with Vasco de Balboa's exploration of the Isthmus of Panama and his discovery of the Pacific Ocean, and with Ponce de Leon's discovery of Florida.

The second wave of Spanish expansion in America was stimulated by rumors of vast treasures hidden in a highly civilized state deep in the interior. In the course of this second wave, the empire of the Aztec ruler Montezuma in Mexico was conquered between 1519 and 1521. This most dramatic and bloody conquest was led by the resourceful, ruthless, and incredibly energetic conquistador Hernando Cortes. There are no heroes in this tale of slaughter and conquest. On one side were about 600 passionate and hard driven Spanish adventurers led by Cortez, who overcame fearful hardships to plunder and ultimately to destroy an ancient civilization. On the other side were the equally courageous but bewildered and less technologically advanced natives.

Other conquistadores extended Cortes's conquest of the Mexican world into North America. Between 1528 and 1536, Cabeza de Vaca circled the northern edge of the Gulf of Mexico and reached the Gulf of California. Between 1539 and 1541, Hernando de Soto cut through the forests of northern Florida and what would later be the southeastern United States and is thought to be the first European to view the great Mississippi River. De Soto's expedition is comparable with that of South American conquistador Franciso Pizarro in terms of bravery, endurance, and sure cruelty afforded the natives. While the great Mississippian cultural centers had disappeared by the time of de Soto's expedition, complex native societies remained scattered throughout the area of his ventures. In fact, de Soto and his comrades were the first Europeans to encounter the still existing large Indian chiefdoms in the southern reaches of North America, and were also virtually the last to see them at their height of development. Undoubtedly, their collapse was caused in part by the economic and social impacts of the de Soto expedition but even more by the introduction of germs and viruses for which the natives had little to no immunity.

Execution of the last Incan Emperor, Atahuallpa (1497–1533), by Spanish conquistador, Francisco Pizzaro, on August 29, 1533

The third great wave of Spanish conquest was led by an illiterate adventurer, Francisco Pizarro, who launched a series of expeditions from Panama through the jungles of Ecuador and northern Peru into the heartland of the elaborate Incan empire, which had been weakened by civil war. By a trick, Pizarro managed to capture the Incan emperor, whom he murdered after extracting a heavy ransom of gold and silver, and then destroyed much of the Incan army and nobility. Next, he proceeded to strip city after city of their treasures, to embroil both natives and conquerors in devastating warfare, and to establish in 1535 the new central city of Lima. From the plundered Incan lands, further expeditions were begun, first into Ecuador, then into Chile and northern Argentina (1535–1537).

Radiating out from these three main lines of conquest (first, the subjugation of the Caribbean Islands and coastal areas; then Mexico and southern North America; and finally the invasion of South America), Spain's empire in the Americas expanded in all directions. By 1607, when England established its first settlement at Jamestown, Spain's American empire extended nearly 8,000 miles, from California to the southern tip of South America. The empire was the largest the Western world had known since the collapse of the Roman Empire. Its only competitor in the Western Hemisphere had been Portugal, which had controlled the coastal areas of Brazil until the union of the Spanish and Portuguese thrones (1580–1640) gave Spain legal jurisdiction even there.

The French in Hot Pursuit

While the Spanish roamed the Southeast and Southwest, the French attempted to concentrate on the mainland further north, nearest to the rich fisheries off the Newfoundland coast. In 1534, Jacques Cartier explored the St. Lawrence Gulf, hoping to find a passage to China.

Samuel de Champlain statue in Quebec City, Canada

A year later he discovered and named the St. Lawrence River, explored the river as far as what is now Montreal, and then wintered at a well-constructed fort near present-day Quebec City. Cartier traded knives and trinkets for the local Indians' furs. The high quality of the furs, as well as the absence of gold or silver, led the French to pursue explorations to extend trade with fur-gathering Indians in the colder parts of North America.

At the time of Cartier's expeditions, the area was inhabited by Iroquois-speaking natives. When the French finally did establish a permanent settlement at Quebec under Samuel de Champlain in 1608, these Indians had been pushed out by Algonquin-speakers from the north. Indian tribes were quick to gain an advantage over each, which only accelerated as the Europeans, looking to secure every advantage possible, played one tribe against another. The Indians, in turn, learned to play the same game, aligning themselves with one European power but switching sides as it benefitted them.

England—Last but Certainly Not Least

England's entry into the age of overseas expeditions was the opposite of Spain's. Where Spain had been swift, England was slow; where Spain had been deliberate and decisive, England was muddled in purpose. For Spain, America yielded riches almost immediately. For England, at least initially, America's balance sheet was deep in the red, and colonists themselves faced a historically dismal period known as the "Starving Times."

While England was a late comer to the party, it had not started out that way. English claims to North America were established in 1497–1498, only five years after Columbus' initial venture to the West Indies. The person responsible was John Cabot, who had been commissioned by Henry VII to explore Newfoundland, roughly the same area that the Vikings had visited some 500 years before. However, neither the crown nor any explorers showed any real interest in developing these distant lands. Suddenly, in the early 1550s, fortunes changed which essentially marked the beginnings of British colonization. The development was complex, and it involved two shifts. The first involved England's economy and the second her relationship with other countries.

England's prosperity in the first half of the sixteenth century was based on the growing European demand for its raw wool and woolen cloth, which were marketed largely in Antwerp, in what is now Belgium. Throughout the reign of King Henry VIII, more and more capital and labor had become involved in this dominant commercial enterprise. As more farmland was converted into pastureland for raising sheep to meet the rising demand for wool, England's financial stability had become increasingly tied to the Antwerp markets. However, by the mid-sixteenth century, Antwerp's wool market was saturated, and merchant activity would have to focus elsewhere.

While England had begun to flex its economic muscles, Spain was the dominant power in the New World. In fact, Spain was then the world's greatest power and its power appeared to be stem from its empire. England, a relatively poor, weak nation, especially in comparison to Spain, needed to meet this challenge. The English, as islanders, were naturally a seafaring people, and they hungered to become like Spain or to at least take what they could from them. Thus, England was about to enter a new phase in its history.

Queen Elizabeth (1585–1603) considered Spain a threat to England's future endeavors. To weaken them while strengthening her kingdom, she authorized expeditions by privateers against Spanish silver shipments from the Americas. In the 1560s, John Hawkins and Francis Drake, part of a group of privateers known as "sea dogs," plundered their way across the high seas to Spain's horror.

Walter Raleigh (1552–1618)

As these overseas enterprises continued, the idea of colonization gradually developed. Much of the English effort at this time went into the search beyond Newfoundland for a northern sea route to Asia called the Northwest Passage. Such an opening, everyone agreed, would enable England to bypass Spain's control of South America and give the English an exclusive direct link to the profitable Chinese market. Unfortunately, despite battling howling snowstorms and dodging towering icebergs, no such link with the Far East was ever found.

Despite obvious disappointment, the English forged ahead with their colonization plans. Directed by the statesman and swashbuckling adventurer Sir Walter Raleigh, a group of settlers in 1585 founded a colony on the Outer Banks of North America, in what was then called Virginia, but today is North Carolina. Raleigh was to join the colony later, but war had broken out between England and Spain, and he was not permitted to leave. The colony survived for about a year, but the settlers encountered hostile natives and were forced to return to England the following year. In 1587, another contingent of settlers—117 men, women, and children—arrived under Governor John White. White returned quickly to England for more supplies, but the threat of open war with Spain and the actions of privateering kept supply ships from reaching the colony. When White finally made it back to the colony in 1590, he found all the settlers

Elizabeth I (1533–1603)

gone. The only sign of the colonists was the marking CRO on a tree and CROATAN on a door. There was no sign of the Maltese cross, the agreed-upon sign for distress. Consequently, White believed that the markings likely meant that the colonists had voluntarily moved to Croatoan Island, where friendly natives were known to live. However, a storm prevented the English from landing there, and the precise fate of these people remains a mystery.

In comparison with the bold and hugely successful first thrusts of the Spanish in America, the English experience reflected a fumbling, failing, almost pathetic affair. Raleigh's Roanoke venture dramatically underscored the limitations that defeated English colonization in the reign of Elizabeth I. Yet it also revealed the basic conditions that would shape the successful English settlements in the early seventeenth century.

Several links of significance had become clear during these earliest and least successful years of England's colonization of America. First, there existed in England leaders who were different from the Spanish conquerors. The Spaniards, "drunk with a heroic and brutal dram," as one Spanish poet later described them, were the sons of poor farmers and townsmen, many of whom were illiterate. However, the leaders of the English New-World quest, such as Sir Walter Raleigh, Francis Drake, John Hawkins, and John White, were the well-educated younger sons of English gentry, bred in secure landed establishments and familiar with the sea from childhood. English law barred younger sons from inheriting family properties, and these men were eager to find a way of reestablishing themselves on the land similar to the genteel conditions from which they came.

Second, it was clear that in England, there was a mass of laborers available for emigration. London, whose population rose from 60,000 in 1500 to 200,000 in 1600, was swollen with unemployed workers, due in large part to the collapse of the wool industry. Officials were convinced that England's well-being was threatened by an idle labor force that consumed more than it contributed. For many, the most attractive remedy was to seek their fortune in a new land.

Third, there was plenty of capital available for investment in overseas ventures, as well as abundant business interest in mobilizing that capital and directing it to profitable uses in colonization. While the early voyages to Virginia were financed by well-to-do gentry, they did not have enough resources to support further, larger-scale efforts. In 1589, Raleigh transferred control of the Virginia enterprise to a London business syndicate that was headed by Sir Thomas Smith, one of the wealthiest merchants of the era. It would be Smith and others like him who would launch the first new wave of colonization in the early seventeenth century.

It had become clear too, in the later years of Elizabeth's reign that her government would play a minor role in the new expeditions. It would legalize exploration and settlement and would have some say in the plans, but would neither initiate nor organize any endeavors. In addition, the English crown had no desire to extend its direct rule over distant territories conquered or settled by Englishmen. The burden of governing the colonies, similar to the burden of financing them, would have to be borne by the organizers. The crown was there, but acting only as a kind of overlay; the governments themselves would be semi-independent self-governing units.

England's war with Spain, which had begun in the 1580s, finally ended in 1604. Peace released the powerful expansionist impulses that had been building up in England for half a century, and the resulting lunge into overseas enterprise in the reigns of James I (1603–1625) and his son Charles I (1625–1649) was spectacular. The famous settlements at Jamestown, at Plymouth, and around Massachusetts Bay were only fragments of a huge effort that reached into many areas of the globe. It involved hundreds of thousands of Englishmen of all descriptions and cost millions of pounds.

As future colonizers looked out at the world beyond England, they saw a single arc of overseas territories suitable for colonization sweeping out from their island. This arc enclosed Ireland, Newfoundland, and the mainland coast of North America south to the Caribbean. It was natural for the English to consider nearby Ireland, which was described in a travel book of 1617 as "this famous island in the Virginia Sea," as the first and primary object of their colonization

Landing of 20 African captives at Jamestown from Dutch man-of-war 1619

efforts in the early seventeenth century. When, in 1607, two of the most powerful Irish earls resisted English authority and ultimately fled the British Isles, the English confiscated their vast properties. They largely cleared this immense territory—which covered six of the nine counties of the northern province of Ulster—of its native population and sold parcels of the land to prospective settlers. After an Irish rebellion in 1641, an estimated 120,000 English and Scottish men, women, and children had settled in Ireland. This migration was six times larger than the famous "Great Migration" that settled New England in the same period. Yet Ulster was the scene of only one of the colonization efforts of the time. Besides Ireland, Virginia, and Massachusetts, English settlements were established on several Caribbean Islands, Newfoundland, South America, and India.

In this global context, the first English settlements on the North American mainland were relatively small undertakings, and their early histories become understandable only in terms of the greater whole. While these American communities would in time have a unique historical importance, originally they shared characteristics common to the rest of the earliest seventeenth-century enterprises. Moreover, of these common characteristics, none was more important than the way in which they were financed.

Whatever their founders' ultimate dreams, these earliest English colonies had to be first financed by profit-seeking joint-stock companies. Eleven commercial companies bore the main financial burden of the settlements that were launched before 1640. They raised the needed capital by selling stock to a remarkable broad range of the English population. Thousands invested, and the funds raised by these investments were, for the most part, managed by men who worked not only within the usual constraints of business operations but also under two very special pressures. These pressures explain much of the hardship and tragedy of life in the earliest settlements.

First, the joint stocks—the initial capital funds—of these ventures were not expected to endure. That is; shareholders did not expect to leave their funds in these companies over a long period and to draw a steady dividend income from them. Instead, investors hoped to benefit from the quick liquidation of the whole enterprise at the end of a single voyage or after a set number of years. It was expected that at such a time, the original capital plus accumulated profits would be distributed to the investors. Whether there would be any further investments beyond the initial one would depend on the business prospects at the time of liquidation. Many of the settlers were in effect employees of the company that had organized the venture, for a stated term of years; thus, they were a lot of pressure to produce immediate profits. If they failed to ship back tangible proof of financial success, they would be cut off and would be forced to fend for themselves. Consequently, the settlers did not carefully explore their surroundings to acclimate themselves to the strange American environment. Instead, they spent much of their time scrabbling for gold in every shallow stream and plunging recklessly into the backcountry to investigate confused native reports of great cities or vast sources of furs or precious metals. The pressures on the settlers were further intensified by the technical fact that the shareholders in these early joint-stock companies had unlimited legal liability. The backers of the settlements were personally liable, without limit, for all debts the settlement companies might incur. Investors were for this reason therefore extremely sensitive to any possibility of failure. They had no choice but to abandon doubtful enterprises as quickly as possible.

The result of these conditions was desperation, starvation, and at times chaos for England's first North American colonists, as well as company bankruptcies. For there were only three possible sources of quick profits for the colonists: First, they might have found valuable resources on the surface of the land, loaded them onto boats, and rushed them back to investors. Second, they might have encountered a docile native population and organized it quickly into labor gangs to dig out the fewer accessible resources. Third, settlers might have discovered new routes to rich, exotic markets. None of these possibilities proved realistic on the coasts of North America. Consequently, after the first shipments, investors withheld life-sustaining supplies from the settlements, and one company after another failed. Sheer accident provided most of the profits that were made at the start. In one incident, the Providence Island Company was lucky enough to capture a Spanish treasure ship worth over 50,000 pounds.

Luck accidents of this kind, however, were rare. Sooner or later almost every one of the companies that had financed settlements in British North America failed, and as they did so, the original investors sought desperately to find secondary sources of profit. Some stockholders, seeking to recover their losses, funded "magazines"—supplies of goods to be sold at high prices to the needy settlers. In fact, the Virginia Company alone created 50 of these private enterprises, but none succeeded long term.

As their financial prospects dimmed, many investors withdrew altogether from the ventures. In these cases, colonists found themselves abruptly cut off from their backers, and for most of them, the transition to self-sustained community life was exceedingly difficult. Even in the best of circumstances, the first inhabitants of Jamestown or Plymouth or

Bermuda would have had a shock in adjusting to the wilderness environment. Forced to search for sources of immediate profit while neglecting the basics of survival, many found the struggle unendurable and succumbed to despair, disease, or relentless harassment of the local native population.

The narratives of the first settlements make for painful reading. There was heroism, but there was also murderous selfishness. Death and misery were everywhere. It is perhaps not surprising that the best organized and most successful of the earliest communities were those in which strong religious beliefs prevailed. For only the otherworldly goals, the fierce determination, and the inner certainty of the Pilgrim and Puritan leaders could withstand the disintegrating effects of the "starving times." As one pilgrim put it, "Weave in faith and God will find the thread."

Conclusion

By the early seventeenth century, life in North America had taken a dramatic turn. Where Native Americans had once population the continent with cultures that were profoundly sophisticated, their numbers had been reduced to a fraction of what they were prior to European exploration and settlement. Those tribes would continue to do their best to maintain a style of life to which they were accustomed, but would face increasing uncertainly as Europeans interacted and sought to gain advantages where they could. A new people had now found their footing in North America. The Spanish kicked it off by exploring the southeastern part of the continent. Following close behind were the French. They explored the area of what is today Nova Scotia and on into the interior north where they traded with native peoples and built settlements. While these nations did their part in the race to subdue the continent, it was the English who made the largest impact. In fact, over the next century, they would come to establish 13 colonies that would permanently alter the course of North America's development.

CHAPTER TWO

European Migration and Colonization

Chapter 2: Key Concepts

- Place yourself in the early Jamestown settlement population. What would that experience have been like and what were the key turning points for the colony reaching long-term stability?

- What is your evaluation of the positive and negative attributes of the puritan society at Plymouth? What lessons can be learned from their approach to colonial life?

- Which colonial region intrigues you the most as a student of history? What are the primary factors behind your reasoning?

Introduction

In the early 1600s, the North American continent and its native peoples would encounter an invasion of Europeans who, beginning with the establishment of Virginia, were obviously here to stay. By a century later, the entire coastal region had been largely transformed. Almost the entire Indian population had been eliminated from the coastal regions. The area now contained a quarter of a million transplanted Europeans and their children and grandchildren, all attempting to re-create the familiar pattern of European life in an undeveloped land. Within this transplanted European population, mainly in Virginia and Maryland, were more than 20,000 African slaves bound to their owners for life. A small proportion of the settlers, perhaps 8 percent, lived in the five main port towns of Boston, Newport, New York, Philadelphia, and Charleston. It was through these main cities that most of the commerce and communications were linked with Europe. The rest lived in village communities of a few hundred people or on isolated family farms or plantations. The newcomers to the American continent came as individuals or were part of private organizations, and the history of this forms not just one but many stories. Yet for all their variety, these stories present a similar pattern of soaring expectations, disappointment and frustration, disaster, and a slow adjustment to reality. However, new forms of society gradually emerged from this process, forms that ultimately would transform a cordial relationship with Great Britain into a one that would be severely tested and finally severed.

Virginia

Virginia's story of settlement is a classic case of grand expectation, hopes shattered, and the emergence of a new world from the ruins. It began in 1606 when the English King James I (1603–1629) chartered the Virginia Company of London. In December 1606, it sent out three ships but did not reach Chesapeake Bay until April 1607. In May, of the original 144 people who left England, 104 survived the hostile Atlantic to land on a low-lying island 30 miles upstream the James River. This place, which came to be called Jamestown, was the first permanent English settlement in North America.

The colony barely survived. During the 18 years of the colony's existence (1606–1624), Jamestown was a disaster for about everyone connected with it. Death was everywhere. Four out of five colonists died of disease or from Indian attacks. The colony survived only because of its leaders' persistence in pursuing empty dreams of profits and because of the financial support they were able to mobilize. Seldom has good money been thrown so extravagantly after bad; seldom have hard-headed businessmen been so mistaken in their expectations of success.

It quickly became clear that the Virginia settlers would not discover easily mined minerals or a northwest passage to Asia, of which they were sure existed. Hope came to rest on the new idea of giving the colony enough settlers and appropriate financial backing to transition the colony from their original pursuits to agricultural products, particularly sugar, cotton, and tobacco. These products could be cultivated and sold to England—a ready and willing buyer.

To establish Jamestown on this permanent basis, the company's London leadership secured a revised charter from the king, which launched a new plan of investment. By the terms of the new charter, the company was transformed into a public joint-stock company for a period of seven years. In February 1609, the company began an aggressive advertising campaign to convince people to purchase shares of stock. One popular way to purchase shares was to pledge personal service in the colony as a settler. Such an "adventurer of person" received one or more shares of stock depending on his or her "quality" (this is, social standing) or special skills. Each share was worth at least 100 acres of land. Those holding shares were given more authority, and a new form of government was created.

However, the colony still struggled. In fact, the year 1609–1610 was so dismal that it acquired the name "the starving time" due to the hundreds of people who perished. Ironically, the woods rustled with game and the rivers overflowed with fish. Inexperienced English settlers wasted valuable time seeking gold when they should have been planting and harvesting corn. It was saved however by the heroic efforts of Captain John Smith, who seized power and basically whipped the colonists into shape. His stay in Virginia was not that long, but he essentially saved the colony and promoted its settlement.

Everett Historical/Shutterstock.com

John Rolfe (1585–1622), Jamestown, Virginia colonist known for introducing the cultivation of tobacco in 1612

Ultimately, the colony was saved by tobacco more than the efforts of Smith. There was a ready, growing market in England, and the price in the early years was so high that profits could be substantial. Profits however were dependent upon a heavy investment of human labor. The seed had to be started in a bed and then transplanted to a field. Weeding was constant, and tobacco worms had to be removed by hand. At a crucial stage of growth, the tobacco leaves had to be cut and then cured. However, despite the words of King James I that tobacco was, "loathsome to the eye, hateful to the Nose, harmful to the braine [sic], and dangerous to the Lungs," it was here to stay.

Once the Virginia Company of London understood that the colony's future depended upon tobacco, it moved to attract more settlers. In 1618, the company adopted the headright system, by which settlers from England who paid for their own passage to the colony and that of others were promised 50 acres of free land for each settler, family member, and imported worker. Wealthy setters imported indentured servants, who contracted to work for a fixed period in Virginia in return for payment of their journey.

Three important events occurred in the year 1619 that would help put the colony on a permanent footing. First, the company began transporting women to the colony to be wives for planters so that families could begin to be established. It was also the year that a

Dutch sea captain, active in the flourishing slave trade between Africa and the West Indies, sold the English settlers 20 or more Africans. Second, although slavery came early to Virginia, many years passed before slaves were numerous. Third, this was also the year that the company created the House of Burgesses, the first legislative body in America, setting the precedent for the establishment of self-government in other English colonies. Landowners elected representatives to the House of Burgesses that, subject to the approval of the company, made laws for the Virginia colony.

Believing that social order required hierarchy, Governor Sir William Berkeley sought to create an elitist society based on inequality. Land policy, in particular, favored the wealthy, while white indentured servants provided labor. Many servants died before their terms of service had ended; those who survived found only limited opportunities to acquire land. In 1675–1676, these resentments, combined with the greed and ambition of the newly arrived Nathaniel Bacon, led to rebellion against Berkeley's authority. Bacon and his land-hungry followers demanded that Berkeley drive the Indians from the frontier in order to open more land for settlement, but the governor did not want an Indian war. In the end, Bacon's Rebellion and its aftermath became a turning point that left Virginia a more stable, hierarchical society, and one more dependent upon slave labor.

EDMUND CHEESEMAN'S WIFE BEFORE GOVERNOR BERKELEY.

Bacon's Rebellion, Virginia 1677. Wife of Edmund Cheeseman faints as Governor Berkeley rejects her plea to spare her husband's life. He was one of 23 rebels executed by hanging

Everett Historical/Shutterstock.com

A member of an old, prominent, and powerful family in England's West Country, Berkeley possessed all the prejudices of his class and region. He was a decorated soldier and a passionate supporter of King Charles II during the English Civil War of the 1640s, and brought strong royalists convictions to the Virginia colony. First and foremost, he held that social and political order required a chain of hierarchical authority. God, Church, and King were at the top of his system; the governor was only a little lower. Next were the gentry, followed by other free people and, on the bottom, indentured servants and slaves. Those of higher rank not only had the right to wield power but also bore responsibility for those below. In return for this patriarchal concern, inferiors owed them loyalty. The lowly were expected to honor their betters constantly, to obey them cheerfully, and to show deference; for example, by lining up according to social rank to enter church on Sunday.

Virginia society was based on preserving and maintaining inequality. The gentry, representing only about 10 percent of the population, held 50 to 75 percent of the wealth, including much of the land, most white servants, and nearly all the slaves. Small-scale famers, another 20 to 30 percent of the population, owned their own land and perhaps one or two white servants. The rest of the population consisted of white tenant farmers, poor white laborers, white indentured servants, and black slaves.

As in England, Berkeley expected the gentry to lead society. He did not believe in or practice equal opportunity, as one's fate was determined by social standing at birth. These ideas enabled hierarchy to be established and order maintained in Virginia. Berkeley once boasted that Virginia had neither schools nor a printing press. He believed both to be curses because education and information might lead ordinary people to challenge elite rule and the hierarchical social order. The gentry enjoyed better education than the masses; they hired private tutors and some sent their sons to higher education institutions in England. The poor and "middling" classes remained unschooled. Even among the landowners, half could neither read nor write.

In the mid-1660s, the gentry used their control of high office to enhance their positions, especially with regard to land grants. Members of the governor's council and the House of Burgesses regularly voted themselves large tracts of land from the colony's vast holding. Back in England, King Charles I pursued a similar policy. In 1649, for example, he gave five million acres to one man. This land grant, which covered five counties, eventually passed to Lord Fairfax, who became the wealthiest Virginian. The elite protected their interest in other ways, too. Berkeley's government continued the head-right system, which allowed anyone to claim 50 acres of land for each English settler brought to Virginia. By enticing settlers and paying their passage in return for a period of indentured servitude, the large planters gained not only labor but also free land. However, the servant, even at the completion of service, had no easy means to obtain land.

During the 1630s and 1640s, during which 60 percent of indentured servants lived out their term of service, about half of the survivors became landowners. Later, the chance for survival grew, but land prices rose and tobacco prices fell, making it harder to save money to buy land. As it became harder for those on the bottom of society to rise socially or politically, the elite increasingly dominated. A number of Virginians moved to other colonies where land was easier to acquire, while others settled on the frontier where farms could be worked without formal ownership. Many former indentured servants became tenant farmers who rented from the great landowners similar to poor famers in the English West Country. This is what Berkeley intended, but it did not please the tenants. They dared not complain though, because deference required that poor people speak of their betters only with great respect. Loose talk by a poor man about a gentleman could result in 30 lashes.

During the 1670s, however, Governor Berkeley's elitist system increasingly came under attack. To avoid an expensive Indian war, the governor had restricted white settlement to areas near the seacoast. This policy not only sustained the lucrative Indian trade that the governor developed for his personal profit but also helped speculators by driving up the price of farmland. Berkeley's land policy irritated indentured servants and ambitious large planters who were not politically connected. The price of tobacco dropped, and the poor economy burdened many with debt and caused tempers to rise.

In late 1675 and early 1676, Berkeley chose to ignore a series of frontier battlers between Indians and whites. The settlers were led by Berkeley's second cousin, the ambitious

Nathaniel Bacon, who had only recently arrived from England. This 29-year-old member of the governor's council was quick to anger and to action. Berkeley refused to attack the Indians, as Bacon requested, for the governor stood to profit handsomely off the fur trade. In response, Bacon raised his own army. In May 1676, Bacon and a contingent of 500 armed men, who included landless free whites, indentured servants, and some slaves, marched into Jamestown and forced Berkeley to commission the troops to fight the Indians. As soon as Bacon left the capital, the furious governor declared Bacon a rebel. Berkeley, however, could rally no troops, and fled. Bacon then marched his forces to the frontier, attacked the Indians, and returned to Jamestown in September. After Berkeley and his supporters retreated, Bacon plundered and burned the capital city. By this time, news of the rebellion had reached England, where an alarmed King Charles II decided to treat Bacon and his accomplices as traitors. The king sent 1,000 troops to Virginia. However, before they arrived, Bacon died suddenly of a fever or perhaps, as his supporters charged, by poisoning. Regaining power in 1677, Berkeley captured and executed 23 of Bacon's most prominent supporters.

Bacon's Rebellion marked a turning point in the colony's history. Afterward, no Virginia officials defended Indians, and officials promoted white settlement of the frontier. The opening of more land drove up land prices, and the small-scale white farmer, whether formerly an indentured servant or not, was considered a positive contributor to Virginia society. However, the most significant consequence of Bacon's Rebellion was its impact on slavery. Africans, as they soon would become the legal property of white landowners, would be less of a threat to social and political instability. However, a new and more pernicious institution was born.

Slavery: the "Peculiar Institution"

Africans who arrived in Virginia before the 1660s were not necessarily slaves, and the differences between black slaves and white indentured servants were blurred. By the 1670s, Virginia had adopted a clear policy of race-based slavery, and large importations of slave labor replaced indentured servants. From 1700 to 1760, great planters used the stability provided by a permanent, naturally increasing slave labor force to gain and maintain enormous wealth, power, and social prestige. Planters displayed their wealth lavishly but also feared poor whites, slave revolts, and land-hungry frontier settlers. The elite kept control because they had all the wealth and power, dominated the society's existing institutions, and admitted talented white newcomers to their ranks.

Although the first blacks were brought to Virginia in 1619, as late as 1670 only 5 percent of the population were black slaves. Even in 1700, they made up only 20 percent. By 1750, however, slaves, mostly African-born, constituted more than 40 percent of Virginia's population. Differences, however, put the two kinds of servants on an unequal basis almost from the start. The English servants spoke the same language as the planters, deferred to them, conceived of themselves as free Englishmen, were protected by English law limiting terms of service, and practiced Christianity. However, Africans spoke no English, were disoriented by their forced removal from their homes in Africa, were sold for whatever terms the market dictated, and were considered heathens. Because Africans were not yet Christian, whites thought that they did not have to be treated with charity, fairness, or equality. By the 1670s, race-based slavery had become entrenched in the colony. Laws banned interracial marriage, required all black slaves to serve for life, and declared the children of enslaved mothers to be slaves themselves.

The growth of the international slave trade, including the chartering of the Royal African Company in 1672, strengthened the institution's growing hold on Virginia. Between 1600 and 1800, European traders regularly visited ports in West Africa, buying as many as ten million slaves for shipment to the Western Hemisphere. During the horrifying Middle Passage, as the trip was called, people were packed so densely aboard ships that as many as one in six did not survive the horrendous crossing. Slave traders were known to be uncaring if not vicious, and even many planters did not like them. Most slaves were destined for sugar plantations in Brazil and the West Indies. Because these plantations had to import food, planters tried to hold down costs by using only highly productive adult male slaves who died quickly and were then replaced. In contrast, Virginian slave owners imported both men and women. Although only 4 percent of the Africans shipped to the Western Hemisphere were sent to North America, their descendants today outnumber the descendants of those sent to Brazil and the West Indies.

For Virginia's great planters, African slaves proved an economic boon. Vast acreages could be worked by a stable, reliable, permanent workforce, one that would never become free and would never be able to seek land ownership. The children of slaves would also become bondsmen for life. If slaves multiplied as planters hoped and expected, then planters would grow ever richer. Virginia society would resemble English rural traditions, in which a permanent laboring class supported a landed aristocracy.

While the great planters largely controlled Virginia society and politics, the immigration of white indentured servants in the 1600s resulted in a substantial population of small-scale white farmers. The elite, however, controlled the colony by their insistence of deference from poor whites, coupled with a growing emphasis on white racial solidarity. The gentry were flexible enough, however, to admit newcomers into their ranks, particularly by marrying their daughters to promising, ambitious young men. Yet, the gentry insisted on dominating all the institutions of society, and they largely went unchallenged. In fact, the Virginia gentry class would produce 10 presidents, including George Washington, Thomas Jefferson, and James Madison.

The elites of Virginia created an entire culture built around slavery, hierarchy, and a particular kind of patriarchal sensibility. Virginia was a colony founded on a taste for wealth, but it also emphasized politeness and gentility. In an often raw frontier society, the elite's good manners were perhaps the only way to hold the society together. The pursuit of wealth, the domination by a few, and pleasant manners became hallmarks of southern culture. People of social standing expected to control most everything in society and politics while exuding kindness to others. People could visit the gentry to settle disputes of a real or perceived wrong. Still, it was still a place where rich white men ruled over all others in a society propped up by the institution of slavery.

Maryland

In 1632, Cecilius Calvert, also known as Lord Baltimore, received a royal charter from King Charles I to establish a colony on the Chesapeake Bay, north of Virginia. It was named "Mariland [sic] in honor of the Queene [sic]" (Queen Mary, 1553–1558). This was the first proprietary colony placed entirely under the control of a single person unlike Virginia that was founded as a company run by its shareholders. The owner or proprietor Lord Baltimore was Catholic, and he established his colony as a refuge for those of the same faith who sought a haven from the religious turmoil then engulfing England.

Cecilius Calvert (1605–1675), the Second Lord Baltimore

Although many original settlers at St. Mary's City were Catholic, Maryland soon lost its Catholic character, as Protestants flooded into the colony. A handful of wealthy Catholic families, however, continued to exert influence. In 1649, the colony passed the Toleration Act that allowed all Christians to practice their religion. Five years later, the Protestants, believing themselves protected by Oliver Cromwell's Puritan government in England, repealed the act. In 1658, Lord Baltimore restored a policy of toleration, but religious strife continued. Like Virginia, Maryland produced tobacco and was home to great planters, African slaves, English indentured servants, and former servants who owned and operated small farms. Maryland imported large numbers of slaves even before Virginia. Therefore, in crucial aspects, Maryland was quite similar to Virginia.

South Carolina

In 1663, King Charles II (1660–1685) gained the English throne after the collapse of England's Puritan government in 1660. He granted eight wealthy supporters, called the lord proprietors, the right to colonize Carolina. Named to honor their king, the colony originally included what later became North and South Carolina. It was planned both to protect Virginia from Spanish movement northward from Florida and to add a distinctive semitropical agricultural area to the ever-expanding British Empire. In 1670, settlers arrived near Charles Town (now Charleston). Many great planters came from the English West Indian island of Barbados, where they used African slave labor to cultivate sugar at great profit. After a brief period of raising grain and cattle to sell to the food-short West Indies, the planters turned the hot, humid swamps along the southern Carolina coast into rice production. Slaves brought the knowledge of how to grow rice. Later, Carolinians grew indigo, a plant used to produce a widely used blue vegetable dye.

The climate of South Carolina was brutal. Europeans died from malaria and other fevers that affected neither the natives nor the Africans (who had gained immunities in Africa). From the beginning, the planters ignored white indentured servants and depended

Georgios Kollidas/Shutterstock.com

King Charles II (1630–1685)

exclusively upon slave labor, both Indian and African. In the early years, native Indian slaves worked the plantations, but the rate of runaways was too high. Planters then purchased Indian slaves from friendly tribes and traded them to the West Indies in exchange for African slaves. The Indian slave trade was highly profitable for some, and the colony's population became mixed. In 1708, there were 5,300 whites, 2,900 African slaves, and 1,400 Indian slaves.

In this multicultural and competitive society, tensions grew as the English encroached on Indian lands and slaves labored under harsh conditions. In 1715, many of the local tribes revolted. In turn the Carolinians, with support from the Cherokee, defeated the Yamasee and Creek tribes. Of the 6,000 whites in Carolina, 400 died. At the end of the Yamasee War, the English in Carolina embarked on a long-term policy of pushing the Indians west, destroying any who remained behind. Slave revolts were always a possibility. In the Stono Rebellion of 1739, a hundred slaves killed 22 whites and then marched toward Spanish Florida. Ultimately, they were defeated in battle by the white South Carolina militia allied with Indians.

South Carolina planters quickly turned to a massive importation of black slave labor. From the failure of Indian slavery until just before the American Revolution, a majority of South Carolina's population was black. In many coastal rice-growing areas, the African population exceeded 90 percent. In these areas, slave communities succeeded in preserving patterns of African culture, including housing types, medicinal herbs, linguistic styles and words, conjuring, and music. Unlike Virginia, South Carolina plantations used the task system, which gave the slave more control over their own time. In this form of forced labor, each slave had a daily assignment, and when it was completed, he or she had the right to spin, weave, fish, or tend to gardens. In Virginia, on the other hand, slaves for the most part worked for the master from sunup to sundown.

During the malaria season, wealthy planter families fled their plantations and moved to the one known healthy location, Charles Town. Protected from malaria-breeding mosquitoes due to the steady flow of the Ashley and Cooper rivers, Charles Town became a populous outpost of English culture and civilization. By 1750, its 8,000 residents made it the only major town in the South. It was a center of urban culture with many accomplished white and black artisans, especially furniture makers.

North Carolina

In 1729, disputes among powerful land speculators forced Carolina to be split into two colonies. North Carolina developed slowly. Geographically isolated, its climate and soil were different from Charleston's. Its coastal areas were too swampy to be habitable, and its barrier islands and the storms off Cape Hatteras prevented ships from reaching much of the mainland, depriving the colony of good ocean transportation. Attracted by good land on ocean-going sea routes, Virginia tobacco planters settled the extreme northeastern portion of the colony, on Albemarle Sound, as early as 1653. Some also came to North Carolina to escape legal problems. These planters controlled North Carolina until the American Revolution.

The border with South Carolina was settled largely by South Carolinians. It was said that North Carolina was "a valley of humility between two mountains of conceit." North Carolina did not prosper until settlement reached the fertile interior. Scotch-Irish and Germans came down from Pennsylvania through Virginia's Great Valley. They were not slaveholders, and because North Carolina lacked numerous large plantations along its swampy coast, the colony always had a greater proportion of small-scale white farmers than its neighbors.

Georgia

The last of the original 13 colonies was Georgia, founded in 1732. General James Oglethorpe was an English reformer. He obtained a charter to establish a colony for England's poor, including those in prison for debt, which was then a crime. Fearing Spanish encroachment, the British government was willing to grant Oglethorpe such a large area of land. To make the colony successful, Oglethorpe adopted several unique policies. First, all settlers including the poor were granted 50 acres of land. Second, there were no large land grants. Instead, actual settlers were limited to 500 acres. These policies encouraged widespread land ownership and forestalled the establishment of the kind of elite that dominated Virginia and South Carolina. Third, there were no slaves. Slaves, Oglethorpe believed, degraded the value of labor, forced poor whites to compete with them, and created an idle, slavehold-

James Edward Oglethorpe (1696–1785), founder of the colony of Georgia

ing elite. Fourth, rum was banned because Oglethorpe firmly believed that alcohol was a main cause of poverty.

However, little came of Oglethorpe's original ideas. The taste and effects of alcohol were too enticing and rum was introduced in 1742. South Carolina planters began to move into Georgia accompanied by their slaves, defying the law. Although plantation slavery became firmly established, the colony's white population formed a higher percentage than in South Carolina, and Oglethorpe's land policy enabled many yeoman farmers to own land. Originally granted a 20-year charter, Oglethorpe considered the experiment a failure and returned the colony to royal control.

New England

In 1620, an English religious group many have called Pilgrims rejected the Church of England and settled at Plymouth in what is now Massachusetts. As early as 1602, Englishmen fished off the northeastern shore of North America. They sometimes traded with the local Indians but in the process transmitted diseases to the Native population. As a result, most of them died before 1620. Native American villages were abandoned, and in a few years, once-productive cornfields were covered with scrubby brush. Many Englishmen concluded that God had killed the heathen Indians to enable the Christian English to replant the fields; it was all part of God's plan. As the Pilgrims journeyed to Plymouth aboard the Mayflower, they signed the Mayflower Compact that provided the colony with a government.

Many members of the rising middle classes demanded changes and reforms to the Church of England. Wanting to purify the church, these reformers called themselves Puritans. The Massachusetts Bay Company was chartered by a group of Puritans in 1629. From 1630 to 1642, as many as 21,000 colonists migrated to Massachusetts, establishing America's first self-governing colony. Drawn largely from the middle classes, the Puritans stressed education. They recreated English ways, including living in villages with outlying fields, a system that discouraged land speculation. The Puritans constituted the largest single group of Europeans to immigrate to America and probably exercised more influence on America's initial development that any other single group.

The Puritans differed from the Virginians in many ways. There were a number of large single European migrations to the America, but the Puritan transatlantic voyage in 1630, consisting of more than 1,000 settlers, was the largest. Unlike Virginia's settlers, the Puritan colonists included many women and children. These family-oriented immigrants reproduced in large numbers, doubling about every generation. The Puritans were remarkably well educated. Two-thirds of the adult males could sign their names—twice the number typical of Englishmen. Because they associated education with religion and particularly with Bible reading, they quickly established schools for both boys and girls. Puritans took their faith very seriously, which was reflected in how they approached learning. They too were responsible for founding a number of colleges. For example, Harvard University then known as "New College" was founded in 1636 principally to train Puritan ministers. Instruction was in Latin, and the all-male student population was required to study Hebrew, Greek, and theology. One in every 40 heads of family was a college graduate. Surprisingly, this was a far higher proportion than in England. No other colony began with so many educated people.

For the Puritans, religion was the key to life. All questions, big and small, had to be answered with reference to the Bible, the church, the minister, and prayer. The colonists put the church at the center, and yet they did not create a true theocracy, that is, a church-run government. Instead, their churches and their government operated along parallel, complementary tracks. While in England, the Puritans claimed that they merely wanted to reform the corrupt, state-controlled Church of England. Once in Massachusetts, however, they created churches that resembled those of the separatist Pilgrims in Plymouth. Indeed, Massachusetts absorbed the Plymouth colony in 1691.

As far as church government was concerned, the Puritans embraced the congregational style that involved the congregation selecting its own minister. This was far different from the Church of England where priests were appointed by bishops, and power flowed from the top down. Although embracing a far more democratic style, decisions could only be made by church members. While all colonists were expected to attend services, not everyone qualified for membership. One had to convince the membership of one's true devotion to the core tenants of the faith. Within the church structure, dissent was not tolerated. There was no freedom of religion. During the 1600s, the government ordered residents who did not wish to practice Puritanism to conform or leave. People who were banished but then returned to the colony ran the risk of being severely punished.

The congregational system of church government made it difficult for colonial officials to restrain a minister who persuaded his congregation to go in a new direction. Roger Williams was such a minister. Williams did not agree with forcing people to attend church who were not Christians. Regulation of religious behavior was akin to "spiritual rape." He believed that only God knows the truth and that governments should, therefore, tolerate all religious beliefs. This view was far too progressive for the Puritans, and he was banished from the colony. He went on to found a new colony at Providence, Rhode Island, which received an official charter from England in 1644. Thus, Rhode Island became the first American colony founded on the basis of personal religious choice.

Roger Williams (1603–1683)

Everett Historical/Shutterstock.com

The Puritans were also involved in the founding of the Connecticut colony. In 1636, Thomas Hooker, a respected but opinionated Puritan minister, led a group into the Connecticut Valley and founded a colony at Harford. Other Puritans, considered to be the most religiously fervent, arrived from England and founded a colony at New Haven in 1638. Having secured a royal charter, these merged together as the colony of Connecticut in 1662.

From Puritan to Yankee

Not everyone in New England shared the uniform religiosity of Massachusetts. Religiously diverse settlements could be found in Rhode Island, which attracted other groups such as Baptists, Quakers, and Jews. Other settlements occurred at Springfield and in the remote areas of Maine and New Hampshire. Massachusetts controlled Maine from 1652 to 1820, but New Hampshire succeeded in organizing separately in 1680.

After 1700, New England became a more secular society and gained greater contact with the broader world. As the British Empire developed, extensive trade grew among England, New England, Virginia, and the West Indies. New Englanders played a prominent role in this trade. From the great trees in abundant forests, they built and sailed ships. They raised grain and horses for export to the West Indies where these items were in short supply. New Englanders netted fish for overseas markets and imported both rum and molasses from which they distilled their own rum. They carried rum to Africa where they traded it for slaves, whom they sold in the West Indies and along the southern seacoast.

Boston and, to a lesser extent, cities such as Salem, Massachusetts, and Newport, Rhode Island became filled with the mansions of the newly rich. People who cared more about making money than saving souls dominated the seaport's economy, society, and politics. The Church of England even erected a building in a prominent location in Boston, while the Revere family turned out silver cups and plates as elegant as any crafted in London. If they saw an opportunity to build a mill, to sell some grain to strangers, or to swap some local produce for imported earthenware plates, they took the chance. New Englanders were, in essence, transitioning from devout, otherworldly Puritans to sharp-eyed, hard-bargaining Yankees.

George Whitefield (1714–1770)

The Great Awakening

By the early 1700s, New Englanders had become less in tune with the intense religious feelings of their ancestors. Though, a sort of renaissance of religious belief began as early as 1733 when the Reverend Jonathan Edwards stirred people with his fire and brimstone preaching at Northampton, Massachusetts. From here, over the remainder of the decade a religious revival spread throughout the colonies. From 1739 to 1741, the great English evangelist George Whitefield preached from the South to New England. These two famous men of God turned the hearts of thousands.

The Great Awakening began with Whitefield. He traveled from Georgia to New England preaching to anyone who would listen. Soon his reputation preceded him. Everywhere he traveled, large crowds turned out. He preached in a new style, extemporaneous and without notes. His message had great emotional appeal. Among his listeners at one New England meeting was Jonathan Edwards, who wept. After Whitefield's visit, a wave of revivals in 1741 and 1742 flooded across New England affecting poor and rich alike. Whitfield was something of a celebrity in the colonies. In New England, the Great Awakening's most important figure proved to be Jonathan Edwards. Although his written sermons showed the dryness, quiet logic, and rich use of scripture associated with Puritanism, his oral delivery was closer to that of Whitefield.

Edwards tended to gaze out across his congregation, his eyes transfixed on the far end of the meeting house, preaching as if God himself were pouring forth from his mouth. Members of Edwards's congregation in Northampton burst out in screams of religious ecstasy, and dozens surged to the front of the church to declare their conversions. Edwards rarely challenged these claims. Important people in Northampton were appalled. Edwards offended their sense of decorum and threatened their status. The creation of a mass, popular church on a wave of emotion might overturn the town's political, social, and economic orders. Therefore, Edwards was dismissed. He went into the wilderness, ministered to Indians, and wrote several volumes explaining his theology. In 1757, he moved to Princeton, New Jersey, where he became the president of a college, now Princeton University, founded by Presbyterians in 1746 to train the clergy.

Jonathan Edwards (1703–1758)

The Great Awakening is considered to be the single most important event in the history of American religion. Although it took place in all the colonies, its most pronounced effect was in New England. The revivals led Baptists to found the College of Rhode Island (Brown University) in 1764, the Dutch Reformed to begin Queen's College (Rutgers University) in 1766, and Congregationalists to start Dartmouth College as an Indian mission school in 1769. Those who tried to maintain orthodox Puritan views were left with an emotionally dead, rigid system of predestined salvation for only a handful of Saints. This was no longer as appealing to Americans living in a more egalitarian society. This sort of evangelical religion emphasized emotion over reason, heart over mind, and individual sentiment over communal decisions. Such a religion risked the dangers of emotional excess, personal eccentricity, and social disintegration. Since the Great Awakening, the two halves of religious experience—theology and reason versus faith and feeling—have been difficult to bring back together. The country has more or less regularly oscillated between periods of rational, secular activity and period of intensely emotional religious revivals.

New York

In 1600, tiny Holland (also called the Netherlands) was one of the richest and most powerful countries in the world. Its wealth came from the hand manufacture of textiles and from worldwide trading and commerce. Dutch merchant ships carried spices to European markets from the East Indies; shipped slaves from the African coast to the West Indies, and sent Dutch, French, and German textiles, knives, and other products throughout the world. After the English began to settle North America, the seafaring Dutch decided to found their own colonies. They were especially interested in trading European goods for Indian furs.

Around 1614, the private Dutch East India Company built a fort at what became Albany, New York, to trade with the Mohawk, a tribe of the Iroquois Confederation.

In 1624, using Henry Hudson's exploration of the Hudson River under Dutch sponsorship as the basis for their claim, the Dutch founded the colony of New Netherland on the site of what is now New York. The Hollanders knew that the English would not recognize this claim. Thus, in drawing New Netherland's boundaries, they made the colony as large as possible to enhance their negotiating position. Their main colony was established on the lower tip of Manhattan Island at a place they called New Amsterdam (New York City). In 1625, they built a crude wooden fort that offered little protection against possible attack by an English fleet. Soon, the Dutch decided to incorporate Manhattan Island, and in 1626, their leader Pieter Minuit bought the island from the local Indians for $24 worth of trade goods.

The seventeenth century saw Great Britain and the Netherlands battle to control both the world tobacco market and the African slave trade. The English hated New Netherland and disliked the Dutch tendency to undercut English merchants by trading with England's American colonies at lower prices. In 1664, an English fleet sailed into the harbor at New Amsterdam and captured New Netherland without firing a shot. At the time, the population was about 9,000 of whom about 2,000 were New Englanders. The English sought to win over the Dutch settlers by allowing them to practice their own religion and retain their property. King Charles II of England gave the colony to his brother the Duke of York, who was the future James II. In honor of the duke, the colony and its capital were renamed New York.

English authorities did not seek to evict any of New York's mixed population. More English merchants settled in New York City, which became largely English, but the area around Albany remained overwhelmingly Dutch as did much of the Hudson River valley. In addition, the fur trade remained in the hands of Dutch traders. The Duke of York permitted, "all persons of what religion sovereign, quietly to inhabit. . . provided they give no disturbance to the publique [sic] peace, nor doe molest or disquiet others in the free exercise of their religion." New York had become the most heterogeneous colony in seventeenth-century North America.

Pennsylvania

In 1681, the Quakers, a Protestant group more formally called the Society of Friends, founded and settled Pennsylvania. The charter was initiated by a wealthy English Quaker named William Penn who was the son of a close friend of the English King Charles II. Penn became the colony's proprietor, a position that gave him great power and influence. It is not clear why Charles II granted so vast a territory in America to Penn, who was a very outspoken religious dissident. However, no doubt one factor was the crown's long-standing debt to Penn's father. The king may also have thought the grant a convenient way of getting rid of these trouble makers. However, Penn's personal relationship with the royal family was probably the decisive factor, and of that very little is known.

The Quakers had suffered severe persecution during their 30 years of existence before the founding of Pennsylvania. They devoted themselves to finding the divine "inner light" within each soul and practiced their faith without the burdens of church, clergy, and formal ritual. They were proud and courageous people who defied state authority to the point of refusing to take ordinary oaths of loyalty. They supported absolute freedom of conscience and were pacifists and political reformers.

Penn planned his colony carefully in order to avoid the mistakes made in earlier settlements. To avoid disputes with other colonies, he had the boundaries surveyed. Carefully negotiating treaties with the various Indian tribes, Penn insisted that whites could settle only on land that he had bought from the Indians. Showing great respect for native culture, Penn even learned the local Indian language in order to avoid interpreter's errors.

William Penn's treaty with the Indians founding the colony of Pennsylvania)

Pennsylvania was the best advertised of all American colonies. Recruitment pamphlets urging emigration to the colony circulated throughout Great Britain and western Europe. A central "City of Brotherly Love," Philadelphia was founded at an excellent site at the junction of the Delaware and Schuylkill rivers, and a well-designed street plan was laid out. By 1682, the population was already 4,000—a remarkable number of people within a few months. There were Dutch, Swedes, and Fins from earlier settlements along the Delaware River. Germans came from the Rhineland who settled Germantown near Philadelphia. Their English neighbors called them the Pennsylvania Dutch—a corruption of *Deutsch*, the German word for "German." The Pennsylvania Dutch included Calvinists, Mennonites who preached pacifism, and the Amish, who clung to tradition and for the most part still do.

Penn gradually lost control of the colony; by 1696, its house of representatives seized the power of initiating legislation essentially forcing Penn to agree to its action. The king could still veto legislation, but Penn could not, and the inhabitants were freed from any special allegiance to Penn or his descendants. For the next half century, an oligarchy of Quaker politicians and representatives who had been elected by a limited voting population would dominate the colony's politics.

Penn had lost control of the colony, but Pennsylvania became a fabulous success. Its politics were contentious, but it was populous and prosperous from the start while being open and attractive to all. Pennsylvania was the distribution center for a mass population of laborers, but it was also a center of provincial high culture. Within a single generation, the colony became the dynamic heart of British North America. In 1723, an eager 17-year-old Benjamin Franklin would leave Boston to seek his fortune in Philadelphia. William Penn had been dead for five years, but his City of Brotherly Love had become a vigorous, thriving community of 10,000 people and a vital part of a dynamic colonial world.

New Jersey and Delaware

New Jersey was originally part of New Netherland and became an English colony in 1664 when the Duke of York gave part of his land grant to two of his friends, about five million acres, which lay between the Hudson and Delaware rivers. A dispute caused the colony to be formally split into two: East and West Jersey. East Jersey, the northeastern portion adjacent to New York, had a varied population similar to that of its neighbor. New Englanders, who had a habit of multiplying and spreading in all directions, created several important settlements, including one called New Ark (Newark).

East Jersey's politics were so controlled by New York that the local residents were relieved when the two Jerseys were rejoined to form a more vigorous, independent colony. From 1702 to 1738, the royal governor of New York was also commissioned separately as the royal governor of New Jersey. West Jersey, the southwestern portion nearest to Philadelphia, was long dominated by Quaker settlers at Burlington who had arrived in 1677. The Quakers retained their local influence longer in that area than in Pennsylvania.

A tiny colony just below Philadelphia, Delaware was founded in 1638 by Peter Minuit and the New Sweden Company. It was named after the Delaware River. The name was derived from Sir Thomas West (Lord de la War) who was the Virginia Company's first governor. As was the case with New Netherland, Delaware fell under British control in 1664. In addition to Pennsylvania, William Penn was given authority over the colony by the Duke of York. Delaware was governed as part of Pennsylvania from 1682 until 1701. The governor of Pennsylvania served in the same capacity in Delaware until the American Revolution. Because Delaware had never been technically annexed to Pennsylvania, it was during the Revolution that the colony was able to reassert its separate status.

Conclusion

The colonization of North America was part of a larger effort by some Europeans countries to broaden the reach of their expanding political and commercial interests. By the early eighteenth century, English settlements had spread from northern New England south into Georgia. While the Dutch attempted to gain ground in New Netherland, the English prevailed there as well with New York. The colonies all shared initial hopes and dreams, but all had to modify their endeavors to succeed in such varied environments.

Distinctions were stark across the colonies, but the greatest divergence of experience was between the northern and southern colonies. In the North, society was dominated by relatively small family farms and by emerging towns and cities. A thriving commercial class developed along with an elaborate urban culture. In the South, there were many family farms as well, but there also were large tobacco, rice, indigo, and cotton plantations. These large farms would come to rely heavily on slave labor. While the colonies were then separated by various economic interests, they too had much in common. Most white Americans accepted common assumptions about racial inequality that caused them to tolerate the enslavement of black men, women, and children. Assumptions of superiority were also directed against native peoples against whom colonists often went to war. Most white colonists (and, in different ways, most nonwhite peoples as well) were deeply religious. The Great Awakening left an indelible mark on these sensibilities. There was also a shared belief among white colonists, embedded in the English Constitution, concerning core principles of law and politics. However, there would soon develop a difference of opinion regarding the interpretation of that constitution, laying the ground work for future hostilities.

CHAPTER THREE

Age of the American Revolution

Chapter 3: Key Concepts

- What were the main factors that turned the French Indian War's aftermath from a positive to a negative for American colonists and damaged their relationship with the British government?

- Which two laws passed by the British parliament do you believe had the greatest impact on the progress toward an American Revolution and what is your reasoning behind these choices?

- What factors made the American military victory over Great Britain most possible? What areas did Great Britain fail to properly take advantage of in a strategic manner?

Introduction

By 1750, the 13 American colonies had settled into a comfortable relationship with their mother country. In fact, the colonies would, in the French and Indian War (1754–1763), help the island nation rid North America of the French. Such wars do not come cheap, and England expected its American cousins to help decrease its heavy debt. This much needed revenue would come in the form of taxes, such as the Stamp Act of 1764, the Townshend Duties of 1767, and the Tea Act of 1773. While the colonists typically complied with trade restrictions, these acts were seen as a direct assault on the colonists' rights as Englishmen. By early 1775, negotiations to settle differences failed, and a military confrontation began. One year later, from what had been unofficial skirmishes, evolved into an outright declaration of independence followed by a war. Five years later, America would emerge as its own sovereign nation and begin a new experiment in democratic government.

The State of the Colonies

By 1750, the North American continent consisted of nearly one-and-a-half-million American colonists allocated along the seacoast of 13 English colonies extending from Maine to Georgia. About one-fifth were slaves of African descent. Another one-sixth were white servants indentured to labor for terms as long as seven years in return for the cost of their journey. Although economic growth had been slow and life hard during the 1600s and early 1700s, the colonies experienced an increase in immigration and greater prosperity after about 1730. The population doubled every 22 years, with a high birth rate, a relatively low death rate, and continued immigration. One-half to two-thirds of the growth came from natural increase. Benjamin Franklin predicted that over the next century, the colonial population would exceed that of England. While the American colonies in many ways benefitted from its association with Great Britain, there were developing signs that the two might be on a collision course.

Over the course of the eighteenth century, the British Empire had increased in size, wealth, and prestige, with opportunities for commerce and trade expanding on a global scale. As part of the empire, the colonists shared in its benefits. Americans already supplied it with numerous raw materials, raising grain and horse or cutting timber for sale to the West Indies. In time, America, too, would become a major market.

As far as governing the colonies, the most powerful person was the governor. While Connecticut and Rhode Island retained ancient charters that allowed the settlers to elect their governor, by 1750, the governor in all of the other colonies was appointed by the king. A governor, in turn, named officials, controlled the military, and spent legislative appropriations as well as funds provided by Britain. The governor had absolute veto power over legislation coming from the colonial assemblies, but he could find himself in trouble if he ignored public opinion. Increasingly, American colonists found themselves governing on their own behalf.

The notion of self-government was supported by the fact that white male Americans enjoyed more actual political rights than their English counterparts. Although in both Great Britain and America a man could vote only if he owned property, the colonists found it easier to gain the small amount of land needed to qualify. In most colonies, a majority of adult males could vote; however, in England, fewer than 10 percent were eligible. In addition, America lacked titled nobility and, as a new country, had little inherited wealth. Indeed, only a handful of colonists, mostly a few landed families in New York and rice growers in South Carolina, had truly great wealth. Even George Washington, reputed to be the richest American at one point, lived in a relatively modest wooden house instead of an ornate stone palace commonly found in England and other European countries.

John Locke (1634–1704), from the National Portrait Gallery in London

Everett Historical/Shutterstock.com

Throughout the eighteenth century, America and Europe came to be influenced by the Enlightenment: a widespread philosophical movement that sought to reorder society along more rational lines. As part of its exploration of different approaches to improving society, both the British and Americans discussed the nature of a just government. Much of this discussion grew out of a general acceptance of the English philosopher John Locke's theory that men were born with "natural rights." These were the things all men are born with and cannot be taken away by a government. In his view, government operated under an agreement to do what was best for the people—or risk being removed by them. Locke's influence on Thomas Jefferson and the Declaration of Independence can clearly be seen with Jefferson's words, "We hold these truths to be self-evident, that all men are created equal, that they are endowed by their creator with certain inalienable rights, among these are Life, Liberty and the Pursuit of Happiness." According to this view, when a people form a government, they give up certain liberties but not ones considered fundamental to their humanity. This concept of natural rights led most English-speaking people on both sides of the Atlantic to conclude that government must be based on the rule of law; otherwise, rulers would trample on rights and establish tyrannies.

It had also become commonly held that power led to corruption, and the English political tradition developed a mixed political system in which power was shared by different branches of government. In Britain, especially after the Glorious Revolution of 1688, power was shared among the king, Parliament, and the courts, which became increasingly independent. In the colonies, power was shared by the governors (appointed by the king's government), governor's councils (usually appointed by the governor), legislative assemblies (elected), and local courts (appointed). Therefore, in America, as in England, power was diffused.

Some Englishmen, however, worried that, even with a mixed government, the political system favored the rich and powerful and especially the king and the nobility. These Englishmen whose elite opponents called Whigs, a derogatory term associated with horse thieves and nonconformists, were strong advocates of limited government and were no friends of English kings who they believed to be corrupt and tyrannical. Not everyone in England agreed with the Whigs. For one thing, some people pointed out, too much liberty could lead to disorder—even to civil war. The purpose of government was to maintain order, and everyone owed allegiance to the government. In this view, the king and especially the Church of England, symbolized proper order. These Englishmen, among whom were many wealthy merchants and powerful rural gentry disinclined toward change, called themselves Tories.

Most Americans were Whigs. Indeed, in a new country where change was common, few people feared disorder. In fact, many came to America to escape what they perceived to be an oppressive political environment. Essentially, Americans were obsessed with liberty. They took to heart the warnings of various English radical Whigs who warned that, unless people were vigilant, a corrupt government would trample on people's liberties. Long before the American Revolution, Americans had been fed a steady diet of political liberalism.

The French and Indian War, 1754–1763

While these conflicts over authority and power would soon materialize into conflict and open rebellion, the chief concern in the mid-1700s was France, Great Britain's chief rival. It too had an empire, including the important colony of New France (today's Canada). French control extended west to the Great Lakes and south down the Mississippi River Valley, which the French had explored in the seventeenth century. The French established relations with the Indians, trading furs with them along the frontier. They also built sugar plantations

Hawkeye. Native Indian, English-French War. Very old and rare wooden antiquity sculpture

along the lower Mississippi River. Slaves built impressive levees along the river to prevent fields from flooding. The French founded the city of New Orleans in 1718, and it developed a Creole culture of mixed French, Africa, and West Indian influences.

Both the French and the English wished to crush each other's empires and take valuable colonies. The two countries were at war from 1689 to 1697, from 1702 to 1713, and from 1744 to 1748. In America, these wars limited frontier settlement, driving up land prices and worsening Indian-colonial relations. Each country was prone to use Indians to attack the other's colonists. Between 1754 and 1763, America itself became a chief battle-ground for the two countries. It was known as the French and Indian War, because it was England's war against the French and their Indian allies. In 1756, the conflict spread to other parts of the world and is known as the Seven Years' War, which lasted from 1756 to 1763.

American colonists and the British military attempted to work together. At this time, the British had the largest and most feared navy in the world. They dominated the Atlantic Ocean, which eased American fears of a French invasion from the sea. Instead, the French and their Indian allies attacked interior frontier areas with sudden and violent surprise. The British and the American colonists agreed that these raids must stop and that the only way to guarantee peace on the frontier was to remove the French permanently from North America. At this time, the colonists only saw themselves as loyal English subjects. In its conflict with the French and their Indian allies, the British supplied the officers, some of the soldiers, and heavy weapons. For their part, the Americans provided armed men and food. The loyalty to England was evident in 1754 when delegates from Pennsylvania, Mary-land, New York, and New England met in Albany, New York to negotiate a treaty with the Iroquois and even to set up a type of unity government to plan a coordinated military strat-egy. However, nothing came of it. No one, the colonists or the British authorities favored a single, unified American government.

The French and Indian War began as a dispute among the English, French, and Indi-ans. In short, all three wanted to control the Ohio Valley. For many years, the Iroquois Confederacy maintained enough power in the region to serve as mediators between the competing European empires. The breakdown of this system coincided with the decline of the powerful Iroquois Confederacy. In the beginning stages of the war, most Indians sided with the French and trusted them slightly more than the English. It was the French, after all, that for many years traded with the Indians on terms that seemed somewhat fair. This French/Indian alliance fell apart after a group of disgruntled Indi-ans attacked surrendering British soldiers after the siege of Fort William Henry. The cus-tomary French gift giving broke down, and after the English resumed the practice with the Indians, native groups increasingly sided with the British. One of the reasons for England's initial failures was its class bias against average colonials and racist view of Indians. The war turned in England's favor once they began treating colonists and Indi-ans as allies instead of subordinates. Colonial interactions with English officers led to mutual hostility. The English thought of colonials as a savage lot who were only slightly better than Native Americans. On the other hand, colonials disliked being treated as second-class citizens of the empire and began to see the British as something different from themselves.

Despite problems working together with inhabitants of the colonies, the British war effort began to succeed. In 1755, Britain's General Edward Braddock marched his troops through the woods to capture France's Fort Duquesne (later renamed Fort Pitt by the English; today, Pittsburgh, Pa). At the Battle of the Wilderness, the French surprised and defeated the British. Although Braddock's soldiers maintained impressive discipline, the French fought Indian-style by shooting from behind trees and other barriers. Braddock died from wounds received in this battle. His aid, George Washington, while getting captured, closely observed the superiority of French fighting methods that would benefit him in the coming revolutionary war. The British would defeat the French on the Plains of Abraham near what is today Quebec City in New France. In the next year, the British took Montreal and seized control of all of New France.

In 1763, as Britain and France made strides toward peace, the former held a strong negotiating position. They demanded and got New France, which they renamed Canada. The numerous French settlers were allowed to remain in Canada under British rule. With the British victory, the French threat had been permanently removed, and now American colonists could move west and settle on new lands. First, the war had been very costly, doubling Britain's national debt. British taxpayers, including wealthy aristocrats, resisted further tax increases. Taxes in the colonies were low, and the English figured that their American brethren should pay a portion of the cost of the war, as they had clearly benefitted from it. Second, the colonists had constantly battled Indians, which continued after the war. From 1763 to 1766, an Indian uprising known as Pontiac's Rebellion, named after Chief Pontiac of the Ottawa, raged across western Pennsylvania, Maryland, and Virginia. Events like this and other threats forced the British to post an army on the frontier, which proved costly. Without the French threat, the English saw no need for such a large frontier presence. If the Indians could be pacified, then the army could be withdrawn. The natives would be peaceful, thought the English, as long as colonists did not move onto their traditional lands.

The British issued a proclamation (known as the Proclamation of 1763), which prohibited frontier settlement beyond the Appalachian Mountains. Americans reacted with much resentment and anger; some were already living beyond the proclamation line, and many land speculators saw their dreams of fortune basically evaporate overnight. Too, America's population was growing rapidly, and the coastal areas were becoming crowded and no longer attractive. British victory in the Seven Years War did not help the cause of Indians in the Ohio Valley. For many years, the Iroquois, the Algonquians, and other Native American groups operated within a network of mutual obligations historians have called "the Middle Ground." This Middle Ground was the area of contestation between Indians and whites whereby neither side could dominate the other. The term described the constant need for compromise in the Great Lakes region that forced both Indians and whites to respect the other's wants. A new culture emerged out of this interplay among the English, French, and Native Americans. Once England triumphed over France in 1763 and greatly limited French influence in the colonies, the Middle Ground began to wither until it finally died after the War of 1812. Indians then lost most of their power once the English viewed them as savage "others" instead of valuable trading allies. Native Americans would never again attain the bargaining power they had during the colonial era. After the American Revolution, the new nation would consistently drive Indians from their lands and onto reservations.

"No Taxation without Representation"

In 1764, only one year after the Proclamation of 1763, Britain's Parliament decided to tax its American colonies. Actually, small fees had been levied for years in the form of import duties. From a British perspective, the main reason for having colonies was to benefit the mother country. Sure, colonists would benefit too from the trade occurring between both parties. However, the relationship could not favor the colonists over the British. The whole arrangement of trade between colonies and its home country was part of the economic system known as mercantilism, and the scenario was crafted to favor the mother country. For example, the British passed the Hat Act in 1733, which allowed the colonists to sell to the British as many beaver skins as they could process, but they were prohibited from making hats. This trade was a British prerogative, and they were prepared to buy large numbers of the American-produced raw material. This was a symbiotic relationship in which both parties benefited, but England would benefit the most, for hats were more valuable than the skins used to make them.

While the colonists were not exactly thrilled with the economic arrangement of mercantilism, they largely accepted it and operated within the system. However, the screws began to tighten on the colonists after the French and Indian War, and it became clear to many Americans that the British were intent on pursuing a more aggressive style of mercantilism that went beyond basic trade rights. In 1764, the British passed the Sugar Act, which placed an import duty not only on sugar but also on a number of other items including paint, wine, and other goods. By placing so many goods on the duty list, Americans were of the opinion that the British were attempting to raise revenue and not to strike a balance between the two parties regarding imports and exports. To make sure that these new duties were paid, Parliament authorized the appointment of many new customs officials and provided for disputes to be sent to special British admiralty courts that did not use juries. This was a new policy, for Americans had traditionally faced their peers in criminal cases. British authorities were aware, however, that American juries were reluctant to convict their own in cases involving smuggling.

The Quartering Act of 1764 was another unpopular measure that enraged Americans. As more fees were subject to being collected, more collectors were needed to ensure that people complied with the law. These revenue collectors were unpopular and were often the target of both verbal and physical assaults. To protect them

Tax stamps for the American colonies from the Stamp Act of 1765

from colonial agitators, the British sent over more soldiers. Soldiers needed a place to stay and Parliament passed the Quartering Act, which required the colonists to provide barracks and provisions. If they refused to comply, the law allowed soldiers to use inns or vacant buildings, including barns. New York's assembly defied the law, and Parliament ordered it to comply or be dissolved.

The British government found that, due to widespread smuggling, the Sugar Act's import duties were raising little money. Consequently, Parliament looked for a way to gain additional revenue from a broad-based tax. The answer was found in the Stamp Act of 1765. England already had such a tax, and it seemed that the colonists would not seriously object to a tax that was also levied against British citizens living in Britain.

The act required that all papers products produced in the colonies—court papers, deeds, licenses, pamphlets, newspapers, playing cards, and other items—carry a stamp that made these products more expensive. Colonists were outraged and initiated serious protests. Drawing on popular Whig ideas about power, the Stamp Act was commonly viewed as part of an orchestrated scheme to deprive Americans of their liberty. Colonists called the required stamp as "internal" tax because it had nothing to do with trade. The rules of the game had been essentially changed, and colonists were not in the least humored by it.

In May 1765, a young Virginia legislator named Patrick Henry introduced resolutions declaring that only the elected House of Burgesses could tax Virginians. Speaking for the Virginia Resolves, as the resolutions were called, Henry compared English King George III to Julius Caesar and Charles I (who had been executed by forces of Parliament in 1649). Shouts of "Treason!" led Henry to reply, "If this be treason, make the most of it." While some English Whigs sympathized with the Americans' claim, the majority in Parliament did not agree with the cry of "no taxation without representation." In fact, Parliament held that Americans were represented by them. This was the theory of "virtual" representation, in which the British Parliament represented all British citizens around the world. Parliament spoke for all people across the empire.

When British officials in America tried to enforce the Stamp Act and other import duties, they were met with acts of defiance that included violent protests and smuggling. In their opposition to British policy, Americans, including many wealthy merchants, created a secret organization called the Sons of Liberty. In the larger towns, these colonial rebel

The American Revolution. The members of the Association of the Sons of Liberty are requested to meet at the City-Hall. A broadside calling a meeting of the Sons of Liberty, New York, 1773

rousers forced officials to swear that they would not enforce these laws. Crowd action in the streets marked a new kind of politics; officials who held the public in contempt soon learned that ignoring mobs could result in broken windows, ransacked stores, and the physical abuse and humiliation of being tarred and feathered.

Colonial protests grew in part because of their revolutionary ideology. The eighteenth century was a period when men deeply contemplated how to improve society. It was a time characterized by humanism and talk of changing the world for the better. Enlightenment theorists such as Locke and Voltaire spoke of natural rights for all men, the obligations of a benign government, and freedom of religion. John Trenchard and Thomas Gordon were among the leading "Commonwealth men" of England; a group who criticized the oppressive use of governmental powers. Enlightenment philosophers and Commonwealth men influenced leading revolutionaries such as Thomas Jefferson and Benjamin Franklin. In fact, by 1776, most Americans had either read or heard about Locke, Trenchard, or others. From these rationalist pursuits of knowledge and perfection grew a growing dislike of the manner in which England governed her colonies.

Printed propaganda from ever more plentiful presses also became important in shaping public opinion and organizing protests. Single-sheet broadsides posted on walls announced meetings and denounced enemies, while pamphlets and newspapers presented longer, rational political arguments. Collectively, these activities tended to ridicule and weaken British authority.

Of course, no import duties could be collected if no goods were imported. Americans thus turned to boycotting English imports. This insistence upon self-sufficiency coincided with economic hard times; it was easy for colonists to swear not to buy imports when they lacked the means to purchase much of anything. At the same time, as Americans dressed in homespun clothing, their pride swelled at the realization that they were capable of producing everything they needed and to rely very little on the mother country.

In October 1765, nine colonies sent representatives to the Stamp Act Congress in New York. At the suggestion of James Otis, the delegates petitioned both George III and the British Parliament to repeal the Stamp Act. They argued that only colonial assemblies had the right to pass "internal" taxes. The protests and acts of resistance and even violence surprised the British. George Grenville, the British Prime Minister, was essentially of two minds. On the one hand, he did not want trouble from the colonies. On the other hand, he was not prepared to give in to American threats and mob action.

A new British Prime Minister, the Marquis of Rockingham, was elected in 1766 and his Whig led government heard the Americans' cry and repealed the Stamp Act. However, even a Whig-led government rejected the American position that Parliament had no right to impose taxes on the colonies. Therefore, in 1766, it passed the Declaratory Act, which upheld the right of the British government to rule its colonies essentially without limits. Despite keeping some import duties on a few products such as sugar and tea, the colonists paid them without much complaint. A lot of damage, however, had been done to the relations between the two parties, and it was only a matter of time before tensions reached another boiling point.

In fact, that point was reached in 1767 under the new administration of Charles Townshend. The new Prime Minister decided that the time was ripe to make the colonists pay more taxes. Paying careful attention to the distinction that the Americans made between internal and external taxes, Townshend persuaded Parliament to pass new and higher import duties on the colonists for paper, glass, paint, and tea. These duties, known collectively as the Townshend Duties, produced an outcry of disdain in the colonies. While traditionally not reacting in a hostile manner to external taxes, the colonists came to see Parliament, through these new duties, as intending to simply raise revenue. This was seen as "taxation without representation" because no American was seated in Parliament.

Soon, American protests were rekindled. One such event occurred in the city of Boston, Massachusetts. It was here that fights between soldiers and local crowds had become frequent. It was a snowy day on March 5, 1770 when a motley crew of colonists gathered at a British customs house that was being guarded by a group of redcoat soldiers. The colonists began throwing snowballs and other projectiles including rocks and bricks. Feeling threatened, the soldiers fired into the crowd. Three persons were immediately killed and two died later from their injuries. Eight British soldiers were arrested and charged with manslaughter, but all were acquitted due to the circumstances of the event. However, the episode was forever etched in the minds of Americans as a prime example of British tyranny. To this day, each year on March 5, the city of Boston reenacts the "Boston Massacre." Local resident Paul Revere made an engraving of the event that presented it as a case of clear murder of unarmed civilians. The image helped spur anti-British sentiment and remains the primary popular representation of the incident.

The Boston Massacre, March 5, 1770, broadside engraved, printed and sold by Paul Revere, 1770

Everett Historical/Shutterstock.com

While the Townshend Duties helped create a wave of colonial resistance, it was the Tea Act of 1733 that made an even bigger splash. By 1773, the East India Tea Company, which was one of Great Britain's largest and most politically influential companies, had fallen on hard times. To aid its faltering balance sheet, Parliament decided to take corrective action by passing the Tea Act. This law allowed the East India Tea Company to sell its tea directly to America without its ships first docking in English ports and paying a fee to the British government. The price of tea, therefore, was able to be sold at a lower price to the colonists. However, the British still retained a tea tax that the colonists were expected to pay. It was assumed though that the colonists would purchase East India tea because the price, even with the tax, was lower than before the Tea Act was passed. However, this was not the case, as Americans sensed an act of trickery. From their viewpoint, the British government was simply trying to exert more control by using a deceitful way to gain higher profits.

Boston Tea Party of December 16, 1773

The Tea Act spread alarm throughout the colonies. In several ports, colonists stopped tea ships from docking and unloading their cargoes. Massachusetts royal governor Thomas Hutchinson, whose family had been given the right to sell the tea, refused to allow ships to leave with its tea. In response, on December 16, 1773, a group of Patriots disguised as Indians boarded a ship anchored in the Boston Harbor, and dumped 342 chests of tea into the harbor in the episode forever known as "the Boston Tea Party." "This is the most magnificent movement of all," exulted John Adams, an ambitious young lawyer from Braintree, Massachusetts. He went on to state, "This destruction of tea is so bold, so daring, so firm, intrepid, and inflexible, and it must have so important consequence, and so lasting, that I can't but consider it an epoch in history."

Adams was right. To the British, the Boston Tea Party was the ultimate outrage. Angry officials pushed for a confrontation over the issue of Parliament's right to legislate for the colonies. England's Finance Minister, Lord North, told Parliament, "We are now to establish our authority or give it up entirely." In 1774, Parliament passed a succession of laws that came to be known as the Coercive Acts. The first act closed the port of Boston until the destroyed tea was paid for. The second act altered the Massachusetts charter and reorganized the government: council members were now to be appointed by the governor rather than elected by the colonial legislature. Town meetings were restricted, and the governor's power of appointing judges and sheriffs was strengthened. The third act allowed royal officials who had been charged with capital offenses to be tried in England or in another colony to avoid a hostile jury. These acts were the last straw; Americans were now convinced that Parliament had no more right to make laws for them than to tax them.

By 1774, many Americans had adopted a new view of the proper relationship between Britain and the colonies. According to this view, Britain was governed by the king and Parliament. The colonies were to be governed by people acting as the king's representatives and by popularly elected colonial assemblies. Parliament had no role to play in governing the colonies. Until the 1760s, in fact, the colonies had largely been governed this way. The sole connection between the colonies and Britain was allegiance to the same king. Many years later, the British government would adopt this formula for the British Empire; however, in 1774, few people in England accepted the idea of colonial self-government.

In response to the Coercive Acts, leading colonists organized Committees of Correspondence that formed a network to exchange information about current events throughout the

13 colonies. These leaders urged the colonies to stand together; otherwise, they believed, the British would play one colony off another and destroy this bourgeoning resistance. These committees organized mass support and began to arrange with elected legislative leaders and militia officers to provide military force if needed.

The Continental Congress and Armed Resistance

To help coordinate these activities, 12 colonies (excluding Georgia) sent representatives to the First Continental Congress in Philadelphia, Pennsylvania in September 1774. This congress pledged to continue the trade boycott, authorized coordinated military preparation, and even sent a conciliatory petition to George III. The atmosphere, however, was anything but tranquil. It was led by the cousins Samuel and John Adams from Massachusetts and by Patrick Henry and Richard Henry Lee from Virginia. However the controversy with Britain might

THE UNITED STATES—CIRCA 1977: stamp printed by the United States shows members of Continental Congress in Conference, circa 1977

end, the Continental Congress would play a decisive role in shaping the colonial response.

In 1775, British officials in America watched events with growing concern. The greatest threat to British rule came from popular defiance backed by local militias. To maintain authority, the British had to crush the colonists' organized opposition. Boston, which the British correctly perceived to be the center of the rebellion, offered an important test case. If there was a suppression of the Patriots, this might serve as a warning to rebels elsewhere. The closing of the port had only worsened relations between the people and the occupying British army. Furthermore, the arming of the militia in nearby towns threatened to leave the British soldiers, called redcoats, trapped inside Boston. Thinking that it was dealing only with mobs led by a few seditious instigators, the British ordered its commander in Massachusetts, General Thomas Gage, to arrest the rebel leaders, break up their bases, and reassert royal authority over the colony.

On April 19, 1775, Gage's army attempted to seize rebel arms and ammunition stored at Concord, a town northwest of Boston. Colonial scouts, including the silversmith Revere, rode ahead of the advancing redcoats, warned patriot leaders John Hancock and Samuel Adams to flee, and roused the farmers of the countryside—the minutemen—to arms. No one knows who fired the first shot at Lexington, but shots between the colonial militia and British troops were exchanged there and later at Concord, where the British found only a few supplies. During their long march back to Boston, British columns were repeatedly harassed by patriot militia. By the end of the day, 273 redcoats and 9 minutemen lay dead. From nearby positions in Charlestown and Dorchester, the colonists quickly surrounded the besieged British in Boston, and this raised doubts that police action would be enough to silence the rebellion.

Two months later, in June 1775, British troops left Boston and moved toward Bunker Hill in Charlestown to confront the rebels. The Americans met them actually at Breed's ill, although traditionally known as the Battle of Bunker Hill, in the first full-fledged battle of the war. The British assumed, as one of their generals John Burgoyne put it, that no numbers of "untrained rabble" could ever stand up against "trained troops." Under General William Howe, British forces attempted a series of frontal assaults on the American position. These attacks were eventually successful, but only at the terrible cost of 1,000 British casualties—more than 40 percent of Howe's troops. In fact the Battle of Breed's Hill (Bunker Hill) would be the most costly military loss, in terms of casualties, in what would become a long war.

European officers assumed that, without training, Americans stood no chance in real battles. They had already demonstrated their disdain for non-regular American soldiers during the French and Indian War. The European way of fighting emphasized tight rows and columns of men under the strict rule of officers. The British believed that men marching and firing in unison could not be defeated. The Americans would also try to fight in this manner throughout the Revolutionary War, with mixed results. However, theywould also use other methods against the greatest military power in the world.

Everett Historical/Shutterstock.com

George Washington (1732–1799 portrait that hangs at his home in Mount Vernon, Virginia

Before it could attempt to hold its own against the British, America had to create an army. The First Continental Congress had given way to the more militant Second Continental Congress, which met in May of 1775. The Congress created a Continental Army, appointed George Washington of Virginia as commander, issued paper money for the support of its army, and formed a committee to negotiate with foreign countries. It was becoming clear that the colonies were seriously questioning the notion of a tiny island governing an entire continent. Did it make sense for Americans to remain part of an empire that would not recognize its right to self-determination? In late 1775, the Congress debated these matters even as it scrambled to provide men and arms for the newly created Continental Army.

By the summer of 1775, the escalation of actions and reactions was out of control. By October of that year, King George III publicly accused the colonies of being in open rebellion and of aiming at outright independence. By December, the British government had declared that all American shipping was liable to seizure by British warships. Truth be known, it was only a matter of time before the

Americans had formally cut their remaining ties to the mother country, though no official American institution had as yet endorsed independence.

American public opinion was mixed about going to war against the British. For one thing, most people considered themselves good British citizens. British culture and government were something most valued and considered something to emulate. For the most part, British Patriots talked about trying to achieve equal treatment within the Empire and not trying to leave it. People tended to blame Parliament and not the king. However, things were starting to change. By the start of the hostilities, people were beginning to believe that the king also was against them.

It was left to Thomas Paine, a onetime English dress maker and school teacher, to express in January 1776 the accumulated American rage against George III. In his pamphlet *Common Sense,* Paine dismissed the king as the "Royal Brute" and called for immediate American independence. *Common Sense* was the most incendiary and popular pamphlet of the entire Revolutionary era. In it, Paine rejected the traditional and stylized forms of persuasion designed for educated gentlemen and reached out for new readers among the taverns and artisan shops.

Statue of Thomas Paine

Unlike more polite writers, Paine did not use lofty Latin phrases that were typically seen in traditional discourse, but he instead relied on his readers' knowledge of the Bible. However, Paine himself was a Deist and not overly religious. He argued that monarchy was not originally part of God's plan. Paine showed that honesty and sincerity was enough to arouse the public to action. Paine also appealed to the American sense of honor. He went as far as to say monarchy itself was wrongheaded and should not be part of America's future.

Declaring Independence and Waging War

In the early spring of 1776, the Continental Congress threw open America's ports to the world and prepared for independence. On July 4, 1776, the delegates formally approved the Declaration of Independence largely penned by Jefferson. In it, the king, who was now regarded as the only remaining link between the colonists and Great Britain, was held accountable for every ill that the Americans had suffered since 1763. The reign of George III, Americans declared "to a candid world," was "a history of repeated injuries and usurpations, all having in direct object the establishment of an absolute Tyranny over these States."

The Declaration of Independence

The Declaration of independence was a brilliant expression of Enlightenment ideals that was inspiring in 1776 and continues to resonate today. Who is not familiar with the phrase, "That all men are created equal; that they are endowed by their Creator with certain inalienable rights; that among these are life, liberty, and the pursuit of happiness." This document expressed and continues to announce a philosophy of human rights, not only for Americans, but to any group believing to suffer oppression. It was essential in giving the American Revolution a universal appeal.

Many of the leading American intellectuals and revolutionaries believed that they were fighting for more than just simple independence. As Paine put it, "the cause of America in great measure is the cause of all mankind." In other words, many believed that it was the hope of all people to be self-governing. This was a very new idea associated with the Enlightenment. For most of History, no matter the type of government, the masses lived under the tight grip of an individual or select group. People were not thought capable of ruling themselves. For these reasons, the first combat at Lexington and Concord is often referred to as "the shot heard around the world." A new age was born, where democracy would begin to replace authoritarianism.On the British front, a British military occupation of Boston was essentially meaningless since a naval blockade could keep the port closed. Accordingly, they decided to carry the war to the other colonies that had supported Boston's resistance. In March of 1776, the British evacuated Boston, regrouped their forces, and returned in July under General Sir William Howe in a massive attack on Long Island, New York with a large force of 32,000 regulars and 9,000 German mercenaries. This was the largest military force ever assembled up to that time in North America. George Washington, on the other hand, had only 19,000 men in arms, including the various militias.

The British strategy was to occupy the major cities—New York, Philadelphia, and Charleston—and to choke off foreign trade that had seemed so necessary to sustain the American economy. From here, British redcoats could make damaging raids into rebel-held areas near the seaports. The Battle of Brooklyn Heights on August 27, 1776 was the first major battle fought after the signing of the Declaration of Independence and one of the largest of the war. Washington was determined to defend the important port of New York City, for if the British took it they would be in a good position to facilitate the actions of the British navy. The battle resulted in 2,000 American casualties, which prompted Washington to comment, "Good God, what brave fellows I must lose." Remarkably, Washington conducted a successful withdrawal to New Jersey, saving most of his army.

While 1776 came in on a positive note, it appeared that it would end in disaster. Washington had lost about every battle, and the enlistment papers of many of his men would terminate at the end of the year. He needed a convincing victory to reverse the momentum.

A change of fortunes would come on the day after Christmas, 1776, as the gentleman soldier from Virginia led a small number of troops across an ice-laden Delaware River to attack a Hessian fort at Trenton, New Jersey. The 900 Hessians who occupied Trenton were ill prepared for Washington's surprise attack and were soundly defeated. This battle gave the Americans new heart, not to mention badly needed supplies, and it suggested that passionately committed colonists could defeat hired foreign troops who cared less about the ultimate outcome of the war and more about their paychecks.

The British military strategy of 1777 was to isolate New England and break the back of the American rebellion. This would be accomplished partially by sending one army under the command of General John Burgoyne south from Canada down through the Hudson Valley by way of Lake Champlain. Another army led by Howe would move north out of New York City. The combined commands of Burgoyne and Howe would gain the British control over the Hudson River Valley, hopefully demoralizing the Americans and dissuading the French from aiding the revolutionary cause. Howe, however, decided that the best option for him was to move on Philadelphia, the seat of the colonial government. Howe's move left Burgoyne essentially on his own, and by the time his army arrived near the town of Saratoga, New York, his army was vulnerable and short on supplies. An American army under the command of native Englishman Horatio Gates surrounded Burgoyne and the British and, after a couple of bloody engagements, surrendered. American General Benedict Arnold was important to this victory. Known

Benedict Arnold (1741–1801), American General, and defector to the British during the Revolutionary War, circa 1770s

as one of the best Patriot generals, Arnold would later betray the Americans and switch sides—making his name forever linked with traitors. The Battle of Saratoga was a turning point in the war. Benjamin Franklin, the then America's ambassador to France, was able to persuade the French to come to America's aid. In 1778, the French boosted the colonial cause through their navy, army, and badly needed military supplies. It is hard to overestimate the value of French support to the future American war effort. The French Navy was especially important, as the Americans had almost no way to counteract the British domination of the seas.

Despite the American victory at Saratoga and the coming French aid, the British remained in control of New York City and Philadelphia. Washington had attempted to defend Philadelphia but was defeated in two pitched battles. After the second engagement on October 4, 1778, Washington led 12,000 of his war weary soldiers out of Philadelphia to about 20 miles to its west to a place called Valley Forge, named for a nearby iron furnace. It was here that Washington and his men would camp for the winter and prepare for spring in which they would fight again. However, it soon became apparent that the winter of 1777–1778 would prove to be a curse before it turned into a blessing. There was inadequate food and clothing, and to make matters worse, diseases such as typhoid, typhus, and pneumonia killed 2,000 of Washington's men. There were desertions and morale greatly suffered. Every day Washington feared that he would have no army left to fight. However, his commanding leadership and help from able commanders such as the Baron von Steuben, a former officer in the Prussian army, turned the tide. Von Steuben's contribution was enormous, for he drilled the soldiers from dawn to dusk, and, over the winter, made boys into men. A new day had clearly dawned for the Continental army.

With a renewed American Continental Army that had become difficult for the British to defeat in the northern colonies, they decided upon a new strategy that would focus on the southern colonies. After winning the south, they would then sweep northward and finalize their victory, and America's revolutionary experiment would end in failure. The strategy began with much fanfare. Savanna, Georgia was captured in late 1778, and Charleston, South Carolina fell in 1780 where three American generals and 5,000 troops were captured. In parts of the southern back country, Tories (British sympathizers) were so numerous that more fought for the mother country than did for the colonial cause. It looked to be a winning strategy, but a series of events brought it into doubt and made winning ultimately an unachievable goal.

In the South, the British won almost every engagement, but they had difficulty crushing the American resistance. The South had even less major cities than the northern colonies. In such a rural environment, with people dispersed all over the countryside, the British could not hold many of its gains. The British would have needed many more men to do so. The British had hoped that their policy toward slavery would help them win over the southern colonies. Cornwallis and others logically assumed that slaves would turn against their masters and fight for the British. In 1775, the royal governor of Virginia, Lord Dunmore, issued a proclamation that any escaped slave would win freedom if he fought for the British. Thousands of blacks did fight in the war, but on both sides of the conflict. The British thought that war would cause chaos in the South and help them win. However, the Dunmore Proclamation was more about trying to increase their war effort that it was about helping enslaved people, and they gained little advantage from it.

British strategy in the South did not accomplish the desired goals. Lord Cornwallis was in command of British forces here. Bolstered by the captures of Savanna and Charleston, Cornwallis was eager to demonstrate British strength by carrying the war into North Carolina. However, his aggressive strategy suffered a blow at the Battle of King's Mountain, North Carolina on October 7, 1780. Of the almost 1,300 Loyalist soldiers, 290 were killed and approximately 859 wounded or captured. In the South, Continental generals such as Nathanael Greene and Daniel Morgan proved reliable. At Cowpens, South Carolina, on January 17, 1781, Morgan led Americans to victory over the British commanded by the nortorious commander Banastre Tarleton. This was a serious setback to Cornwallis' strategy, but it would not be the last. Cornwallis also overestimated the level of Loyalist support in the South. British plunder of the backcountry, particularly by Colonel Tarleton, drove countless Georgians and Carolinians to take up arms against the redcoats. Colorful leaders such a Francis Marion, "the Swamp Fox," organized bands of Patriots outside of the regular army to harass loyalists and British forces. The war in the South became a series of guerilla skirmishes, which gave the colonists a home-field advantage.

Deciding to abandon his southern strategy, Cornwallis marched his redcoats north toward Yorktown, Virginia so that his army could either be resupplied or be evacuated if the need arose. Yorktown was an ideal place to create a base of operations. It was on high ground and surrounded by water. However, the Americans had gained control of the rivers on both sides of Cornwallis's position, and he was not able to escape inland. British supply ships did arrive, but were late and were engaged by a French naval fleet. The French won the day, and the British general was cut off from an Atlantic escape route. On October 19, 1781, Cornwallis realized his hopeless situation and surrendered his army of 8,000 troops to Washington. Although the war dragged on for several months, everyone knew that Yorktown meant American independence.

George Washington hand colored engraving with vignette of the British surrender at the Battle of Yorktown, 1781

A peace treaty was not immediately forthcoming, as the details had to be negotiated and discussed. However, by September, 1783, both sides reached a deal, and the Treaty of Paris was signed. According to the terms, in the west, the United States territory reached to the Mississippi River; on the south to the 31st parallel; and on the north, roughly to the present boundary with Canada. The French, although they greatly aided the American war effort, gained very little except the satisfaction of seeing their greatest European and international rival lose. America, on the other hand, had defeated Europe's greatest military power.

The British could have continued the war, but they never put the full weight of their military mighttoward winning it. They had always thought of the American rebellion as a nuisance more than a prescription for success. However, the American cause was mighty, and greatly underestimated. Too, the British were more preoccupied with their European enemies—especially France. Thus, they decided to stop fighting and concentrate on their many other possessions around the world. After all, North America was never its most profitable set of colonies.

Conclusion

While the American colonies initially valued and cherished their identities as British, the actions of their mother country were not becoming of a permanent, cordial relationship. When the relationship turned sour over perceived injustices and violations of rights, British policy did not heal the fracture. In fact, such parliamentary acts such as the Coercive

Acts and Tea Act resulted in further damage. It was not long that most Americans believed that the best course was to separate entirely from Great Britain and emerge as an independent country. However, it would take a war to turn a yearning into a reality. While success on the battlefield would propel a young country forward, winning the peace would require just as much trial and effort.

The road to making America an actuality and not just a dream, composed of abstract, lofty Enlightenment ideals, did not instantly materialize after Yorktown. Historians have even questioned whether this even constituted a real revolution. One thing though that marked this Revolution as unique was that Americans essentially already had what they were fighting to preserve: local, representative government and opportunity. Americans were familiar with some level of democracy. There was opportunity for land not known in Europe. At the same time, slavery was still intact. Thus, the true meaning of what the Revolution meant and how it would change the future of the former colonies lay in the future.

CHAPTER FOUR

A Country Emerges, 1783–1800

Chapter 4: Key Concepts

- Why is it important that the new constitution had a system of checks and balances? What are the most vital characteristics of this system?

- Why is it important that a Bill of Rights became a part of the new constitution? Which two amendments are the most vital in your view and why?

- Which American statesman had the biggest impact during this time period and how would you explain your reasoning behind this choice?

Introduction

The American Revolution initiated a period of great promise. New economic opportunities emerged along with a spirit of freedom and equality. However, many divisive issues remained. One was slavery. How could a county justify holding in bondage almost one million people when its Declaration of Independence stated that, "all men are created equal?" This glaring inconsistency is more than apparent today, but it was also not lost on the revolutionary generation. Another crucial issue centered on the proper function of a federal government. While many were supportive of a decentralization of power toward the states, it was apparent to others that the Continental Congress was too weak. It seemed likely that the nation needed to revise, at least, the current methods of governance. In the end, with the signing of a national Constitution, a new era would begin. While many were apprehensive about the powers it gave to the federal government, others saw it as the framework best needed to help steer the country along the road of stability, harmony, and eventual greatness.

The Advent of Republicanism

The Revolutionary War itself was a both a disruptive and a creative force. It touched nearly everyone in one way or another. Like all wars, it destroyed familiar channels of trade and produced new sources of wealth. During the eight long war years, perhaps as many as 100,000 men served in the Continental army and state militias. All these soldiers had to be clothed, fed, housed, armed, and transferred from place to place. Over this time span, Congress and the state governments were involved in large mobilization efforts that had powerful and far-reaching effects on the American economy. Hundreds of military and government officials bought millions of dollars' worth of goods from food and wagons to blankets and uniforms—anything and everything needed to fight a war. A British naval blockade of American shipping affected the inability to purchase many goods from abroad, so most things that people needed had to be grown or made by Americans. Consequently, American farmers and artisans were drawn into producing for these huge new government markets on a scale never before experienced in the colonies. By the 1780s, many ordinary Americans were enthusiastic about the possibility of raising their standard of living.

The new American economy was accompanied by a swelling population. In fact, the 1780s saw the fastest rate of population growth of any decade in American history. This swelling population resumed its movement westward after being delayed in the late 1770s by occasional

James Madison (1751–1836)

Everett Historical/Shutterstock.com

warfare against the British and Indians. By the early 1780s, there were more than 20,000 people living in the Kentucky territory, and within a decade it had become more populous than most of the colonies had been at the time of the Revolution.

This spectacular growth and movement of people further weakened traditional ways of society. Such a mobile population, one Kentuckian told James Madison in 1792, "must make a very different mass from on which is composed of men born and raised on the same sport. . . They see none about them to whom or to whose families they have been accustomed to think themselves inferior." These tendencies were intensified by the ideology of republicanism that was in every way a radical ideology for the times. It meant more than simply dispensing with a monarchy and replacing it with an elective system of government. A moral and idealistic dimension was added; an elite class of nobility that directed, dominated, and orchestrated society was replaced with a republican spirit of broad, individual property-holding. It stressed devotion to the common welfare of the people. Several of the states—Massachusetts, Pennsylvania, and Virginia—even adopted the title "commonwealth" to clearly express this new dedication to the public good. Unlike monarchies, which maintained power through the manipulation of the ranks of people dependent on them, republics had to be held together from below by the people themselves. Were Americans capable of ruling themselves? Did they have the same community-oriented spirit of the ancient republican citizens of Greece and Rome?

The individual ownership of property, especially land, was believed to be essential for a healthy republic, both as a source of independence and as evidence of a permanent attachment to the community. In Europe, corruption and dependency were thought to be common because only a few people possessed property. However, as one Carolinian wrote in 1777, "the people of America are a people of property; almost every man is a freeholder." Jefferson was so keen on this point that he proposed, in 1776, that the new Commonwealth of Virginia granted 50 acres of land to every citizen.

Another important aspect of republicanism was the emphasis placed upon equality, one of the most powerful and influential concepts in American history. Equality was the necessary basis for the anticipated harmony and public virtue of the New World. Many felt that the endless squabbling over position and rank and the bitter factional politics in the colonies had resulted from the artificial inequality of colonial society. This inequality, Republicans said, had been created and nourished largely through the corrupting influence and patronage of the British government. In a republic, individuals were no longer tied to be what their fathers had been. Ability, not birth, would define a person. Republics would still have an elite, but it would be a natural, and not an artificial, one. The Republican elite would not resemble the luxury-loving, haughty aristocrats of the Old World. Instead, it was thought that leaders would be men like George Washington, who seemed to many Americans to perfectly embody the ideal republican.

Some more radical, equality-minded citizens attacked distinctions of all kinds, including membership in private social clubs and the wearing of imported fine clothing. In this new republican society, no one would admit being dependent on anyone else. Ordinary citizens now claimed the right to the titles such as "Mr." and "Mrs." that had once belonged only to the members of the gentry. Foreign visitors were stunned by the unwillingness of American servants to address their masters and mistresses as superiors and by the servants' refusal to admit that they were anything but "help." For many Americans, living in a free country meant never having to tip one's cap to anyone.

Since republicanism depended on a knowledgeable citizenry, the Revolution immediately inspired educational efforts of about every conceivable kind. Americans formed numerous scientific organizations and medical societies and produced many scholarly magazines. Gentleman-scientists and amateur philosophers gave lectures and wrote essays on everything from raising sheep to ridding noxious, dangerous odors from wells. They also prepared detailed plans for educational structures ranging from elementary schools to a national university.

In 1776, America had only nine colleges, but by 1800, 16 more were enrolling students. By the early 19th nineteenth century, colleges—mostly religiously inspired and relatively short-lived—were being created by the dozens. Yet in the decades immediately following the Revolution, most of the high hopes of the Revolutionary leaders for the establishment of publically supported educational systems were not fulfilled largely because of penny-pinching legislatures and religious jealousies. Even in New England, which had a long tradition of public education, privately supported academies sprang up after the war years to replace the older town-supported grammar schools. Nevertheless, the republican ideal of the state's fundamental responsibility to educate all its citizens remained alive and was eventually realized in the educational reform movement of the next century.

Perhaps the institution that was most directly and substantially affected by the liberalizing spirit of republicanism was slavery. To be sure, the enslavement of nearly half a million blacks did not end at the Revolution, and this failure, amid all the well-intentioned talk of liberty and equality, became a glaring and hypocritical inconsistency of the Revolutionary era. Nevertheless, the Revolution did suddenly and effectively end the social and intellectual climate that had allowed black slavery to exist in the colonies for more than a century without it being seriously questioned. The colonists had generally taken slavery for granted as part of the natural order of society. Bondage and servitude existed in many forms in pre-Revolutionary America, and the colonists had felt little need to question or defend slavery any more than other forms of the recognized social order. Now, however, republican citizenship suddenly brought into question all kinds of personal dependency. For the first time, Americans were compelled to confront the institution most often taken for granted. They had to recognize that slavery was a deviation, a "peculiar institution," and that if they were to retain it, they would have to explain and justify it. Northerners were not as committed to slavery

Portrait of Thomas Jefferson

Everett Historical/Shutterstock.com

as southerners nor was it as widespread or deeply rooted in the society or economy. The institution was open to political pressure, and it slowly began to disappear. In the decades following the Revolution, most northern states moved to end slavery. By 1830, there were fewer than 3,000 slaves out of a northern black population of more than 125,000. The Revolutionary vision of a society of independent freeholders led the Continental Congress in the 1780s to forbid slavery in the newly organized Northwest Territory between the Appalachian Mountains and the Mississippi River. The new federal Constitution of 1787 promised an end to the slave trade after 20 years and many hoped that this would be the beginning of the end of the institution of slavery.

In the South, however, despite initial criticism by Thomas Jefferson, James Madison, and other enlightened social thinkers, slavery was too deeply entrenched to be abolished by legislative or judicial action. Southern whites, who had been in the forefront of the Revolutionary movement and were among the most fervent spokesmen for its liberalism, now began to realize for the first time that the South was different from the rest of America. In the 1790s, slave insurrections on the French West Indian island of Santo Domingo, together with the tales of horror brought by thousands of fleeing white refugees to American ports, created fears about the future stability of America's slave society. By this time, the South had to reconcile the American claim that people everywhere had a right to seek their freedom with slavery.

From the Articles of Confederation to the Constitution

Despite the successes of the Revolution, including the promise of republicanism, and new economic opportunities, it was not but a few years after the Declaration of Independence was signed that many Revolutionary leaders came to question the way America was headed. State legislatures, many believed, not the governors, were the political authorities to be most feared. Some of the legislatures were pursuing reckless economic policies by printing too much paper currency. All of them had absorbed executive and judicial duties. It began to seem that the legislative power of the people was no more trustworthy than the detested royal power of old. Legislators were supposedly the representatives of the people who had elected them. However, as Jefferson wrote in 1785 in his <u>Notes on Virginia</u>, "173 despots would surely be as oppressive as one."

The idea of a constitution serving as fundamental law immune from legislative changes began to grow. In fact, some state judges were active during the 1780s, imposing restraints on acts passed by legislatures. Judge George Wythe of the Virginia Supreme Court stated in 1782, in addressing the Virginia legislature, "here is the limit of your authority; and hither shall you go, but no further." Few, however, were willing to go this far, for it appeared obviously un-republican. However, the precedent was set.

The growing economic instability throughout the 1780s, that the state legislatures had helped create through their large loan debts, created chaos, debate, and an uncertain future.

Recognizing that they had printed too much money, Massachusetts decided to slash their "loose" money policy that left many debtors in a difficult position of having to pay off debts without adequate money. As the dwindling money supply brought a general decline in commerce, artisans and farmers found it hard to sell their goods. Economic production dwindled and the standard of living fell. As a result, there was an economic depression. Farmers unable to pay off their debts were in deep trouble. Some Massachusetts farmers were actually thrown into prison for their debt problems. Others

Political cartoon about the ratification of the U.S. Constitution, including events such as Shays' Rebellion

faced the prospects of losing their homes and farms. Daniel Shays, a celebrated Revolutionary War veteran, led a rebellion of approximately 2,000 against Massachusetts courts while forcing some of them to temporarily close. He hoped to create an even larger crisis by marching his motley crew of angry farmers on the state arsenal at Springfield in February of 1787 to seize its weaponry, but a state militia was summoned that defeated them. While Shay's Rebellion was not successful, some of its sympathizers soon won legislative elections that highlighted the growing friction between the bankers and creditors of eastern Massachusetts with the debtor farmers of the western part of the state. Shays Rebellion also emphasized the need, according to some, for a stronger central government that could protect states from domestic insurrection, for the Articles of Confederation had no such power.

By 1786–1787, many influential Americans began to see that a new blueprint of government was needed, not only to address the weaknesses of the Articles of Confederation, but also the perceived democratic despotism and inefficiency of the state legislatures. Creating a new government was no longer simply a matter of cementing the Union, creating a better apparatus for negotiating foreign affairs, or of satisfying the demands of particular interests. It was now a matter that would, as James Madison declared, "decide forever the fate of republican government."

It was in 1777, with the American Revolution raging, that the Articles of Confederation were adopted. Under this framework, the Continental Congress recorded some notable achievements including the Treaty of Paris in 1783, which ended the war and secured American independence. Another noted achievement was the Northwest Ordinance of 1787, which provided for the surveying, settlement, and formation of states in the territory bounded by the Appalachians, the Great Lakes, and the Mississippi and Ohio Rivers.

The Articles of Confederation. First page of a 1777 printed version of the Nation's first constitution

One notable provision funded public education through land sales. Slavery was also prohibited. The act also pledged to honor Indian treaties but was soon violated.

Despite these notable achievements, the Articles of Confederation proved weak. This government, which consisted of little more than a congress appointed by the states, could not perform some crucial functions. It lacked the power to collect taxes. It could only beg money from the states, which often ignored its pleas. It also could not control interstate commerce, which proved to be an extreme deficiency.

If American farmers were prohibited from selling their surplus crops to Europe, not only would the industrious character of the farmers be undermined, but the United States would be unable to pay for manufactured goods imported from Europe. Therefore, the nation would be compelled to begin large-scale manufacturing for itself. According to Madison, Jefferson and like-minded others, these developments would eventually destroy the farmer-citizenry on which republicanism was based and create in America the same kind of corrupt, rank-conscious, and dependent society that existed in Europe.

Yet the mercantilist empires of the major European nations remained generally closed to America throughout the 1780s. Ambassadors John Adams in Great Britain and Thomas Jefferson in France made strong diplomatic efforts to develop a new international commercial relationship based on free trade, but these efforts largely failed. The French were unwilling to take as much American produce as had been expected, and Britain effectively closed its markets to competitive American goods while selling Americans what it had produced. The Confederation lacked the authority to retaliate with its own trade regulations, and several attempts to grant Congressional control over international trade was lost amid state and regional jealousies. The Confederation Congress watched helplessly as the separate states attempted to pass conflicting trade acts. By the mid-1780s, for example, Connecticut was levying heavier trade duties from Massachusetts than on those from Great Britain. It was truly a chaotic situation, and one that needed immediate resolution.

It was to address this concern and others that in February of 1787, Congress asked the states to send delegates to Philadelphia to revise the Articles of Confederation. Convening in May in the Philadelphia State House (Independence Hall), all answered the call except for Rhode Island who feared losing the power to impose import duties. It was generally expected that the convention would simply revise the Articles of Confederation. However, when the 55 delegates arrived, they instead scrapped them and began work on a completely new framework of government.

The Virginia delegation took the lead and presented the Convention with its first working model. The Virginia Plan, as it was commonly known, was largely the effort of the 37-year-old James Madison, who more than any other person deserves the title of "Father of the Constitution." He was a slightly built, soft-spoken man who often dressed in black. He was not trained for any particular profession, but was widely read, had a sharp and questioning mind, and was a devoted public servant. He understood clearly the historical significance of the task at hand. Moreover, because Madison decided to make detailed notes of the Convention, future generations have learned so much of the proceedings that summer in Philadelphia.

Madison's Virginia Plan called for a general government that would be not a confederation of independent states but a national republic in its own right. It would exercise direct power over individuals and be organized as most of the state governments, with a single executive, a bicameral legislature, and a separate judiciary. It provided for a national legislature with the authority to legislate "in all cases to which the states are incompetent" and to veto or negate, "all laws passed by the several states, contravening in the opinion of the national legislature." The Congress was to have two houses, both based on state population. The lower house was to be elected by the people, while the upper house was to be elected by the lower house from among men nominated by state legislatures. This would obviously give a big advantage to the states with the largest populations. The Virginia Plan also supported the creation of a single strong executive elected by Congress.

The Virginia Plan was opposed by the New Jersey Plan that was supported by the smaller states. As with the Virginia Plan it gave the federal government the power to tax and to regulate interstate commerce, but it overall gave the federal government fewer powers than that proposed by Madison and the Virginia delegation. Regarding Congress, instead of a two-house legislature allocated by population, the New Jersey Plan proposed only a one-house legislature with each state having the same number of legislators.

After a long and bitter four-month debate amidst a scorching Philadelphia summer, a compromise was reached. As temperatures and tempers cooled, 39 of the original 55 delegates signed the Constitution. According to an ailing Benjamin Franklin who had to be carried to the convention every day, "There are several parts of this Constitution which I do not at present approve, but I am not sure I shall never approve them." In the end, Franklin signed the Constitution because he expected "no better and because I am not sure that it is not the best." Franklin lived only three more years, but long enough to see the Constitution ratified by the necessary number of states along with the beginnings of America's new form of government.

The Constitution was signed by the delegates largely because of the compromises reached. One such compromise concerned the composition of Congress. The split

Alexander Hamilton (1755–1804)

between the Virginia and New Jersey Plans was mended with the "Connecticut Compromise." The agreement stated that each state was given two senators in the upper house of the legislature called the Senate, and the lower house, now referred to as the House of Representatives, would be based on population. Another compromise had to do with counting slaves as part of a state's representation. Southern delegates wanted representation to be based upon total population including the slaves. Northern delegates opposed allowing states to be added to the totals numbers of people in southern states. Finally, it was decided that three-fifths of the slaves would be counted for the purpose of representation. This became known as the Three/Fifths Compromise.

The convention also decided on a single strong executive. The president was to stand alone, unencumbered by an executive council except one of his own choosing called his cabinet. With command over the armed forces, the authority to direct diplomatic relations, the power over appointments to the executive and judicial branches, and with a four-year term of office and no limits set on how many terms served, the president was a high official who, as Patrick Henry later said, could "easily become a king." The Virginia Plan had proposed that the president be elected by Congress to ensure the president's independence, and because the people were not trusted to make the best decisions. The Constitution provided for the establishment of local "electors" who were equal in number to the representatives and senators from each state. These electors would cast ballots for the president.

The fear of tyranny was one of the most salient republican ideas influencing the framers of the Constitution. The colonies had just recently fought and won a war to rid them of a foreign tyranny, so they certainly wanted to protect themselves against creating a government that echoed any similarities. Not wishing to give any one institution too much power, the Constitution divided it among three branches: the executive, legislative, and judicial. At every turn, the process of checks and balances prevented any single branch from exerting too much power.

For a bill to become a law, it had to pass both the House and Senate and then be signed by the president. However, the president could veto the bill if he wished. The veto, however, could be overruled by a two-thirds vote in each house. The president appointed the cabinet and all judges, but the Senate had to approve the appointments. Federal judges were independent of political sway as they served for life, but both judges and the president could be removed from office by Congress using the impeachment process. The president negotiated all treaties, but they had to be ratified by the Senate. The Constitution also promised to settle the decade's economic problems. The federal government would have the sole right to coin money and to regulate both interstate and foreign commerce.

The document was written broadly so that it could evolve according to the needs of the country. Basic rules were clearly stated, but the specific details were left to later generations of Americans to debate and negotiate. The amendment process and the fact that it has and continues to be reinterpreted in the light of changing political and economic conditions is a testimony to its uniqueness.

To Ratify or Not: The Federalists/ Antifederalists Debate

While the Constitution offered a revolutionary blueprint for how a government should function, not all of the delegates approved. In fact, only 39 of the 55 delegates signed it. Those who did called themselves Federalists. Those who did not support the Constitution, who were labeled the Antifederalists, feared that the document created too powerful of a central government at the expense of the states and individual freedom.

The Federalists were well organized and prepared to defend the Constitution. Alexander Hamilton, James Madison, and John Jay published 85 essays in various New York City newspapers under the pseudonym "Publius." Most of the essays were written by Hamilton and Madison. The Antifederalists believed that the new Constitution betrayed some of the principles of the American Revolution. It would increase taxes, weaken the power and independence of the states, and, in general, endanger individual liberty. Of all of their complaints, the most significant one centered on protecting individual liberty, such as the right to freedom of religion and speech and the right of due process. They insisted that the only way they could support the Constitution was to have the natural rights of the people specifically spelled out, and only then would there be any guarantee that those liberties would be protected. In response, the Federalists pledged that a listing of specific rights of the people would be added to the Constitution once it was ratified.

The Bill of Rights. The first 10 amendments to the U.S. Constitution were adopted by the House of Representatives on August 21, 1789 and ratified December 15, 1791

In 1789, as the Antifederalists demanded and the Federalists had promised, the first Congress passed a Bill of Rights that consisted of 10 amendments to the Constitution. The most important, the First Amendment, provided that Congress could not interfere with religious choice or with the freedom of speech—including that of the press and assembly. The Second Amendment provided for the right of militiamen to keep and bear their own arms. The Fourth through Eighth Amendments required search warrants, due process, a speedy trial, trial by jury, and reasonable bail. The 10th Amendment gave the states powers that were not specifically granted to the federal government.

The George Washington Administration, 1789–1797

With the Constitution in force, it was time to decide on the first president. In early 1789, the first Electoral College, appointed by legislatures in some states and elected by the voters in others, met and unanimously elected George Washington the first president of the United States. There was no contest. Massachusetts was the home to vice president John Adams and New York City was chosen as the site of the nation's capital. Adams was chosen in part to balance the administration between representatives of both the southern and northern colonies. Despite ardent opposition from some of the Antifederalists, most of the states quickly ratified the Constitution. It took only 9 of the 13 to vote for ratification for the Constitution to become the law of the land. It took about six months for the ninth state, New Hampshire, to vote for ratification, which meant that in July of 1788 the Constitution was in force. New York and Virginia soon followed suit but only after intense debate. North Carolina did not ratify until November 1989, and Rhode Island, the most resistant, finally bowed to pressure and voted to adopt the Constitution in May 1790.

Washington was a very popular public figure. In the Revolutionary War, he had showcased some skills that would be needed as president. He was effective at mediating between bickering rivals, handling both military and political disputes, and was adept at successfully navigating through bureaucratic red tape.

Benjamin Franklin (1706–1790)

The new president's first and most important task was to set the tone of the government. Washington strongly believed in republican government as opposed to monarchy or aristocracy, but he also insisted on order and proper decorum. He found himself caught between the Federalists who wished to bolster the dignity of the new republic by adopting some of the ceremony and majesty of monarchy and those who were opposed of anything that smacked of an aristocracy. Some Federalists in the Senate tried to make "His Highness" the proper title for addressing the president. Because the future of the new republic was so unformed and doubtful, this issue seemed loaded with significance. While Washington agreed that some title was necessary to show proper respect for the office, he also understood that most Americans would not support any honorific that reminded them of what they had risked their lives to end.

While Washington was at the helm of this new ship of state, Alexander Hamilton was the moving force. As a military aide to Washington during the Revolutionary War, he had earned the president's admiration and trust. In fact, despite his short stature, Hamilton impressed just about everyone with whom he met. He was quick-witted and very knowledgeable about public finance. This was very important in a time when America was still learning how to create a strong economy. One of the main problems facing the new country was that it owed a lot of money to creditors, both foreign and domestic, who had provided needed loans to the war effort. There also was the issue of the now worthless paper money left over from the days of the Articles of Confederation.

Hamilton firmly believed that the new government needed the support of the wealthy and powerful, and to get them invested in the long-term success of the government required them being convinced that the government's success was theirs, as well. In other words, the rich and powerful would only support the government if they were convinced that they would personally benefit. To that end, Hamilton wanted the government to assume as much credit liability as possible. If the government failed, then no one would get their money back. In other words, no one would benefit from a bankrupted government. In addition to paying off the government's war debts, he also saw that the states' Revolutionary debts be "assumed" (taken over by the federal government). Many people now had a big stake in seeing that this young government flourished.

Hamilton also proposed that the federal government would create a national bank. It would be managed at the federal level, but much of its funds would come from private investors. This reflects his desire, as with the war debts, to have wealthy people properly invested in the country's future. The bank would extend loans to businesses, provide a safe place for federal funds, and enable the government to more effectively collect and deposit taxes and facilitate expenditures. Last but not least, Hamilton's methods would provide financial stability for the nation's infant banking system.

For the government to begin paying off its new-found debt, it had to have the necessary funds. Some of the money would come from public land sales, but this was not sufficient to meet all financial obligations. One form of revenue was a tax (tariff) placed on imports, which Hamilton saw as not only a way to raise revenue but also to protect domestic industries from foreign competition. The other tax was an internal tax on alcoholic beverages that would be most strongly felt by backcountry distillers and small farmers who converted much of their corn and rye into whiskey. Part of his justification for this tax was that he wanted to ensure that all citizens, however far removed from the urban centers, felt the weight of the new national government. In 1794, some western Pennsylvania farmers rebelled against this hated internal tax, and in response the government raised nearly 15,000 militia troops and quickly disbursed the uprising. It would be known as the Whiskey Rebellion. The show of force was essential as President Washington declared because, "we had given no testimony to the world of being able or willing to support our government and laws."

A Nation Turns Outward: U.S. Foreign Affairs

While putting down an internal domestic rebellion that did not prove to be a great difficulty for Washington and company, foreign relations tended to be slightly more challenging. Both Great Britain and Spain maintained positions on the borderlands of the United States. There, they traded and plotted with the Indians, who still occupied huge areas just across from the Appalachian Mountains. From its base in Canada, Britain encouraged the Indians to join forces and resist American encroachments. In the South, Spain, which held the Florida's, New Orleans, and the Louisiana territory, refused to recognize American boundaries. It controlled navigation down the Mississippi River, and offered protection to the Creek and Cherokee Indians of the Southwest. Much of the diplomacy of the early Republic was devoted to the removal of these barriers to western expansion.

In 1790–1791, Indians inflicted several defeats on American soldiers, mostly militia, in the area along the present boundary between Ohio and Indiana. The worst came in November 1791 with the annihilation of troops under the command of the Northwest Territorial governor, which gave the Federalists the opportunity to overhaul the War Department and to create a regular standing army. With a reorganized professional army, General Anthony Wayne, in 1794, smashed the Indians at the Battle of Fallen Timbers, near present-day Toledo, Ohio. In the Treaty of Greenville in 1795, the Indians ceded much of the Ohio territory to the United States. This, in turn, would put pressure on Britain to evacuate most of its posts in the same area that they had occupied since the Revolution.

By 1794, tensions were running high between the United States and Great Britain. The British continued to hold onto their posts in the Ohio Valley area, and the British Navy was harassing U.S. merchant ships. The French had initiated their own revolution in 1789, which eventually engulfed many European nations in war, since many had come to oppose the republican sentiments exercised by the French. The new revolutionary government believed that this new experiment in republican government would ultimately succeed only if oppressed peoples throughout Europe were freed from their tyrannous monarchs. This was a frightening prospect even for the British, for while it had secured a limited monarchy in the late seventeenth century, the French Revolution was too earth-shattering for their liking.

John Jay (1745–1829), first Chief Justice of U.S. Supreme Court (1789–1795), engraving 1859

Everett Historical/Shutterstock.com

As tensions escalated between France and Great Britain, the British Navy began to harass U.S. merchant ships as they traversed the Atlantic. British actions not only strained relations between the two countries, but it also elevated tensions between the Federalists and the Republicans (formally known as the Antifederalists). The Federalists made strong attempts to overcome the natural sympathy most Americans had for France—their former ally in the Revolutionary War and now a sister republic. However, to the Federalists, Britain seemed to be a bastion of stability in the midst of worldwide chaos. While Republicans called for stiff commercial retaliation against Britain for its seizing of American ships and occupation of posts in the Northwest, the Federalists hoped to halt war with Britain through negotiation. In the spring of 1794, Washington appointed John Jay, chief justice of the Supreme Court, to be a special minister to Great Britain.

The treaty that Jay negotiated with Britain in 1794 demonstrated both the Federalists' fears of France and their reliance on the former mother country. Britain agreed to evacuate the Northwest posts and to open parts of its empire to American commerce, especially ports in the West Indies. The United States agreed to grant Britain more favorable trade conditions than it gave to any other nation. In doing so, the United States could no longer discriminate against British shipping that was the one great weapon that the Republicans were counting on to weaken the imperial power's hold on American commerce.

The treaty shocked and angered the Republicans. They pointed out that the treaty would benefit the merchant class while taxing everyone to pay for it, and Jay was even burned in effigy. However, hostility against the treaty soon abated upon news of Wayne's victory at Fallen Timbers and with the British agreeing to evacuate their northwestern outposts.

Good news also came in the form of another treaty negotiated by the envoy to Spain, Thomas Pinckney. Known as Pinckney's Treaty, it opened the Mississippi River to U.S. navigation and permitted Americans to store goods duty-free in New Orleans. It also set the boundary between the United States and Florida at the 31st parallel. The treaty was also a sign of Spanish weakness. Seeing the United States makes peace with Great Britain, and fearful of an Anglo-American alliance, Spain resigned itself to the possibility of increased American encroachment across the river and sought peace with the young country.

All three episodes, the victory over the Indians at Fallen Timbers, and the Jay and Pinckney treaties, made U.S. westward and southern expansion a reality. Consequently, western land prices were on the rise and the export trade blossomed. While some Republicans remained obstinate in their opposition to these Federalist victories, a majority of Americans were optimistic about the future.

Despite these Federalist victories, George Washington had grown tired and frustrated with all the political infighting. In 1796, longing for a return to his beloved plantation at Mount Vernon, New York, Washington decided against seeking a third presidential term. His decision would set a precedent for all future chief executives until Franklin Roosevelt's third term election in 1940. In leaving, he penned what has become known as his Farewell Address. His frustration centered on the bickering that had engulfed the country, especially in his second term. In his view, scoring political points against one's rivals had taken precedent over doing what was best for the country. He also warned against establishing permanent foreign alliances that he believed could easily lead to war. America would be much better off remaining neutral, he urged. This isolationism basically became the foreign policy position that subsequent administrations would pursue for the next century or so.

The Federalists Remain in Control: The John Adams Administration, 1797–1800

With the strong hand of Alexander Hamilton guiding the party, the Federalists advanced forward Washington's vice president John Adams as its choice for president in the election of 1796. The Democratic Republicans (former Republicans) supported former

Secretary of State Thomas Jefferson. The voting of the Electoral College was close with Adams winning only by three electoral votes (71-68). Under the constitutional rule then in place, Jefferson, who had the second highest number of votes, became vice-president.

The Federalist government's pro-British policies as expressed in jay's Treaty now drove the French into a series of attacks on American shipping; they even refused to trade with the United States until the new American connection with Britain was broken. President Adams dealt with the crisis in 1797 by sending a special mission to France. The French government, using agents whom they designated as X, Y, and Z, tried to extort a payment from the American diplomats as a precondition for negotiations.

Alien and Sedition Acts of 1798

Enraged by French action, Adams declared that the two countries were in a state of Quasi-War, but refused to ask Congress to make it official. However, he did lend his support to Congress' passage of acts in 1798 aimed at silencing Republican opponents who were ardent supporters of the French. Many leading Jeffersonian newspaper editors were foreign born, and the Federalists now enacted a new Naturalization Act. It increased the period of residency required for citizenship from 5 to 14 years, and those who failed to meet the requirement faced the threat of deportation. A companion Alien Act gave the president the authority to deport any noncitizen deemed a threat to public safety. It also enabled the government to arrest and imprison any person from a country involved in war against America. The Sedition Act was intended to prevent an internal insurrection. It barred "malicious writing" that attacked the reputation of any government official. The law was so loosely written that it could be applied to almost anyone.

The Democratic Republicans attacked the Alien and Sedition Acts as despotic and unconstitutional. In their view, these laws violated both the First Amendment's protection of free speech and the 10th Amendment's limitation of federal power. In 1798, Jefferson secretly drafted a series of resolutions, which the Kentucky legislature adopted. That same year James Madison framed a similar set for Virginia. Taken together, these came to be known as the Kentucky and Virginia Resolutions. These resolutions proclaimed the right of their states to judge for themselves the constitutionality of federal acts. In other words, the state had the right to decide whether or not to abide by a federal law. While this sounds simple enough, the underlying issue was difficult and rather complex. The Constitution had not clearly spelled out how a law might be declared unconstitutional. The Kentucky and Virginia Resolutions suggested one method, but it could produce the awkward result that some federal laws might be enforced only in parts of the country. Some people suggested

Everett Historical/Shutterstock.com

as an alternative that the Supreme Court might rule upon a law's constitutionality, which was a position that the court would later adopt.

The Country Resets: The Election of 1800

The Federalists had occupied the executive branch since 1789. The party was not unified with the idea of the renomination of John Adams, but seeing no good alternative, Adams became their candidate. The Democrats, as they now increasingly called themselves, had come close to winning with Jefferson in 1796 and decided to go with the gentleman from Virginia once again.

It was a dirty campaign. The tensions over foreign affairs, including the Alien and Sedition Acts, poisoned the political atmosphere. Federalists were suspicious about how the Democrats railed against elite and moneyed interests, and the Democrats were fearful that the Federalists were too willing to sacrifice individual freedoms. Jefferson himself became a topic of disagreement. He expressed belief in God but discussed the subject in ways that made some conservative believers uncomfortable. Writing to his nephew in 1787 he said, "Question with boldness even the existence of a god; because, if there be one, he must more approve the homage of reason, than that of blindfolded fear." Federalist newspapers raised questions about Jefferson's relationship with his slave Sally Hemings, who was three-fourths white and his deceased wife's half-sister. Jefferson denied the allegations, but more recent genetic testing suggests that Jefferson might well have fathered Hemings's children.

As was the case with Adams and Jefferson in the 1796 election, the original Constitution authorized the Electoral College to vote for two names for President. The person who garnered the most votes became president and the person with the second highest votes became vice president. In this election, both Jefferson and Burr received the same number of votes, which threw the election into the House of Representatives. The Federalists were more inclined to support Burr while the Democratic Republicans backed Jefferson. In fact, no one achieved a majority of votes until the 36 ballot when Alexander Hamilton intervened in the process in favor of Jefferson. Burr never forgave Hamilton for the slight, and in four years, the two would meet face to face in a duel in which Hamilton was mortally wounded. To prevent a similar problem with the Electoral College, the country adopted the 12th Amendment to the Constitution, which allowed the electors to designate their presidential and vice-presidential choices separately in their ballots.

Conclusion

The young country of the United States of America had emerged from its war of independence from Great Britain confident that bright days were ahead. The manner in which it made the necessary compromises to that end spoke volumes of its leaders' level of dedication and commitment. However, there were signs of trouble that some could not help but take notice. As he exited the political scene to return to farming, Washington worried that government guided by those who truly served the public interest could easily devolve into a state of winner take-all politics. In fact, upon his retirement he stated, "The alternate domination of one faction over another, sharpened by the spirit of revenge, natural to party dissension, which in different ages and countries has perpetrated the most horrid enormities, is itself a frightful despotism." The 1790s witnessed a steady escalation of suspicion and distrust among those pledged to serve the people. However, all was not bleak. While Americans were divided over many issues, there was a sense that as the nation grew, it could, under the right leadership, meet the challenges before it. In fact, the next presidential contest, often referred to as the Revolution of 1800, would demonstrate that the country could withstand bitter political factionalism and merge back onto the American road imagined by its revolutionary generation.

CHAPTER FIVE

Jefferson's America, 1801–1829

Chapter 5: Key Concepts

- What is your evaluation of Thomas Jefferson as a president during this period?

- What is your assessment of the chief legacy of the War of 1812?

- How would you evaluate the relationship between White Americans and Native Americans during this period?

From the days of the Constitutional Convention to the beginning of a new century, the country was guided by a Federalist vision of a strong central government presided over by a traditional, gentlemanly elite. However, by 1800, it was becoming clear that a different view was gaining momentum. American life was changing and the Federalists seemed a little out of touch. When Jefferson took the oath of office, hogs ran through the streets of the new city of Washington, but the new president seemed little concerned about that or the many unfinished government buildings. To him and many like-minded Democratic-Republicans, the unrefined and unfinished nature of the new capitol city suited the proper roles of national government: to be small in size and modest in its guardianship of the people. Over the next three decades, wide constituencies of Americans continued to believe that they could escape the dangerous tendencies of growth and rapid pace of development that led to war and internal corruption. Public discussion and local political policymaking reflected Americans' yearnings for a republican citizenry. However, expansion into new frontiers, the growing use of national government to create opportunities and divide resources, and continuing international controversies all threatened to erase the republican ideals that framed American political culture.

Enter Thomas Jefferson

Thomas Jefferson took the oath of office on March 4, 1801. At the time, the U.S. Capitol building in the new capital city of Washington, D.C. was unfinished. While the country had been torn by political factionalism, the very thing that George Washington warned against in his Farewell Address, Jefferson stated that, "We are all Federalists, we are all Republicans." While Jefferson may have sincerely believed that his vision of America was one in which all would unite, his policies and personal preferences were such that many Federalists found them problematic.

Stocksnapper/Shutterstock.com

Thomas Jefferson, President and one of the founding fathers of United States

Believing that most of the evils afflicting humanity in the past had flowed from the abuses of the political establishment, the Republicans in 1800 deliberately set about to carry out what they believed was the original aim of the Revolution: to reduce the dangerous power of government. They envisioned a central government whose authority would resemble that of the old Articles of Confederation more than the powerful type of government the Federalists desired. Washington and Adams, like the English monarchs, had personally delivered their addresses to the legislature "from the throne," but Jefferson chose to submit his in writing. He made himself easily accessible to visitors. However, his preference for proper decorum was quite unconventional. Once, when Jefferson first received the British ambassador to the United States at the White House, the president wore only a bathrobe. Reflecting on the incident, the ambassador stated that Jefferson had received him, "with a most perfect disregard to ceremony both in his dress and manner."

Jefferson, however "low brow" his bathrobe incident may have been, was a man with a cosmopolitan flair.He loved to entertain, and his dinner parties became quite famous. Jefferson liked to serve fine food and French wine. In fact, many bottles of wine bought today include Jefferson's famous quote: "Good wine is a necessity of life for me." He even served ice cream after dinner, which was then a novelty in the United States. Guests included members of his cabinet, congressmen, diplomats, and visiting dignitaries. Conversation could turn to almost any subject since Jefferson's interests included politics, philosophy, agricultural experiments, exotic languages, the violin, architecture, horticulture, literature, and many other things.

Political Changes

While the Federalist government that Jefferson inherited was minuscule by today's standards, he believed that the federal bureaucracy had become "too complicated, too expensive," and offices under the Federalists had "unnecessarily multiplied." Thus, the Democratic-Republicans reduced the number of government officials. All tax inspectors and collectors were eliminated. The Federalist dream of creating a modern army and navy like those of Europe disappeared. The military budget itself was cut in half. The army, stationed in the West, was left with 3,000 regulars and only 172 officers. The navy consisted of only a half-dozen frigates and a few gunboats that helped to deal with pirates in the Mediterranean Sea. The benefits of a robust standing military force, Jefferson believed, was not worth the cost either in money or in the threat to liberty that this kind of establishment posed.

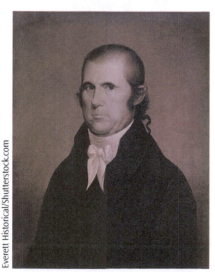

John Marshall (1755–1835), the Chief Justice of the United States

Although Jefferson maintained the Bank of the United States, its influence was diminished. State and local banks resented the privileged and restraining authority of the National Bank. By 1811, the federal government had diluted the bank's powers to control either the society or the economy. Most of its money had been distributed among 21 state banks. In addition, the proliferation of state-chartered banks allowed them to issue their own paper money. This occurred despite the Constitution's prohibition against the states' issuing bills of credit.

The federal debt was also a major focal point of Jefferson's attention. Alexander Hamilton and the Federalists regarded the permanent federal debt as a principal source of support for the government. If the government owed people money, then people had a personal stake in making sure that the government succeeded. However, the Democratic-Republicans took the position that an indebted government burdened future generations and allowed it to have too much influence. Their aim was to create a new kind of government, one that was diminished in power and scope. In many ways the changes initiated by the election of 1800 were revolutionary. During the opening three decades of the nineteenth century, particularly after Jefferson retired from the presidency, the U.S. government was weaker than at any other time in its history.

Changes in the interpretation of law also occurred during the Jefferson administration. Before he left office, John Adams made several moves to assure Federalist power and weaken the incoming Republican government. In one of them, Adams appointed ardent Federalist William Marbury as Justice of the Peace of the District of Columbia. New Secretary of State, and Republican, James Madison refused to carry out the appointment once Jefferson became president. As a result, Marbury appealed to the Supreme Court in order to receive his position. Chief Justice John Marshall authored the majority opinion in the case that has become known as Marbury v. Madison. In the decision, the Supreme Court ruled against Marbury, but most importantly, they established the supremacy of the judicial system to review laws and test them against the Constitution. In other words, Marshall believed that the Supreme Court could make judicial rulings on if laws violated the Constitution. Therefore, the judiciary, alongside the legislative and executive branches, became solidified as an equal part of the federal government's power structure. Marbury v. Madison is one of the most important Supreme Court decisions in History, and the precedent of judicial review has since become an accepted part of the practice of law. Marshall was instrumental in creating a strong Supreme Court.

"Go West Young Man"

While Hamilton and the Federalists had looked eastward across the Atlantic to Europe for their image of the destiny of the United States, the Republicans fixed their eyes on the vast lands in the West. Only by moving westward, Jefferson believed, could Americans maintain their republican society of independent yeoman-farmers and avoid the miseries of the concentrated urban working classes of Europe. Jefferson was indeed the most expansion-minded president in American history. He dreamed of Americans with republican principles eventually swarming over the continent and creating an "empire of liberty." But, even Jefferson did not anticipate how suddenly Americans would take the road to the West. The population grew from almost 4 million in 1790 to more than 7 million in 1810 and nearly 10 million by 1820, with most people moving west. By the 1790s, the population in some of the tidewater counties of Virginia was declining. The population advancement over portions of the Appalachian Mountains had been a trickle before the American Revolution, but after 1800, it became a flood.

Happenings in Europe ultimately helped to spur American settlement beyond the Mississippi. Napoleon Bonaparte was a very successful and aggressive Emperor of France. Secretly, he negotiated the transfer of the Louisiana Territory from the crumbling colonial

Napoleon Bonaparte

holdings of Spain to France. Bonaparte's control of Louisiana worried Jefferson and other Americans. This is especially true after Bonaparte vowed that America would have no access to the port at New Orleans. It was the busiest port in the country and vitally important for shipping goods to the heartland of the nation. Naturally an admirer of all things French, Jefferson wondered if he would have to change his allegiance. "The day that France takes possession of New Orleans," Jefferson wrote, Americans would have to "marry ourselves to the British fleet and nation." In other words, Jefferson could envision a future when Americans had to align with the British in order to counteract the French threat.

The situation was not as dire as it must have seemed. As it turned out, the French under Bonaparte were not committed to having long-term plans for the Louisiana Territory. Several factors led the French to take this position. In their colony of Haiti, slaves rebelled under the leadership of Toussaint Louverture. The colony was almost completely composed of slaves from Africa. In the uprising, slaves killed almost all of the white Haitians or forced them to leave. A French army failed to contain the rebellion, and the rebels won and held the island nation. This and other considerations distracted Bonaparte away from Louisiana. The French emperor, above all, was focused on defeating Britain and her allies in a war that was certain to come in Europe. Generally, the French looked toward Europe and not westward at the Americas. The Haitian Revolution was a distraction to Bonaparte that he did not want to repeat in Louisiana. After all, the British navy was likely to harass the French in North America and limit their dominance of the colony. Thus, Napoleon decided that Louisiana was more of a nuisance than an asset.

Jefferson sensed that New Orleans, at least, could be had at the right price. Between 1801 and 1803 America's Foreign Minister to France, Robert Livingston, worked to secure a deal for America to gain Louisiana. Jefferson also sent James Monroe to assist Livingston in the middle of 1803. The main concern was to gain access to the port of New Orleans. Perhaps the French would sell the city or allow Americans free use of it, Jefferson hoped. To the surprise of everyone, the French government inquired if America would be interested in the whole of Louisiana. Livingston, Monroe, and Jefferson had reason to be shocked. Louisiana, stretching from the Gulf of Mexico to Canada, was larger than the former English colonies that then composed the country. Not authorized to make such a gigantic deal, Livingston and Monroe at first wondered whether to proceed with negotiations. In a time before easy communication, there was little means to ask Jefferson for his approval. They decided that it was best to act independently and consider a deal for all of Louisiana.

In April 1803, the American and French diplomats settled on a price for the Louisiana territory. In the end, America bought Louisiana for $15 million with the caveat that Catholics there would be granted citizenship. For the time, and now of course, this was not a cheap price. Yet, when one considers the number compared to the land gained, it was one of History's great bargains. The Louisiana Purchase was at once great news to Americans while instigating criticism of Jefferson and his party. It had no precedent in American History. Some, including Jefferson himself, wondered if it was constitutional. The masses did not care that much. To the average person, the acquisition of a vast land meant opportunity. People wondered about the potential of Louisiana. Some scoffed that it would not be of much use to Americans. Still, Louisiana offered potential and wonder to a new nation restless for land. After some debate, the Senate approved the treaty to add Louisiana to the country's holdings.

Jefferson had already approved a plan to explore the West of the North American continent before the purchase of Louisiana. Though not exactly legal, it was not surprising considering the temperament and outlook of Jefferson. A child of the Enlightenment, Jefferson had a natural curiosity about all things. He thought it advantageous to gain knowledge of all lands. The president wondered about the wildlife, the scenery, plant life, and everything about the natural world beyond the Mississippi. In a practical sense, Jefferson thought about potential trading opportunities with other nations. After the addition of Louisiana, Jefferson had even more reason to explore western lands.

Jefferson commissioned the creation of a group who would explore Louisiana on behalf of the American government. The small band would be officially known as the Corps of Discovery. Army captain Meriwether Lewis was selected as the leader with William Clarke the second in command. Lewis was thought to be capable with some scientific knowledge and familiarity with Native Americans. Clarke, though not a scientist, studied at Jefferson's vast library before the trip. To the president, the Lewis and Clarke Expedition had both scientific and practical goals. The explorers were to catalogue plants and animals while cultivating relationships with different Native American groups. There were 29 people among the company led by Lewis and Clarke. Among them was a female Native American guide named Sacagawea and Clarke's slave, York.

Meriwether Lewis (1774–1809), co-leader of the Lewis and Clark Expedition

In May 1804, Lewis and Clarke departed westward from St. Louis. It was an exciting and dangerous time. Western territories were not entirely unknown. Other Europeans had written about their encounters with the people and natural life that existed there. It was the hope of Jefferson to establish friendly relationships with the Native Americans. He even had coins minted, with his likeness, to offer Natives both as a gesture of good will and to symbolize they now lived under the authority of America. On a number of occasions, the company faced starvation or the threat of war with Native Americans. This was especially true of the Sioux, who Clarke described as the fiercest of nations that he encountered on the trip. In November 1805, the expedition reached the Pacific Ocean. Lewis and Clarke returned to St. Louis in late 1806.

Aaron Burr, ca. 1810

The Lewis and Clarke explorations led to many positive outcomes while predicting potential problems associated with western settlement. It was discovered that the Great Plains were teeming with wildlife. However, as was hoped, no continuous waterway was found that led to the Pacific Ocean. They created hundreds of maps that offered the beginnings of understanding the geography of the West. Lewis and Clarke documented many new unknown species of plants and animals. Some feared that the Corps of Discovery would find a barren or unusable land—but this was not the case. In all their encounters with natives, Jefferson hoped that Lewis and Clarke would begin a friendly coexistence between them and the white settlers who would eventually come to settle Louisiana. However, the journals of Lewis and Clarke are filled with instances of miscommunication and frustration between Native Americans and the expedition. Natives did not recognize them as the first wave of what would become an overwhelming number of white settlers. In addition, most of them did not consider Jefferson's government to hold any sort of dominion over their present and future existence. In the coming years, conflict in the western lands between those who had lived there and the newcomers would only increase. Most American Indians did not hold the same concept of land ownership as did those of European descent. Even when there were good intentions on both sides, violence often occurred in the West.

Aaron Burr

Americans were emboldened to explore the opportunities represented by the Louisiana Purchase. This was especially true after the publication of the journals of Lewis and Clarke. Since the spread of their published account, Lewis and Clarke have been lionized as great heroes of the early republic period. For former Vice-President Aaron Burr, Louisiana was only the beginning of American expansion. Burr was fascinated by the new nation gaining new lands. He believed that people who lived in Spanish-held lands in the West were eager to break free and form an independent republic. Some believe that Burr's intention was to create an empire in the West separate from America. By 1806, he had assembled thousands of men—though what they were supposed to do is not certain. James Wilkinson of the U.S. Army at first conspired with Burr but ultimately turned him into the government. Jefferson considered these actions as treasonous and ordered Burr's arrest. By this time, the would-be revolutionary had become an enemy of his own party. Jefferson was committed to making sure that Burr was convicted. The Supreme Court found no evidence to convict Burr, and he was released. Chief Justice Marshall argued that no actual incidents of treason had taken place and talking about doing something did not constitute a real offense.

This was not the first time that Burr blurred the law for his own interests. He was nothing else if not a man committed to increasing his political power through any means. In 1804, Burr ran for the governorship of New York. Secretly and separately, both Jefferson and Hamilton worked to ensure his defeat. Hamilton was especially strident in his opposition to Burr. Though not a supporter of Jefferson or the Republicans, Hamilton had a unique dislike of Burr. Hearing that Hamilton had personally insulted him, Burr challenged him to a duel. Usually, two men worked out their differences before an armed fight actually took place, but this was not the case this time. In July 1804, Burr and Hamilton met in New Jersey to complete the duel. As a result, Hamilton was shot by Burr and then died. Both New York and New Jersey issued warrants for Burr's arrest. Americans were outraged by the death of one of their founding heroes in Hamilton. Yet again, Burr escaped punishment for his actions. Though, he was politically ruined and never achieved the kind of power and influence he desired.

Trouble Brewing with Europe

Despite Burr, and a few critics of the constitutionality of the Louisiana Purchase, Jefferson's popularity was on the rise during his first term. The Louisiana Purchase challenged Jefferson's well-known preference for a strict interpretation of the Constitution. Yet, here, and in many cases, the president was willing to forego this standard and amend his views. No doubt, people viewed his first term as successful mostly due to the Louisiana Territory. In 1804, Jefferson easily won another four years in office as president.

Jefferson entered office with the intention of continuing the practice of American non-involvement in foreign affairs, but Europe increasingly tested the legitimacy of isolationism. As a true believer in Enlightenment philosophy and a founding father, Jefferson envisioned a prosperous America without the wars and alliances that had long entangled Europe in warfare. With Jefferson, there was always a tension between his idealist vision and the practical matter of running the country. However, there were brewing issues in Europe that the government could not ignore. In the early century, imperial France embroiled the European continent in war. Principally, the major contest was between the interests of Britain and France. For Jefferson, France was always the preferred ally, but Britain's naval power and industrial strength far surpassed that of America. Thus, there were reasons to be friendly with both nations. Both England and France forbade Americans to trade with their enemy combatant. It seemed that Jefferson might have to choose between the two.

Both England and France violated the neutrality of American shipping. Though, England presented the most direct threat. Basically, the British could board and take whatever they wanted from American ships in the Atlantic. They often did so, even close to the eastern American coast. The British sometimes claimed that the Americans had recruited deserters from their navy and took these sailors back by force. The French, as well, targeted American ships bound for Britain. There was little Jefferson could do, as he and others complained but had little means to stop any of these practices. During Jefferson's second term, the French were the masters of the European mainland, while Britain dominated the Atlantic.

Jefferson compounded the problem while seeking a way out of the situation. After several incidents of attacks on his nation's people abroad, Jefferson told seafarers they could not enter foreign ports without his express permission. Basically, Jefferson ended the practice of trading with Europe. In effect, the government had entered into a self-imposed embargo with its two most important trading partners. Some wealthier American businessmen could find ways to smuggle goods to and from Europe. However, most people who engaged in trading suffered. Farmers also were dismayed, because they depended on goods made by the British and French. Most were united against the Jefferson Embargo. The president hoped it would remove the problem that threatened to draw the new nation into a war. Yet, it was shortsighted and disastrous. The embargo resulted in a depression until it was repealed.

The embargo was the worst decision of Jefferson's tenure as president and represented the shortcomings of his national vision. Historians consider his second term as not nearly as successful as the first. The act also demonstrated that the president did not have a full understanding or appreciation for the priorities of northeastern merchants. Here, the Federalist presence was strong. These were people committed to creating and sustaining trade networks with Europeans. They were the merchants who already did not trust Jefferson. Even Jefferson's beloved agrarians could not live under the conditions of the embargo. As it turned out, America was not yet strong enough to go its own way without the help of the major European powers. Also, the dream of a nation of small farmers could not wholly exist unless business coincided alongside it.

The world was changing, and during and after the Jefferson administration, Americans searched for solutions. It was not only Europeans who took advantage of American weakness on the high seas. States along the Barbary Coast of northern Africa engaged in piracy of American ships. Among these semi-independent states were Algiers, Tripoli, Tunis, and Morocco. This began to be a problem soon after the end of the Revolution, but for a while, the French protected American sailors. This ended, however, and Americans had little means to protect themselves and their cargoes. Many sailors were held hostage while both the governments of John Adams and then Jefferson negotiated for terms. In short, pirates wanted ransom payments in return for the safety of American citizens. A small-scale war resulted. Colonel William Eaton, a few marines, and few hundred mercenaries marched across the desert to capture the city of Derna in Tripoli. It worked and was forever memorialized in the marine battle-hymn: "from the shores of Tripoli. . . " The First Barbary War did not eliminate piracy but did show that Americans could successfully defend their interests abroad.

Enter James Madison

As Jefferson left office, many problems remained for the next administration. For one, Republicans were internally divided on the question of who would become their next presidential candidate. Eventually, they chose James Madison who won the election of 1808. The Republicans had swept into office in "the Revolution of 1800" with promises to restore the country to the true intentions of the founding fathers. Yet, the last few years had been controversial with a slow economy. Some opposed Madison only because he was Jefferson's handpicked protégé. In the years to come, the Republicans would have to adjust to meet the demands of world politics.

One pressing problem Madison faced was the issue of impressment. British law authorized seizing American citizens, called impressing them, into military service during a time of crisis. Certainly, there was something of a crisis in Britain, as they faced the huge armies of Napoleon in the competition for European dominance. The problem was that when the British encountered American merchant ships, they often forced American civilians into their service. They often claimed that these men were deserters from the British navy, and this was sometimes the case. However, some who were impressed were Englishmen who had immigrated to the former colonies

James Madison (1751–1836), U.S. President (1809–1817)

of North America. In sum, it was hard for the British to tell the difference between those who could be impressed and ordinary American citizens. They often did not care, anyway. This outraged most Americans, as they had fought a war to be out from being under their former colonial masters. In 1807, near the coast of Virginia, the British ship *Leopard* demanded to search the American frigate, *Chesapeake*. When the Americans refused, the *Leopard* fired and killed three Americans. People were angry—especially since the incident was so close to home. It appeared that the British insisted on making another war on America.

The new president did not intend to ignore Britain and France's blatant mistreatment of Americans. Madison's goals were to augment his predecessor's policies, avoid war, and protect his country's interests through diplomatic means. Through different measures, Madison attempted to reestablish trade with Europe without including Britain and France until they discontinued practices like impressment. One bill, passed in 1810, once again allowed trade with the two major European powers but threatened to stop if the rights of American sailors were not respected. None of these types of policies were effective, however. In June 1812, Madison finally asked Congress for a declaration of war against Great Britain. If America truly wanted to be independent, it seemed war was the only option left.

The possibility of war and the reality of it between Britain and France caused political arguments between the Federalists and Republicans. The party of Jefferson was known for a fondness for France and its culture. Even after the bloody French Revolution, many Republicans believed in the lofty, Enlightenment-inspired ideas of the early revolutionaries. Federalists were more associated with the conservatism and business-oriented British. The Federalists, especially those in New England, admired British strength and hoped to build an American society based on their model. Republicans, on the other hand, were suspicious of the British who they still thought of as tyrants. The drive toward war alienated and angered most Federalists. For one, northeastern merchants realized that a war would disrupt their trading as much or more than British policies. They also hoped to emulate the British and not become their permanent enemy. Despite the protests of the majority of Federalists, America prepped for war.

The War of 1812

Aside from practical economic concerns, the War of 1812 was also about upholding American honor. If the Revolution established legal independence, the second war with Britain was about seeking practical freedom and membership into the community of free, autonomous nations of the western world. Cleary, Britain did not recognize America as the latter. Many, it seemed, thought that their former colonies could be manipulated back into the ranks of the empire. In fact, the British hoped to encourage Native Americans to attack frontier settlements in order to stir internal wars. Doing so might allow the British to swoop in and reestablish themselves in North America. Aware of what the British were doing, this only contributed to the sense that American honor was at stake.

During the War of 1812, the principal region of contestation between Native Americans and white settlers was the Northwest Territory. This was the region composed, roughly, of the present-day Midwestern states. Years before 1812, the roots of a conflict were sewn that later took place as part of the war with the British. Tenskwatawa was a Native American holy figure who began to see visions and make predictions condemning white Americans while calling them "evil spirits." He gathered a large following, and the group included members of several different tribes. Tenskwatawa preached that native peoples should abandon white culture and return to purely traditional ways. His prophetic declarations often seemed to come true—making him a powerful cultural figure within Native American communities. Soon, a war erupted that was then absorbed into the War of 1812.

Tenskwatawa's more famous brother, Tecumseh, led the military arm of the movement to fight back against white encroachment on Native American culture and lands. In 1809, Governor William Henry Harrison of the Indiana territory negotiated a sale of American-Indian lands to the government known as the Treaty of Fort Wayne. A number of different tribes agreed to the deal, but Tecumseh was not happy. He tried to create a pan-Native American movement whereby no tribe could sell to whites without the agreement of all of them. Tecumseh was a persuasive and fearless leader, and he traveled all over the country convincing Native Americans to join his faction. He was oftentimes unsuccessful. However, Tecumseh and his followers did help instigate "Tecumseh's War" in 1811. Historians often denote that this war ended in November with the Battle of Tippecanoe in Kentucky. At this battle, Harrison led an army on behalf of the government and defeated Tecumseh. However, Tecumseh continued to fight for his vision in Canada until his death in 1813. Others continued his legacy during the War of 1812—most notably the "Red Sticks" of the Creek Nation.

The future of Native Americans was but one of several issues at hand during the War of 1812. Many Americans feared a general Native American uprising. It could result in an independent confederacy of nations within the interior of the country. The British, most assumed, would certainly support a movement with any possible method. Americans also reckoned that the British might try to reclaim other lands lost due to the Revolution. On the other hand, the British wanted to ensure that the Americans did not try to seize any of their holdings in Canada. The war would be fought on the seas, in Canada, along the eastern coast, in the Northwest Territory, and in the South.

America was unprepared for war and the British were stretched too thin to devote too many resources to fighting overseas. The British had a few thousand soldiers in Canada. For the empire, the most important concern was defending itself against France in the Napoleonic Wars. These series of battles consumed most of Europe. The vaunted British navy, at least most of it, was being used to blockade mainland Europe. As they did during the Revolution, America lacked much of a regular army and pinned its hoped, initially, on militias. The Republican Congress took steps to create a larger navy, but Americans were mostly dependent on privateer sailors who were not officially apart of the military. For the most part, the American military was poorly led and organized.

Americans hoped that their superiority of numbers could lead to the occupation of British Canada. American General William Hull meant to lead a force toward Canada in 1812 but instead returned to his base in Detroit. There, a British army surrounded and captured the Americans without any actual combat taking place. Other campaigns that aimed at Canada failed in 1812. In general, militiamen were often uncooperative and reluctant to follow orders. Though, the Americans found an early success, in one of the most well-known battles of the War of 1812, on Lake Erie in September, 1812. Commandant Oliver Hazard Perry's American navy defeated their counterpart led by Britain's Robert Barclay. After the battle, Perry famously messaged William Henry Harrison that "we have met the enemy, and they are ours." The victory assured that Lake Erie would be secured for the American side. Yet, hopes of taking Canada were far-fetched and never likely to happen. As it turned out, British Canadians mostly saw Americans as an enemy instead of a friend.

The War of 1812, British forces burning Washington, D.C

Everett Historical/Shutterstock.com

In August 1814, the British escalated their war effort. In Europe, Napoleon had been forced to leave his throne thus temporarily ceasing war. As a result, a few thousand hardened British veterans of the Napoleonic Wars were transferred to North America. The experienced British regulars easily defeated American forces in Maryland and set their sights on

Washington, D.C. From a British perspective, the enemy capitol was basically defenseless and could be easily taken. On August 24, the British set fire to much of the city. Among several buildings, the White House and Capitol Building were destroyed. The Library of Congress and the halls of Congress were burned. The British looted and did whatever they wanted until a storm forced them out of the city. In all, Washington D.C. was occupied for a period of about 24 hours.

The next main target of the British was nearby Baltimore, Maryland. The city had a valuable port, and unlike the capitol, was well-fortified and protected. The plan was for a combined land and naval campaign meant to capture and or destroy the city. Most of the fighting took place around Fort McHenry, as the British navy fired their cannons from the sea. The night of September 14 would become the pivotal and most remembered part of the Battle of Baltimore. After a furious bombardment during the night, Americans awoke to see their flag still flying on the grounds at Fort McHenry. American Francis Scott Key was inspired to write a song about it that eventually became the national anthem. "That the flag was still there" must have been disheartening to the British. After all, the fort's heavy guns did not have the range to cause much damage to the British, so it seemed likely that McHenry would fall. The British never could coordinate a land attack and decided to leave Baltimore altogether, however. Thus, it appeared that the Americans had won this round.

Enter Andrew Jackson

America enjoyed its greatest success due to Andrew Jackson in the South. Jackson assembled an army composed mostly of militia and allied Native Americans. Many of his actions during the War of 1812 concerned quelling the uprising within the Creek Nation. The Creek War began as an internal conflict between those Native Americans who wanted to obey their tribal councils and the Red Sticks who were inspired by Tecumseh toward a militant posture toward whites. Jackson was summoned to intervene against the Red Sticks in order to prevent a possible larger rebellion among Native Americans. A decisive battle occurred along part of the Tallapoosa River in the Mississippi Territory that was called Horseshoe Bend in March 1814. Jackson led roughly 3,000 men against Chief Menawa's 1,000 members of the Creek Red Sticks. It was an overwhelming victory for the Americans. Most of the rebel Creeks died, though some escaped to fight another day. In August of the same year, the Creeks would be forced to sign the Treaty of Fort Jackson that gave America 23 million acres of land. Most of it would later form the state of Alabama. The Battle of Horseshoe Bend would begin Jackson's rise to national prominence.

After Horseshoe Bend, Jackson turned his attention toward the city of Pensacola in Spanish West Florida. Many of the defeated Creeks sought refuge in the city. In addition, both Spanish and British soldiers were stationed in Pensacola, and generally West Florida had become a safe haven for any groups who desired to resist the authority of the American government. Jackson's army arrived near Pensacola in November of 1814. Without engaging his enemy, Jackson managed to convince the British to retreat without putting up a resistance. The Battle of Pensacola was not much of one, but it was another success for Jackson. He then focused on going to Mobile before a larger crisis forced the Americans elsewhere.

Jackson learned that the British were planning a major invasion of New Orleans. Jackson had a natural dislike of the British that went beyond that of the average American, and he was determined to prevent the British from succeeding. As a man from humble origins, he thought of the British as arrogant and their military officers, especially, as elitist. He once remarked, "I owe to Britain a debt of retaliatory vengeance," and "should our forces meet I trust I shall pay the debt." At the Battle of New Orleans, the Americans were outnumbered. Jackson, though, had increased his numbers through recruiting anyone willing to fight—including French-American Jean Lafitte's small band of pirates. Though arriving on New Year's Day, 1815, the British elected to wait for reinforcements before attacking the Americans. This gave Jackson time to assemble an impressive line of earthwork forti-

fications in order to defend New Orleans. On January 8, 1815, Jackson's army won the most impressive, one-sided victory of the entire war and likely of any to that point in American History. Attacking American fortifications outside the city, the British suffered roughly 2,000 casualties in a matter of minutes while Jackson lost only a few dozen. The Battle of New Orleans was a complete disaster for the British. Jackson, or "Old Hickory" as he was sometimes called, entered New Orleans as a conquering hero to the cheers of an admiring public.

The Battle of New Orleans, January 8, 1815, lithograph by Nathaniel Currier, 1842

Jackson became the most important military figure since George Washington, but as it turned out, the Battle of New Orleans was not necessary to the outcome of the War of 1812. Diplomats from both countries met in Belgium and signed the Treaty of Ghent on December 24, 1814. The agreement ended the War of 1812, gave back all American lands taken by the British, and did little else. The treaty did not address the impressment of American citizens into British service. However, after the defeat of Napoleon, there was little need neither for the impressment of Americans nor even for the British to continue the war. Much like with the Revolutionary War, the British could have kept fighting but chose it better not to do so. It helped that the American navy achieved an important victory at the Battle of Plattsburg on Lake Champlain in September. As a result, the British were forced to abandon their invasion and retreat to Canada. At New Orleans, however, neither side had learned of the treaty and believed the war was not yet settled. In fact, most Americans learned of the Treaty of Ghent and the results of the Battle of New Orleans at about the same time. So, Americans figured that Jackson was the hero who won the war and drove the British back across the Atlantic.

The Era of Good Feelings

Roughly at the same time Jackson was planning the New Orleans Campaign, New England Federalists were meeting to discuss their grievances with the current state of the nation. Federalists convened in Hartford, Connecticut from December 15, 1814 until January 5, 1815. The Federalists talked about New England making a separate peace with the British. During the war, merchants in New England, who were the core of the Federalist Party, saw their trading with Europe practically disappear. They had not wanted war in the first place. Federalists also had long been disgruntled with what they perceived as the Democrat-Republicans moving toward western expansion. They rightly predicted that western expansion would mean the spread of slavery, and in turn Federalist power in Congress would weaken. The party saw the country was moving in a direction that did not favor their interests. Some at the Hartford Convention even considered leaving the country to create an independent republic of New England states. However, historians tend to doubt there was significant momentum for secession. They also proposed that a president could not follow another who was from the same state (owing to the dominance of Virginians in presidential elections.) They also supported a policy that states could overrule congressional laws deemed unconstitutional. Publishing their thoughts, the whole nation learned what these Federalists stood for and believed in.

The Hartford Convention suffered from incredibly bad timing. By the time the Federalists sent representatives to Washington, D.C. in February, news of both the Treaty of Ghent and Battle of New Orleans had reached the country. This left the Hartford Federalists in an awkward and unenviable position. The masses, as usually is the case, were very happy with an administration that had prosecuted a successful war. Federalist proposals seemed at best petty complaining. Americans, especially those in the Southwest, accused members of the Hartford Convention to be treasonous. After the War of 1812, the Federalist Party lost power and ceased to be a force in national politics. Time had passed them by, and the Federalists almost became extinct.

It was partly the demise of the Federalists that sparked the period historians call the Era of Good Feelings. The War of 1812 made Americans feel very good about themselves. From feeling dishonored and unable to fend for itself before the war, America now felt pride and patriotism. After all, the fledgling nation had now twice defeated the powerful British Empire. It had doubled in size due to the Louisiana Purchase. The Democrat-Republicans had won and ruled, though not without internal debate and discord, for many years to come. It was a time of relative peace compared to the years of struggle, war, and political uncertainty. America was on its way toward developing a vast countryside into an international power. In 1816, James Monroe easily was elected to the presidency and served two terms. The Virginian was an ally of both Jefferson and Madison and continued the Democrat-Republican dominance of the White House along with his native state's hold on the office of president. In 1817 and 1819, Monroe made goodwill tours of America where he stirred support from most. Most notably, Monroe went to New England, the home of Federalism, to promote unity between all sections of the nation.

In addition to harmony, Monroe wanted to project American strength to the international community. In the wake of the Napoleonic Wars, the government feared that imperial powers would now turn their attentions to re-establishing colonies in the New World. Monroe was especially leery about the prospects of nations that were committed to monarchy, like Spain, conquering weaker ones in the Western Hemisphere. The Monroe Doctrine stated that the West was closed to future colonial settlement by the world powers. It further offered a threat of American intervention should any nation disregard the

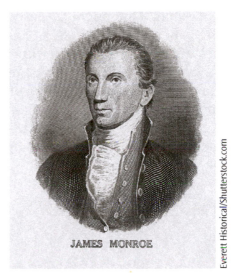

JAMES MONROE

U.S. President James Monroe

edict. Monroe also promised to keep America out of the affairs of Europe. Essentially, the Monroe Doctrine defined the Old and New Worlds as two distinct civilizations that should remain separate. By doing so, the president intimated that the future of the West would be free, democratic governments without Old World authoritarianism. The Monroe Doctrine was offered with the blessing of Britain, as it wanted to ensure it would have an advantage as the world's preeminent empire. It sent a clear message that America was seeking to graduate into the fraternity of influential, powerful nations. The Monroe Doctrine served as the primary diplomatic position of America throughout the nineteenth century, and beyond.

Apart from diplomacy, the Era of Good Feelings was characterized by a comprehensive plan to develop and government the nation known as the American System. Its chief proponent was Kentucky Senator Henry Clay, and it was partly based on Alexander Hamilton's economic policies. In general, the American System was meant to create economic growth while supporting the creation of a more modern country. Those like Clay supported a tariff on imports that would protect the consumption of American-made goods. Not everyone supported the tariff—especially those in the West and South who purchased foreign goods. As part of the system, a national bank would be strengthened and made permanent. In addition, many argued for improvements in internal infrastructure like the building of roads, canals, and bridges. Not everyone approved of the American System, but it became the blueprint for the future of America.

Division on the Rise

One way to view politics during the Era of Good Feelings is the triumph of Jeffersonian ideals. With most people identifying as Republicans, the shadow of Jefferson remained strong all over the country. National politicians often invoked Jefferson as the ideal American statesman. One might say, as well, that the Era was a return to the American preference to avoid political parties. At least, this was the case on the surface. Washington and others, after all, had pleaded with Americans not to follow the European way of competitive, squabbling political factions. Yet, in practical terms it remained a question if the country was moving toward or away from agrarianism, strict constructionism, and limited government. In fact, the American system was not that compatible with any of these principles. Americans continued to debate on these and other issues. Monroe hoped that significant factionalism would not develop, yet it is inevitable that it would be given disagreement about policy.

The Missouri Compromise of 1820. This legislation outlawed slavery above the 36' 30 latitude line in the remainder of the Louisiana Territory

Politics during the Era of Good Feelings was affected by a growing sectionalism. The Louisiana Territory was the first battleground for the debate about slavery's future in western lands. Those who feared slavery's power, like the Federalists, understood that the institution could dominate the political landscape. When Missouri was set to become a state, Clay took the opportunity to settle the issue of slavery's existence in Louisiana. Clay, one of the great politicians in American History, worked toward creating a framework that would appease both northerners and southerners. He worked with other Congressmen to pass a series of bills that became the Missouri Compromise. As part of the deal, slavery would be allowed in Missouri, but all other states above the 36°30′ parallel carved out of the Louisiana Territory would become free states. In addition, part of Massachusetts would become the new state of Maine. In this way, the Missouri Compromise meant there would remain an even number of slave and Free states while, it was hoped, solving future questions about slavery by creating a border between where it could and could not exist. Instead of ending conflict, however, the Missouri Compromise only led to more fierce debate in the years to come. Thomas Jefferson feared the worst, and his words were prophetic. Jefferson wrote, "this momentous question, like a fire bell in the night, awakened and filled me with terror. . . A geographical line, coinciding with a marked principle, moral and political, once conceived and held up to the angry passions of men, will never be obliterated; and every new irritation will mark it deeper and deeper."

Sectionalism was on the rise, as was the kind of political strife the Democrat-Republicans hoped to avoid. The presidential election of 1824 marked a turning point back toward party factionalism and severe partisanship. The Democrat-Republicans split into different factions after the era of Monroe. Each represented different party interests and/or sections of the country. In the end, four candidates within the party ran for the presidency: John Quincy Adams, William Crawford, Henry Clay, and Andrew Jackson. Prominent South

Carolinian Senator John C. Calhoun contemplated entering the race but chose to seek the vice-presidency, instead. It appeared that Jackson had the most widespread popularity before the election. Jackson and Adams, the son of former president John Adams, were the top two candidates, but neither won a majority of electoral votes. Thus, the House of Representatives had to decide who would become the next president. Clay persuaded his allies to support Adams who was given the presidency. Adams and Clay were more alike in their political positions than either was compared to Jackson. The military hero was a political outsider with strongly held views that did not always fit the mold of the mainstream Democrat-Republicans.

Jackson believed the election was stolen from him, and the stage was set for a new era in American politics. Jackson supporters called the Election of 1824 the "Corrupt Bargain." They believed that Clay and Adams had conspired against Jackson even though he won the most electoral votes. As it happened, Jackson was strongest in the South but had large pockets of support all over the country. Jackson was not a man to forgive or forget a grievance, and Adams and Jackson shared a mutual hatred of each other. As it turned out, Jackson's time on the public stage was far from over. Running again in 1828, Jackson defeated Adams and became president. The campaign was nasty, bitter, and personal. The civility of the Era of Good Feelings was over. Built around or in opposition to Jackson, two new parties would define the political landscape of the next decades.

Conclusion

It is questionable how long Jefferson's America could be said to exist. Americans sometimes forget how much Hamilton influenced the country in the long term. Perhaps, it was because he died so young and never became president. Jefferson himself augmented his views over time and adapted to the realities of running and expanding the country. In fact, it was expansion, with the Louisiana Purchase, that likely defines his presidency more than anything else. With more territory, came the need for some type of regulation and control over it. Thus, the government grew larger than Jefferson had originally wanted in his American dream. Staying out of foreign affairs, a typical attitude of a "founding father" like Jefferson, was an impossibility. What emerged in the wake of 1812 created the conditions that led America down the road to its next stage of development. At this point, Americans were hopeful about the future and hungry for land and opportunity. It was not yet apparent that sectionalism had an incredible power to negate Americans' positive momentum.

Perhaps, the most lasting legacy of Jefferson has simply been that Americans, in every period of History, have referenced him as a model of the ideal republican. Jefferson was an Enlightenment—soaked idealist who wrote on so many topics one can mold him into anything. Conservatives, Liberals, Socialists, Anarchists, southern sectionalists, and Patriots of all persuasions have spoken of themselves as the true heirs of Jefferson. The idea of the independent agrarian as the ideal American increasingly grew less attainable as farming grew less profitable for individuals and corporations took over. Yet, the spirit of the

Jeffersonian ethic was replaced by the idea of Americans as innovative, energetic, entrepreneurs. Ironically, this would describe Jefferson more than would any notion of him as an agrarian. Perhaps Jefferson would be disturbed by the reality that America became a nation of debtors, city dwellers, and wage labor. There is still much to be said for Jeffersonian idealism along with its obvious shortcomings. Jefferson once wrote "dependence begets subservience and venality, suffocates the germ of virtue, and prepares fit tools for the designs of ambition." On this, Jefferson had a strong argument.

CHAPTER SIX

Jacksonian America

Chapter 6: Key Concepts

- What are the characteristics of Jacksonian America?

- What would make Andrew Jackson a great president and what would make him a not-so-great president?

- Why do you think historians refer to this period as Jacksonian America even though Andrew Jackson only served eight years in office?

Few could have anticipated that Andrew Jackson would become an important figure in society much less define a period of American history. When the American people looked at Jackson, many of them saw themselves. If the orphan child from the frontier could become wealthy and successful in politics, then anyone could replicate his example. Jackson's rise to prominence coincided with a new course that Americans blazed. This path led the American people toward more democracy. **Jacksonian Democracy** came to mean several things: expansion of the franchise, the spoils system, preserving the Union, ending monopolies, aiding the common man, and acquiring more territory. This road to democracy, however, was not open to all Americans. Only white males benefitted from the democracy espoused by Jackson. Females, Native Americans, and African-Americans would be excluded from the democracy championed by Jackson and their conditions in American society did not improve. Jacksonian Democracy defined the period of American History during the 1820s, 1830s, and 1840s.

Henry Clay and Internal Improvements

An 1816 Congressional report noted that it costs $9 to ship a ton of goods from Europe to the United States. The report then noted that in America, as a result of a poor system of roads, $9 could only ship a ton of goods 30 miles. If the infrastructure of the country could be improved, then the cost of shipping would decrease. Farmers, manufacturers, merchants, and all citizens would benefit from cheaper prices. Henry Clay of Kentucky was among the first to recognize this. A westerner, Clay perceived that the West would have much to gain from a system of roads and canals built with federal dollars.

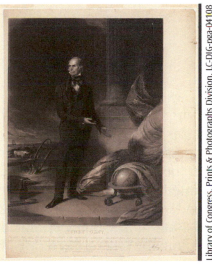

Library of Congress, Prints & Photographs Division, LC-DIG-pga-04108

Clay's call for federal dollars to finance these projects was met with lots of resistance. Some states, like New York, which had built the Erie Canal on its own, now did not want to be taxed to benefit other states. Many southerners regarded federally sponsored internal improvements as unconstitutional. When Congress passed bills appropriating funds for national works, presidents vetoed them. This meant that these expensive projects would have to be built with either state or private funds. New York succeeded with the Erie Canal, but most other states who tried to replicate the example of New York, failed. The smashing success of the Erie Canal meant that no New York legislator in Washington would vote for a federally funded canal, since their state had built one out of its own pocket. In spite of Clay's pleas, a national system of federally funded roads would have to wait until Dwight Eisenhower became president.

The Union League's portrait collection includes likenesses of numerous American political leaders. A notable example is John Neagle's portrait of Henry Clay, painted for his 1844 presidential campaign.

Industrial Capitalism

Improvements in transportation and assistance from the federal government through tariffs enacted in 1816, 1824, and 1828 brought about the rise of industrial capitalism in America. The first factory was created in 1793 to produce cotton textiles in New England. Although the factory had appeared, most manufacturing in America after the Revolution and until the War of 1812 was done at the household level. Families worked together to produce their own fabrics, shoes, and other necessities of life. If they produced a surplus it would be sold at a local market. A New England entrepreneur named Francis Cabot Lowell established a textile factory in Massachusetts. Lowell urged his fellow associates to pool their resources together so that they could create a new factory where the entire process of cotton production would be done under one roof. Specialized workers with specific knowledge and expertise would be set up into units that would be run by executives. Running water would be the form of energy to drive the machinery in the factory. The success of this model allowed it to spread to other areas of the North and West. Cotton manufacturing soon became the leading industry in America.

What worked in cotton fabrics was soon borrowed by other industries. Woolen, iron, alcohol, and weapon industries replicated the factory system of cotton manufacturers. Eli Whitney, who had failed to become rich even though he had created the cotton gin due to a loophole in the patent laws of the time, now developed the concept of interchangeable parts. Before interchangeable parts, if a trigger malfunctioned or broke on a rifle, then the gun was now useless. But with machine manufactured parts, a busted trigger could now simply be replaced. To an amazed audience, Whitney disassembled 10 rifles, mixed up the pieces, and then put the rifles back together, and all of them worked.

Corrupt Bargain

A Virginian had occupied the White House since the election of 1800. As the country moved closer to the presidential election of 1824, Americans from other states felt that it was time for a change. Several states now began putting forward their favorite sons as candidates for the presidency. In Tennessee, Jackson's supporters believed that his military fame warranted presidential consideration. Jackson entered a crowded field of presidential contenders. The candidates all had distinguished records of service to their country. Secretary of State John Quincy Adams of Massachusetts entered the race and campaigned on his diplomatic record. Secretary of the Treasury William H. Crawford appealed to southerners due to his calls to cut federal spending. The Speaker of the House, Henry Clay of Kentucky, also joined the competition. Clay based his bid on his economic nationalism. Unlike the other three aspirants, Jackson was known throughout the country. His other rivals were known only in their home states or regions. Adams was strong in New England. Crawford had lots of support in the South. Clay was the western candidate. Only Jackson, because of his victory over the British at New Orleans, had a national following.

Jackson and the other candidates could not actively campaign or solicit votes in 1824. They all had to act disinterested and only run if persuaded by others. When the people went to the polls, they tended to support Jackson. But several states still did not let the people choose presidential electors. In the states that allowed the people to select electors, many states had property requirements that prohibited many Americans from voting. When the votes were counted, Jackson had the most popular and electoral votes, but he did not have a majority of the electoral votes. This meant that just as it had in 1800, the House of Representatives would have to choose the next president.

A Foot Race

Since he had the most popular and electoral votes, Jackson and his supporters felt confident that the members of the House would elect him. However, the Speaker of the House, Henry Clay, who had finished fourth in the presidential election of 1824 and therefore could not be considered by the House, had other ideas. Clay regarded Jackson as unqualified for the presidency. He said, "I cannot believe that killing 2,500 Englishmen at New Orleans qualifies for the various, difficult, and complicated duties of the Chief Magistracy." Clay now decided to support Adams and encouraged his own friends in the House to do the same. On the first ballot, Adams was popular enough to win the presidency. Adams then appointed Clay to the position of Secretary of State, which many regarded as the stepping stone to the presidency. Jackson and his friends immediately cried **bargain and corruption,** because it looked like Clay had negotiated away the presidency for the reward of the office of Secretary of State. The voice of the people had been ignored. "So you see," Jackson announced. "The Judas of the West [Clay] has closed the contract and will receive the 30 pieces of silver. His end will be the same."

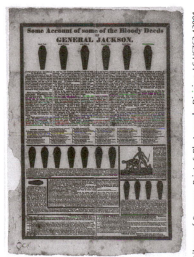

Coffin Handbill

The Campaign of 1828

Adams's alleged theft of the presidency prompted Jackson and his followers to begin the campaign for the 1828 race. Jackson's supporters built a broad coalition that included the "planters of the South and the plain Republicans of the North." Jackson remained a national candidate who appealed to all Americans regardless of their class or section. Adams made some blunders that also aided Jackson. In his first message to Congress, Adams laid out a bold and visionary program for the country to adopt: a national university, a national observatory, and federally sponsored internal improvements. If the people did not agree with what their elected representatives wished, Adams announced, then members of Congress should not be "palsied by the whims of their constituents." According to Adams, if the people did not approve of his vision for the country, then elected leaders should ignore them.

As the country prepared to pick a president in 1828, Jackson and his followers felt comfortable about their chances. Jackson would sweep the South carrying the states of Virginia, North Carolina, South Carolina, Georgia, Alabama, Mississippi, Louisiana, and Tennessee. Jackson's followers recognized that the issue of the tariff could be used to win votes here. In 1828, they introduced a new tariff bill into the House of Representatives. This bill offered increased protection on items that benefitted the states of New York, Pennsylvania, Kentucky, and Missouri. For instance, a high duty on raw wool would help wool farmers in New York; a high duty on iron would aid iron manufacturers in Pennsylvania. A high duty on hemp was welcomed by hemp growers in Kentucky because it was used to make rope. Increased rates on pelts and furs assisted trappers in Missouri. The Jackson men also designed the tariff to injure New England manufacturers who were loyal to Adams. A high duty on molasses was included to make it unprofitable to manufacture rum. Therefore, the people would choose to drink the whiskey of the West instead of rum produced in New England. A high duty on raw wool hurt woolen manufacturers in New England because they now had to pay increased costs for the raw product. Also, the high duties on hemp and iron hurt New England shippers because this increased the prices of rigging on ships and also on chains and anchors. John Randolph of Virginia noted correctly that the tariff of 1828 related "to manufactures of no sort, but the manufacture of a President of the United States."

John Quincy Adams

This was a risky strategy for southerners, as they had the most to lose if the bill became law. Increased protection to American manufacturers would mean higher prices that they would have to pay for goods. George McDuffie of South Carolina disliked this strategy and equated it with "fighting the devil with fire." The bill, which southerners dubbed the **tariff of abominations**, passed the House and Senate and then was signed into law by Adams. They called it the tariff of abominations because it set the average rate for imported items at just under 50%. Southerners charged that the bill would force them to pay higher prices for manufactured goods.

The election of 1828 proved to be one of the nastiest in all of American history. Both sides engaged in mudslinging. Jackson's supporters charged that Adams had lavishly spent the taxpayers' money on White House improvements. They also suggested that Adams, while he was a diplomat in Russia, had acted like a pimp since he had allegedly procured American virgins for the Russian czar! The Adams men argued that Jackson's temperament made him unqualified for the presidency. They reminded voters how Jackson had ordered the execution of six of his soldiers for desertion during the War of 1812. This was plain for many to see in the notorious Coffin Hand Bill, which had six coffins and the title: "a short account of some of the Bloody Deeds of General Jackson." Other campaign posters and literature articulated the same theme—Jackson could not be trusted with power. But the nastiest charge was leveled not at Jackson or Adams but rather at Jackson's wife Rachel. Jackson married Rachel in 1791. Rachel and Jackson had believed that her first husband had divorced her. However, Rachel's first husband had failed to file the necessary paperwork. Jackson and Rachel learned about this a few years later and also realized that they had been living in adultery. Rachel completed the divorce to her first husband and then remarried Jackson. The sordid affair might have been neglected, but an Adams supporter learned of the story and published it. How could Jackson cry "bargain and corruption" when he and his wife had lived in sin, supporters of Adams asked.

When not defending his marriage, Jackson and his followers presented him as a son of the American Revolution. If elected president, they promised, he would usher in reforms and restore the constitution and country to its original purity. Jackson's patriotism and service to his country prompted the people to overlook the charges leveled against him by the Adams forces. Jackson won in a landslide. But soon after the election tragedy struck the president-elect. Jackson's wife died. The new president blamed his political foes for causing her death.

The Spoils System

Once Jackson came to Washington, government workers feared the worst; because it had been widely rumored that Jackson would fire workers and replace them with his friends. One worker, expecting to be removed from his office, committed suicide before he could be fired, while others locked themselves in their offices in an attempt to retain their position. The reign of terror that had been feared did not happen as predicted. Instead, Jackson removed not more than 20% of all federal office holders. When his friends in one state urged him to fire a postmaster because that man had voted for Adams, Jackson refused once he learned that the men had fought and had received a wound in the American Revolution.

While Jackson claimed that the removals and his idea of rotation of office would bring more efficiency to the federal government, his political opponents saw something more sinister. In their eyes it looked as if Jackson only sought to reward his friends and punish his enemies with federal offices. On the floor of the Senate in 1831, a Jackson supporter named William L. Marcy seemed to confirm these fears. When Jackson's foes grumbled over some of his appointments, Marcy declared, "to the victor belong the spoils." Jackson had inaugurated a policy that came to be known as the **Spoils System**. Offices would be awarded not on merit, but rather on one's political connections and affiliation. The Spoils System remained in effect until the Pendleton Act of 1883 commenced the Civil Service System.

The Jackson Administration

Jackson's administration got off to a rough start. This stemmed from the men he appointed to be members of his cabinet. Few had much faith that Jackson's official advisors would be able to handle their responsibilities. One appointment in particular, Secretary of War John H. Eaton, caused Jackson numerous headaches. Right before Eaton assumed his duties, he married a recently widowed young woman named Peggy Timberlake. Her husband had only recently died and custom dictated that a female was supposed to be in mourning for a period of time, but Peggy rushed off and married Eaton. Washington society was aghast at this unethical behavior. The leading females regarded Peggy as a loose woman of low morals. Therefore, most members of Washington society refused to socialize with the new couple. If the Eaton's announced they were attending a party, then other respectable Washington residents would refuse to attend. Instead of discussing the major issues before the country, Jackson's cabinet debated the expectations of a proper woman and whether or not the cabinet secretaries and their wives should dine with the Eaton's. When the press found out about this **Eaton Affair**, they charged that, since Jackson could not govern his own cabinet, he was unfit to govern the nation. The Eaton Affair would not be resolved until 1831 when Jackson fired his cabinet.

Since Jackson could not get advice and counsel from his cabinet, he turned to an unlikely source. The president began soliciting advice from members of Congress, newspaper editors, government officials, and private citizens. This informal group of advisors convened in the White House periodically and entered through a door in the kitchen. Therefore, Jackson's informal group of advisors became known as the **"Kitchen Cabinet."** Many men were a part of the Kitchen Cabinet at various stages of Jackson's presidency, but the primary members included: Martin Van Buren, Francis P. Blair, Amos Kendall, Thomas Hart Benton, and Roger Taney. The men who comprised Jackson's kitchen cabinet were men of modest means. Although some had become successful, everything that they had gained they had gotten through hard work and perseverance—just like Jackson. These men like Jackson all had an intense dislike for the national bank, and when the president decided to challenge it, they offered him support that he could not get from his official cabinet.

Andrew Jackson

"The Rats Leaving a Falling House"

Indian Removal

Although Jackson is regarded as one of America's better presidents (he usually ranks among the top 10), Jackson had a very poor legislative record. Congress ignored most of Jackson's recommendations for legislation. Jackson's biggest legislative accomplishment also turned out to be his most controversial: Indian Removal. Jackson asked Congress for legislation that would allow the federal government to remove Native Americans off of their ancestral lands and force them to relocate to areas west of the Mississippi River. The **Indian Removal Act of 1830** passed and Jackson signed it into law. Jackson now began urging Native Americans to relocate to areas to the West of the Mississippi River. Most tribes recognized the futility of resistance and acquiesced. Only the Cherokees, located mostly in Georgia, decided to fight Jackson and the federal government. They did so through the courts. In the 1832 case of *Worcester v. Georgia*, the Supreme Court, still led by John Marshall, issued a ruling saying that Native Americans were a separate nation and could not be forced from their lands. When Jackson learned of this decision, he supposedly snapped, "John Marshall has made his decision, now let him enforce it." Jackson seemed to be suggesting that he would ignore the decision of the Supreme Court.

Unable to get assistance from the Supreme Court, the Cherokees now had few options available to them. If the federal government did not forcibly evict them, then the state of Georgia would. In 1835, a small number of Cherokees signed a treaty with the federal government that became known as the **Treaty of New Echota**. In return for leaving Georgia, the Cherokees would get title to lands west of the Mississippi River and would be compensated for their holdings in Georgia. Also, the Cherokees would be paid $5 million. Although many doubted the legality of this treaty since only a small minority of the Cherokees themselves supported it, Jackson sent it to the Senate for ratification. The Senate ratified it by a single vote.

The Treaty of New Echota commenced the final chapter in this tragic story. Just as Jackson left the presidency, federal troops began arriving in northern Georgia to ensure that the Cherokees left their lands. These troops would escort the Cherokees to the area of present day Oklahoma. The federal government had arranged for supplies to be provided for the Cherokees. However, many men accepted the contracts but failed to provide the Cherokees with food, blankets, and clothing on their journey. They simply took the money and forgot about the Cherokees. The Cherokees were marched out of Georgia during the winter of 1838. Unknown before removal, this would turn out to be a brutally cold winter. Disease and hunger began decimating the Cherokees. By the time they crossed the Mississippi River, around 4,000 Cherokees had perished on what came to be known as the **Trail of Tears**.

Nullification

In November 1828, vice president John C. Calhoun anonymously drafted a document known as the *South Carolina Exposition*. Calhoun contended that the protective tariff system only aided northern manufacturers. According to Calhoun, high tariffs gave northern

Daniel Webster

manufacturers a monopoly over the domestic market. With this monopoly, northern manufacturers forced southern farmers to buy manufactured goods at increased prices. Furthermore, since these tariffs were aimed at keeping British goods out of America, the British might retaliate by putting their own tariff on America's biggest export—cotton. A British tariff on cotton would ruin southern planters such as Calhoun.

In order for an agricultural state like South Carolina to protect itself from the majority of the North, the state declared it could nullify a federal law. A state could nullify a federal law through a nullifying convention, Calhoun argued. The convention apparatus was very important for Calhoun because the states had ratified the constitution in conventions. Once a state voided a law then the other states would have to hold conventions of their own to determine whether this was justified. If three quarters of the rest of the states regarded the law as constitutional, then the nullifying state could either accept and rescind the ordinance, or secede. Calhoun believed that there was already a precedent for nullification in the Virginia and Kentucky Resolutions of 1798. Most Americans had difficulty following Calhoun's complicated logic, but they all grasped that nullification might lead to secession and secession almost certainly meant civil war.

Calhoun and his allies in South Carolina expected Jackson to agree with them and to support nullification. After all, Jackson was a cotton planter and slaveholder from Tennessee. However, Jackson did not condone nullification. When asked to give a toast at a dinner commemorating the birthday of Thomas Jefferson in 1830, Jackson used the occasion to announce his opposition to the Nullifiers. Jackson stood up, raised his glass, stared directly at vice president Calhoun, and said: "Our Federal Union, it must be Preserved." Calhoun responded with: "Our Federal Union, next to our Liberty most dear."

The Nullifiers in South Carolina pushed ahead with their calls to nullify the tariff. In 1831, Calhoun publicly endorsed the doctrine. George McDuffie, who had opposed the southern strategy over the tariff of abominations, announced that the tariff took 40 bales of cotton for every 100 that a farmer grew. McDuffie's forty bale theory represented bad economics but excellent propaganda. It crystallized how the tariff taxed the people of the South. With support building for nullification throughout the state, the supporters of nullification won control of the state legislature in November 1832. The state of South Carolina then nullified the tariff. Jackson reacted with outrage. "Disunion by armed force is treason," Jackson announced. Jackson also talked openly of hanging his own vice president. According to Jackson, the will of the majority must prevail. The president also prepared to lead an army into South Carolina to ensure that tariff duties were collected. Jackson's problem became that if he marched an army into South Carolina, he would have to go through Virginia and North Carolina. While these states did not approve of nullification, they also did not think that the president could coerce a sister state into obeying a disputed law. If Jackson marched an army south, it could lead to a civil war. Clay proposed a new tariff bill, which would reduce the rate of protection gradually over 10 years. Northern manufacturers would have a decade's worth of protection and southerners would have low tariffs eventually as well. Jackson signed this compromise proposal and tranquility prevailed.

Second Bank of the United States

In 1816, Congress had chartered a Second National Bank (2BUS). By the late 1820s, the bank had become very successful and powerful. It controlled most of the other state banks. In some ways it functioned like a central bank or even the Federal Reserve System. The bank's growth during the 1820s had come as a result of the policies of its new president, Nicholas Biddle. He adopted a series of new policies that had made the bank extremely profitable for its shareholders and had become wealthy as a result. Many Americans resented the power of the national bank. Some Americans, mostly in the South, still regarded a national bank as unconstitutional. Many westerners resented the bank because of the Panic of 1819. In addition, some New Yorkers disliked the bank since its headquarters in Philadelphia made that city the financial capital of the country. These foes of the bank became a powerful force when they coalesced. They became even more so when Jackson announced that he did not support it.

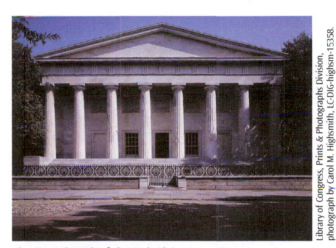

The Second Bank of the United States

Library of Congress, Prints & Photographs Division, photograph by Carol M. Highsmith, LC-DIG-highsm-15358.

In 1832, Jackson planned on running for a second term. His opponent, Henry Clay, needed an issue to differentiate himself from the president. Clay seized on the bank issue. He urged Biddle to recommend a re-chartering of the Second Bank of the United States even though its charter would not expire until 1836. Both the House and Senate passed a bill to re-charter the bank. On the day the bill arrived at the White House, Jackson was sick from one his old dueling wounds. The color in his face was ashen. When he received the bill, the color suddenly returned to Jackson's face as he was now flush with anger. "The bank is trying to kill me," he said, "but I will kill it."

Jackson assembled his advisors and they crafted a veto message. This message became the personification of Jacksonian Democracy. Jackson viewed the national bank as unconstitutional even though numerous presidents and the Chief Justice had declared a national bank to be legal. But the real reason why Jackson disliked the bank came from the class of individuals that it aided. According to Jackson, the bank only sought to aid the aristocracy.

GENERAL JACKSON SLAYING THE MANY HEADED MONSTER.

"General Slaying the Many Headed Monster"

"It is to be regretted that the rich and powerful too often bend the acts of government to their selfish purposes," Jackson declared, "but when the laws undertake to add to these natural and just advantages artificial distinctions, to grant titles, gratuities, and exclusive privileges, to make the rich richer and the potent more powerful, the humble members of society—the farmers, mechanics, and laborers—who have neither the time nor the means of securing like favors to themselves, have a right to complain of the injustice of their Government."

Clay and Biddle decided to use Jackson's veto message against him. "It has all the fury of a chained panther biting the bars of his cage. It is really a manifesto of anarchy, such as Marat or Robespierre might have issued to the mob," Biddle exclaimed. The two foes of Jackson printed and distributed copies of the veto to the people expecting that the people would side with them and the bank over Jackson. However, the veto resonated with the people. Most Americans concurred with Jackson that the bank aided the few at the expense of the many. "The veto works well," Jackson informed a friend, "instead of crushing me as was expected and intended, it will crush the bank."

Clay and Biddle wanted the **election of 1832** to be a referendum on the bank. In many ways the election hinged on the question of whether the bank should be continued or destroyed. But another issue interjected itself into the campaign of 1832—the political power of Masons in America. Masons had arrived in the United States during the colonial era. Numerous politicians belonged to Masonic lodges, but the Masons came under scrutiny when William Morgan, a former member, proposed to write a book and reveal their secrets. Morgan disappeared under mysterious circumstances in western New York, and he was never seen again nor his body ever found. The public assumed that he had had been murdered by the Masons. When a jury filled with Masons and a Masonic judge failed to impose stiff penalties on the men suspected of killing Morgan, Americans argued that a conspiracy was afloat. In the wake of Morgan's disappearance, Americans began charging that Masons had taken control of the American government. When they looked to the upcoming presidential election in 1832—the two leading candidates, Clay and Jackson, were both Masons. To save American democracy, foes of Masons formed a new political party—the Antimasons. They nominated William Wirt as their presidential candidate. Wirt received over 100,000 popular votes and carried the state of Vermont. Owing to the furor over Masons, membership declined dramatically. Before Morgan disappeared, there had been over 100,000 Masons in America, but by 1840, there were less than 40,000. In spite of the fear of a conspiracy by Masons to take control of the government, Jackson won a second term in 1832 over Clay and Wirt in a landslide.

Since the bank had tried to influence the election of 1832, Jackson feared that it could still secure a new charter by bribing enough members of Congress to override a presidential veto. Jackson now decided to order the removal of all federal funds in the national bank. Funds would now be placed in what came to be known as "pet banks." These banks were run by men loyal to Jackson and these men could now make loans on whatever terms they wanted since they were no longer under the control of Biddle. With federal funds no longer coming into the vaults of the bank, Biddle decided to curtail all loans that it had made and also to call in all outstanding loans. This policy decision would give the bank more money, but it also created a credit crisis throughout the country, which is exactly what Biddle wanted. If Jackson could not see the importance and power of the bank then Biddle would show him. By creating this economic panic, Biddle hoped to force Jackson to surrender.

Everyday Americans poured into the White House. They all urged Jackson to restore the deposits and allow the bank to operate unfettered. Many said that the situation was similar to the Panic of 1819, but Jackson would not be intimidated. When one group of New York businessmen urged Jackson to allow the bank to be left alone, Jackson exploded in rage. "The abominable institution, the monster! I've got my foot upon it and I'll crush it. Is Andrew Jackson to bow the knee to the golden calf as did the Israelites of old? I tell, if you want relief, go to Nicholas Biddle," Jackson retorted. Biddle's decision to create a financial crisis had only convinced Jackson that his course was right and that the bank was dangerous. As it turned out, Biddle had given himself a self-inflicted wound by creating this crisis. "The question was," James K. Polk asked in the House, "whether we shall have the republic without the bank or the bank without the republic."Increasingly more politicians and average Americans were now siding with Jackson against the bank. In 1836, the Second Bank of the United States closed its doors for good.

Whigs and Democrats

Beginning in 1832, Jackson's supporters officially began calling themselves **Democrats**. Some of Jackson's followers had used this term as early as 1828, but the Democratic Party was officially born in 1832. The Democratic Party had followers from every part of the country. Democrats believed in states' rights and limited government involvement in the lives of the people. The Democrats opposed any measure that resembled a government favor or handout. Therefore, most Democrats, but not all, opposed a protective tariff, a national bank, and federally sponsored internal improvements. They favored hard money and cheap prices for western lands. The Democrats drew large amounts of support from urban workers in the northeast and southern slaveholders. The notion of limited government appealed to both of these groups. The Democratic Party was also sympathetic to slavery and its extension. A government of few powers would not be able to interfere with

"King Andrew the First"

slavery, which appealed to southerners, but also to northern workers who realized that if slavery was abolished then former slaves would now compete with them for jobs. Many Democrats saw slavery as an issue for state governments and not the federal government. As a result, the protection of slavery linked both northern and southern Democrats. Jackson always remained the central figure in the Democratic Party and was seen as its leader. Other leading Democrats included Martin Van Buren, James K. Polk, and Thomas Hart Benton.

The opponents of Jackson had at first called themselves National Republicans, but this did not work in the long term. Beginning in 1834, the opposition party renamed themselves as **Whigs**. At first, the only thing that linked all of the Whigs was a personal dislike of Jackson. They took their name from the English Whig Party, which had fought to maintain the supremacy of a democratically elected legislature over the king. Whigs viewed Jackson as a tyrant. His vetoes had thwarted the wishes of the people, they charged. The only reason why Democrats supported Jackson, Whigs maintained, was because Jackson bribed them with offices. At every opportunity, Whigs believed, Jackson was accumulating more and more power. Eventually, Jackson would become equivalent to a king. "We are in the midst of a revolution, hitherto bloodless, but rapidly tending toward a total change in the pure republican character of the government, and to the concentration of all power in the hands of one man," Clay announced in a Senate speech that symbolized what the new Whig party stood for. "The Whigs of the present day are opposing executive encroachment and a most alarming extension of executive power," Clay declared.

Eventually, the Whigs developed a positive program. They stood for a national bank, a highly protective tariff, and federally sponsored internal improvements. The Whigs believed that government had a moral duty to help society make progress. Whereas the Democrats saw government regulation and involvement in the economy as a bad thing, the Whigs believed that this was the duty of government. The leader of the Whig Party became Jackson's biggest enemy: Henry Clay. Other prominent Whigs included John Quincy Adams, Daniel Webster, William H. Seward, and Abraham Lincoln. Seward and Lincoln later became key Republicans. Like the Democrats, the Whigs had followers in every part of the country. Merchants and entrepreneurs in the Northeast typically supported the Whig Party. Evangelical Christians voted for Whig candidates, as well. Even some of the biggest and wealthiest slaveholders in the South were Whigs because of the party's position on improving the country's infrastructure. Improved roads and canals would allow slaveholders to get their crops to a market at a cheaper price and allow them to increase their profits.

Specie Circular and Panic of 1837

In 1835 and 1836, the federal government accumulated a surplus of revenue. This surplus had been acquired because of a boom in land sales in the western states. Speculators had begun to buy large tracts of land in the West with paper money that had been printed by the pet banks. They hoped to buy these lands at a low price and then sell them at a much higher one. Jackson frowned on this and issued an order that became known as the **Specie Circular**. This order said that all land sales in the West had to be conducted with some form of specie which meant either gold or silver. The Specie Circular had the desired effect. Americans spent almost $25 million on public lands in 1836 but that number fell to just under $7 million in 1837. Then in 1838, they spent only $4 million on western lands. Jackson had stopped a speculative boom. However, it had started to drain specie from the East to the West.

"Specie Claws"

As Jackson pondered what to do regarding the western lands, the nation prepared for another presidential election. By 1836, the Whigs were strong enough to field candidates for the presidency. Instead of selecting a single nominee, the Whigs decided to run three candidates. A northern Whig, a southern Whig, and a western Whig would each run in the hopes that no candidate would achieve a majority of the electoral votes, which would force the House of Representatives to pick the president. In the House the Whigs could then unite behind a single candidate. This strategy failed to work. The Democrats nominated Martin Van Buren, and with Jackson's blessing, he won a majority of the electoral votes and the presidency in the **election of 1836**.

Just two months after Van Buren became president, banks in New York City suspended specie payments. This meant that they would no longer redeem paper bank notes for hard money. Banks in other cities soon began to follow the example of the New York banks. The **Panic of 1837** had begun. Many Americans said the same thing, "It is 1819 all over again." It was believed that during the panic years of 1837 until 1843, 33,000 businesses and firms failed involving a loss of $440 million. A slave in Mississippi was worth $1,500 in 1836, but in 1837, he was now worth $250. Lands in North Carolina that were sold for $50 an acre were now sold for less than $5 an acre. In some western states, loans could only be taken out with an interest rate of 50%. Internal improvement projects stopped because funding could no longer be procured. In a few areas it was said that since money was so scarce a barter type economy took hold. In every major city destitute mothers could be found begging for food for their children.

The Whigs blamed the panic on Jackson's and Van Buren's misguided financial policies. Had the Democrats not destroyed Biddle's bank, they argued, the panic would not have begun. For the Whigs, the only remedy was to charter a new national bank. Van Buren and the Democrats had a different idea. Since they blamed the Panic of 1837 on speculators who had taken funds from banks and made risky investments, Democrats proposed to separate the federal government from the banking industry once and for all. They called for the creation of the **Independent Treasury**. Under this system, federal funds would no longer be put in pet banks but rather would now be placed in treasuries located in major cities. Bankers would no longer have access to federal funds. For Democrats, the federal government would "divorce" itself from the banking industry. Whigs mocked this proposal. They charged that it might prevent future panics, but how would it help the Americans who were currently suffering? From 1837 until 1840, Whigs and Democrats battled over a new national bank and the Independent Treasury. Since the Whigs wanted to tie the government to the banking industry and the Democrats wanted to divorce it from that industry, the two parties found themselves at opposite ends of the spectrum on this issue and could not compromise. The big loser became the American people.

The panic dragged on into 1840, which was an election year. The Whigs decided to nominate a single candidate in 1840: William Henry Harrison. The Whigs had plenty of issues to use against Van Buren, a man who they now referred to as "Martin Van Ruin." The Whigs linked the recent financial crisis to Van Buren. A vote for Van Buren would mean four more years of economic hardship. Whigs often chanted, "Van, Van, Van—Van's a used up man." But the best Whig slogan came to them by accident. One Democrat had said that Harrison would be happiest living in a log cabin and drinking hard cider. Whigs seized on this because it suggested that Harrison was a man of the people from the frontier. Most Whig rallies would include a hastily constructed log cabin where the people could get drunk. While the Whigs touted Harrison's humble origins, they also charged that Van Buren was a dandy who used expensive perfumes every day and had his meals cooked by a French chef. Harrison, on the other hand, had worked for everything that he got and lived a simple lifestyle in a log cabin. The **election of 1840** hinged more on hoopla and slogans than issues. Whigs sang numerous songs during their rallies including "Tippecanoe and Tyler too." This reminded voters of Harrison's great victory at the Battle of Tippecanoe in 1811 and linked him to his running mate John Tyler. In the end, Harrison won in an electoral landslide. The 1840 election confirms the march of democracy that had begun in 1824. In that year, only 1.1 million Americans voted in the presidential election. In 1840, 2.4 million Americans voted for president. In 1860, 4.7 million Americans would cast a vote for president.

The Accidental President

Harrison delivered an inaugural address that lasted for more than an hour and a half. He discussed how the country needed to create a new national bank. Harrison gave his address in the middle of a freezing rain storm. Shortly after, he developed pneumonia and on April 4, 1841, Harrison died. New President John Tyler was a Whig, but he was a states' rights Whig from Virginia who had been put on the ticket to give it balance between the northerner Harrison and the southerner Tyler. The new president did not agree with the majority of the Whig party on the issues of the day. Since he was the first vice president to become president because of another's death, he became known as the "accidental president" or "His Accidency."

When Congress passed a bill to create a new national bank, Tyler vetoed it. They passed another to make it conform to Tyler's objections but again he vetoed it. In the spring of 1842, the government found itself on the brink of bankruptcy. Whigs decided to raise money by increasing the tariff. When they passed a bill which raised the tariff Tyler again resorted to a veto. Whigs now cut all ties with Tyler while some Whigs even recommended impeaching the president. In August of 1842, Tyler signed a bill increasing the tariff only after it conformed to his wishes. But many

"Death of William Henry Harrison"

saw the Whigs as unable to fulfill their promises. The hard times from the Panic of 1837 lingered on into the early 1840s. As a result of the political infighting among the Whigs, the Democratic Party, which stood on the brink of extinction following the election of 1840, was poised to make a comeback in 1844.

Manifest Destiny

"I have observed this march of civilization advancing from the seacoast, passing over us like a cloud of light, increasing our knowledge and improving our condition, insomuch as that we are at this time more advanced in civilization here than the seaports were when I was a boy," Thomas Jefferson said in 1824.

Jefferson did not know it, but he seemed to be prophesizing a key moment in American history. As a result of the tough financial times and recurring outbreaks of diseases such as cholera, many Americans made the fateful decision to travel west. The unsettled lands west of the Mississippi offered Americans a chance to begin their lives anew. As land became scarcer in the East, western lands could be obtained at low prices for Americans who wanted to replicate the agrarian lifestyle of their forefathers. "Go west Young man," soon became the slogan of the day.

Angel of Progress

Other Americans saw something nobler in settling the West than material betterment. For these Americans, the people had a moral duty to spread American ideals of Christianity and democracy from the Atlantic Ocean to the Pacific Ocean. A New York newspaper editor and Democrat named John L. O' Sullivan coined the term **Manifest Destiny** to articulate their belief that God favored American expansion across the continent. Since God supported it, nothing should stand in the way of the inevitable march of progress of American institutions. The idea of Manifest Destiny provided an alibi for America's expansion across the continent.

In 1846, American officials sought to acquire the Oregon Territory. Since 1827, the United States had a joint occupancy agreement with Great Britain over Oregon. Now the United States terminated that agreement and announced that it want all of the Oregon territory up to the area of present day Alaska. A common refrain from American expansionists became **"Fifty-four forty or fight!"** because the United States sought territory all the way up to the 54th parallel. The British prepared their military for a potential war but cooler heads prevailed. The United States and Great Britain worked out an agreement whereby the United States would acquire the Oregon territory up to the 49th parallel. This line represents the present day boundary between the United States and Canada.

Westward Trails

The primary destination for these emigrants was California. Americans journeying west had to travel a distance of over 2,000 miles. The trip, which typically began in western Missouri at Independence, would last as long as six months. It began in the spring when the rainy season ended, and it had to be completed before the snow blocked the passes in the Sierra Nevada Mountains into California. California bound Americans had to cross the windswept plains and then trek through a series of mountain ranges and deserts. This was all done in a covered wagon. Emigrants had to watch the stock of supplies because they were mostly alone except for their fellow emigrants. The trading posts along the route were few and far between. Settlers also had to be wary of attacks from Native Americans during their voyage. Diseases and malnutrition claimed thousands of lives along the western trails. Yet, the promise of an unencumbered and better life gave these pioneers faith.

While these pioneers felt they were following the American dream it turned into something more for one group of travelers during 1846 and 1847. The **Donner Party** decided to take a potential short cut in their trip to California. Instead of saving them time, the proposed path actually added four more weeks onto their trek. When the Donner Party arrived at the base of the Sierra Nevada Mountains in California, they found that the pass had been blocked by an early snowfall. They then had to spend the winter of 1846 and 1847 trapped in the mountains. With no food available and having to endure six blizzards, some members of the Donner Party resorted to cannibalism in order to survive. News of the Donner Party spread back east and stymied emigration into California for a few years.

Annexation of Texas and the Mexican War

Although Tyler is usually regarded as a failure as a president, he scored at least one major victory. Texas won its independence from Mexico as a result of the Texas Revolution of 1835–1836. Mexico, however, refused to recognize the independence of Texas, and the Mexican army stood poised to reclaim it. As Mexican troops prepared to reconquer a lost province, the British government made overtures to make Texas a colony in the British Empire. This alarmed southern slaveholders because Great Britain had taken the lead in the global crusade to end slavery. Southern slaveholders did not want an antislavery nation on their southern flank. Therefore, the slaveholding Tyler began discussions to have the United States annex Texas. Tyler and his Secretary of State, John C. Calhoun, had concluded a treaty whereby the United States would annex this huge land. However, when Calhoun submitted the treaty to the Senate, he included a letter in the packet. In this letter, Calhoun discussed how making Texas an American possession would be a great benefit to slaveholders. Calhoun also discussed all of the benefits of slavery. Northerners were appalled. It seemed as if gaining Texas was solely for the benefit of slaveholders. Northern Senators rejected the treaty by a large majority.

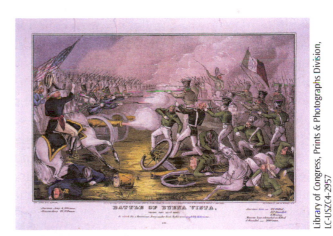

"Battle of Buena Vista"

Library of Congress, Prints & Photographs Division, LC-USZC4-2957

However, the **annexation of Texas** had suddenly become the main issue in American politics. Former president Martin Van Buren wanted the Democratic Party's nomination in 1844, but he announced that he opposed the addition of Texas. When the Democrats held their convention in 1844 they abandoned Van Buren and nominated James K. Polk of Tennessee instead. Polk had announced that he favored the immediate annexation of Texas, and this made him acceptable to most Democrats who craved more territory for the United States. The Whigs nominated Henry Clay, who said that if the United States annexed Texas it would lead to a war with Mexico so therefore, he was opposed to annexation. Polk won a narrow victory over Clay in 1844.

As Polk prepared to become the new president, Tyler was able to add Texas in 1845 through a Joint Resolution of Congress. By the end of the year Texas had entered the Union as a slave state. Mexican officials severed diplomatic ties with the United States. The potential for war now loomed large. Mexico did not like that a former province had become a part of the United States. However, Mexican officials rejected the boundary that Texas claimed. Texans insisted that the southern border of their state was the Rio Grande River. Mexico believed that the border was the Nueces River, which was about 90 miles north of the Rio

Grande. Polk sent American troops to the Rio Grande River. On April 25, Mexican troops attacked American troops north of the Rio Grande. Polk learned of the attack on May 9. He reported to the Congress, "Mexico has passed the boundary of the United States, has invaded our territory and shed American blood on American soil." To make sure that few Whigs would vote against a declaration of war, Democrats included in the declaration a bill appropriating funds for the troops already in the field and to raise 50,000 volunteers. Any Whig who voted no would be seen as injuring the troops already fighting. The trick worked. The House approved the measure by a vote of 174 to 14. It then passed the Senate by a vote of 40 to 2. Only a handful of Whigs opposed to slavery had the courage to vote no.

At first, the **Mexican-American war** was very popular throughout the country. General Zachary Taylor won a series of victories against Mexican troops in northern Mexico. "Old Rough and Ready," as Taylor's troops called him, was a blunt leader. When Mexican leader Santa Anna told Taylor to surrender to him Taylor's response was: "Tell him to go to hell!" Against long odds, Taylor won a series of victories that prompted the Whigs to embrace him. They now began discussing Taylor as a candidate for president even though he had never voted in an election before. Back in Washington, Polk became jealous of Taylor's success and ordered most of Taylor's troops to serve under the command of General Winfield Scott. Since Polk had promised the people that the war would be quick and decisive, it now became unpopular, particularly in New England. In Congress, an obscure Illinois Whig demanded to know the exact spot where the opening shots had been fired since he suspected, along with many others, that Polk had ordered American troops onto Mexican soil to provoke a war. That obscure Congressman was Abraham Lincoln. As Americans debated the war, Scott landed his forces at Veracruz and marched toward Mexico City. Marines entered the "Halls of Montezuma" on September 14, 1847.

The fighting ended in the September of 1847, but an official peace would not be reached for several months later. As negotiations dragged on, Polk and others began arguing that the United States should acquire all of Mexico. The acquisition of more territory would offset the high costs of the war. The man that Polk had selected to negotiate a settlement with Mexico, Nicholas P. Trist, had been selected because Polk thought that Trist would simply do as Polk wanted. Polk soon discovered that Trist had an independent streak. When Polk issued an order removing Trist from the negotiations, Trist ignored the order. He concluded a treaty with Mexican officials on February 2, 1848 and sent it to Washington. It arrived 16 days later, an incredible accomplishment which demonstrated the improved transportation networks in America. Under the **Treaty of Guadalupe Hidalgo**, the United States acquired 500,000 square miles of territory. This represented all of present day California, Nevada, and Utah; and parts of present day Arizona, Colorado, and New Mexico. A disgruntled Polk sent the treaty to the Senate where it was ratified.

Many northerners believed that Polk had gone to war against Mexico for the benefit of southern slaveholders. Some of Polk's other actions as president seemed to suggest to northerners that he only cared about aiding the South. When Polk became president, he filled many offices with northern Democrats. However, Polk appointed mostly men who supported slavery. Northern Democrats who opposed slavery were excluded from patronage positions by Polk. In 1846, Congress passed the Walker Tariff that reduced rates on imported goods to a level not seen since 1816. Manufacturers believed that this low tariff would ruin them. In 1846, Congress passed a bill to improve harbors along the Great Lakes. Even John C. Calhoun, the most vocal proponent of strict constructionism in America, voted for this bill. Polk, however, saw this as unconstitutional and vetoed it. Also in 1846, Polk vetoed a bill that would have appropriated federal dollars for American shippers who had lost their cargo due to attacks made by French privateers in the 1790s. For northerners, Polk's presidency seemed to be benefitting only the South.

Angered by Polk and his policies that aided only the South, northerners struck back in 1846 shortly after the start of the Mexican-American War. When Polk asked for a $2 million appropriation to purchase land from Mexico, an obscure Democrat from Pennsylvania named David Wilmot offered an amendment or proviso to this request. The **Wilmot Proviso** required that any territory taken from Mexico must exclude slavery. The appropriation bill passed the House with the Wilmot Proviso attached to it. It passed because almost all northerners, regardless of party, voted for it while almost all southerners, regardless of party, voted against it. The Senate was not able to vote on the bill with the Wilmot Proviso since it was set to adjourn. However, the Wilmot Proviso, which had brought the question of slavery in the territories to the forefront, would reappear in the upcoming years. The question of slavery in the territories would now become the main point of contention in American politics.

California and the Gold Rush

Even before the United States had officially acquired California, gold was discovered there in early 1848. This discovery occurred not far from where the infamous Donner Party met their fates. Word of the discovery quickly travelled back east and a **gold rush** began. Over a 100,000 people ventured to California hoping to make their fortunes. But the emigrants to California were not just white Americans from the East. Europeans from Great Britain, France, the German states, and China flocked to California. They worked in the mines, built railroads, and operated businesses in California. This helped to make California a very cosmopolitan part of the United States. However, many white emigrants in California did not welcome these different groups. They passed laws which sought to deprive these newcomers of the right to vote. California even imposed a tax on foreign miners. The goal was to make it so expensive for them to look for gold that they would have no choice but to leave the state.

The discovery of gold, however, had unintended consequences. With so many residents of California, the people there now petitioned Congress to be admitted as a state. Californians wanted to enter the Union as a free state. This would upset the balance between the North and South because the areas that did not allow slavery would have two extra votes in the Senate. When the request of the people of California became known in Washington near the end of 1849, it began a crisis that would nearly result in civil war.

Conclusion

Jacksonian America was a time of conflict, expansion, and change. Many of the debates that would define and divide people for the following decades arose during the period named after "Old Hickory." Americans showed that democracy could survive and adapt after the passing of the Revolutionary generation. Pioneers and politicians expanded the territory of the United States. There was much hope for the future. In spite of economic panics in 1819 and in 1837, the economy was poised to boom as a result of the discovery of gold in California. But the men and women who lived during the Age of Jackson failed to solve the problem of slavery. Ending this scourge would divide Americans in the 1850s and precipitate the greatest crisis in American history.

CHAPTER SEVEN

Social Reform

Chapter 7: Key Concepts

- What prompted so many reform movements before the Civil War?

- What would you consider to be the most important reform movement?

- How did these reforms and the changes that took place in America help to bring on the Civil War?

During the first six decades of the nineteenth century the American people saw a series of quick and unsettling changes take place. When Abraham Lincoln left Springfield, Illinois to deliver his Cooper Union speech in February 1860, it took only three days to make the journey by a series of railroads. Forty years earlier, it would have taken three weeks at the minimum to travel that same distance, and in 1840, it would have still taken Lincoln 11 days to make the trip. The change in how Americans travelled and the speed by which they received their news resulted from the **market revolution**. Before the market revolution, farmers and manufacturers grew crops or produced goods for sale at a local market. It led to the rise of urbanization, the arrival of industry, new roles for women, a renewed interest in religion, and the appearance of a middle class. Many welcomed these changes with open arms. Others saw these changes with a foreboding sense of anxiety. Those who were fearful of these apparent changes vowed to reform their country. They drew inspiration from the Enlightenment, the Bible, and the Declaration of Independence. The market revolution helped to draw the North and West together while it isolated the South.

The Second Great Awakening

American religion was in a state of decline at the beginning of the nineteenth century. Several members of the founding generation did not belong to an organized church and instead were Deists. They believed in a Supreme Being, but this Creator did not involve himself in the affairs of the world. What He did, however, was give man the gift of reason. Man, according to Deists, should rely on reason and science rather than the Bible. In Cane Ridge, Kentucky, in 1801, a religious revival commenced. Within a few days, perhaps as many as 25,000 people had attended this camp meeting. What began in the backwoods of Kentucky quickly spread to other parts of the country. The **Second Great Awakening** had begun. Whereas the First Great Awakening sought to bring religion to those whose faith had waned, the Second Great Awakening wanted to bring religion to those who did not belong to any church or had never been exposed to religion. The camp meeting or religious revival became the medium to bring religion to the unchurched. Itinerant ministers would deliver open-air sermons

A Religious Camp Meeting

Library of Congress, Prints & Photographs Division, LC-USZC4-772

and would work their audiences into frenzy. At the end, it was hoped that the people who had gone to these camp meetings would join a church.

During the Second Great Awakening, the fire and brimstone approach of the Puritans in New England and their successors gave way to a more democratic form of Christianity that was open to the masses. Instead of a vengeful God that had predetermined one's fate, preachers and ministers now saw a compassionate God. The most successful of the preachers associated with the Second Great Awakening was Charles G. Finney. Originally a lawyer, Finney turned his back on the law to become a preacher. "I have a retainer from the Lord Jesus Christ to plead his cause, and I cannot plead yours," Finney allegedly told a legal client. True to his word, in 1830 and 1831, Finney began revivals in New York State. He had his biggest success in Rochester, New York. Finney also devised a mechanism to exert extra pressure on his audiences. Finney developed the "anxious bench." Sitting before the audience at the front of a meeting or church service, a sinner would be urged to repent and rededicate his or her life to Christ.

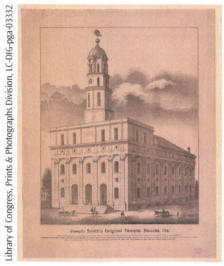

Joseph Smith's Original Temple. Nauvoo, Illa.

Early Mormon temple

The Second Great Awakening drew many Americans into churches and also spawned new religious denominations. One of these denominations was the **Millerites**. William Miller, a Baptist from New York, studied the book of Daniel and calculated that Christ would return in March of 1843. When the millennium failed to take place, Miller adjusted his calculations and predicted the return would occur in March of 1844. After this day came and went without the reappearance of Christ, Miller now announced that the millennium would begin on October 22, 1844. Unfortunately for Miller, as he and his followers sat on hilltops and prayed in churches, nothing occurred on October 22. Miller died five years later but the Millerites evolved into the Seventh-Day Adventists.

Most Deists, if they attended a church service, attended the **Unitarian** church. Unitarians believed that God existed in a single form as opposed to the holy trinity. Unitarians saw God as a loving man capable of compassion and not the malevolent ruler of the Calvinists. Predestination was replaced by the idea of salvation through a series of good works. Educated and intellectually-minded Americans tended to be Unitarians. Practicing Unitarians included influential politicians like John Quincy Adams, John C. Calhoun, Ralph Waldo Emerson, and Daniel Webster.

Another religious group that emerged during the Second Great Awakening was the **Mormon** Church. In Palmyra, New York, Joseph Smith witnessed a brilliant light in a wooded area. "Two personages" appeared claiming to be God the Father and Christ the Savior. Three years later, another "personage" appeared and revealed to Smith that a series of golden plates had been buried and these plates contained a lost section of the Bible telling of a group of Israelites who had lived in America. Smith found the plates, and with the assistance of a magic stone he translated them into English. He published the deciphered texts in 1830 as the *Book of Mormon*. Then in April of that year, Smith founded the Church of Jesus Christ of Latter-day Saints.

Quantifying the exact number of Americans who became Christians during the Second Great Awakening can only be estimated. A recent estimate suggests that by 1860, 75% of all Americans had become affiliated with some church. The majority of new church members during the Second Great Awakening were females. Many preachers had argued that it was the duty of the mother to bring her family back to God. Excluded from advancement in most other aspects of life during the opening decades of the nineteenth century, women found acceptance in religion. This paved the way for the beginning of the women's rights movement that would reach a crescendo in New York State in 1848 not far from where Finney had wowed audiences. The "camp meeting" concept of religious revivals would be borrowed by interest groups in the upcoming years. Manufacturers, merchants, farmers, and reformers would hold conventions that resembled a camp meeting. The biggest and longest lasting influence of the Great Awakening became its inspiration for Christians to reform the United States of America. The reform movements of the early to mid-nineteenth century, included: making alcohol illegal, improving conditions for prisoners, stopping public executions, aiding the poor, and helping the disabled. The most important reform effort, abolishing slavery, also drew its inspiration from the Second Great Awakening.

The Burned Over District

The construction and route of the Erie Canal had brought numerous settlers into central New York State. This led to a series of boom towns all along the canal. The cities of Utica, Rome, Syracuse, Rochester, Lockport, and Buffalo all developed at a rapid rate due to the Erie Canal. The large majority of these new settlers hailed from New England. While their Puritan ancestors had sought to create a city on a hill, their heirs sought to remake the United States of America and commenced their work in Western New York.

New York proved to be fertile ground for reform and outbursts of religious revivals. Since so many revivals occurred along the canal corridor, the area came to be known as either the "infected district" or more commonly as the "**Burned Over District**." The fires of religious revival burned brightest and hottest in this part of the country. The "Burned Over District" spawned numerous reform movements. The temperance movement was strong here too. The Mormons and Seventh-Day Adventists can trace their origins to the Burned Over District. The Seneca Falls Convention for women's rights took place in this region. Many abolitionists started their campaigns for freedom and equality in this area, as well.

Class Consciousness

In the years after the American Revolution, American workers, mechanics, and artisans, enjoyed a modestly comfortable lifestyle. These men owned their own tools, set their own hours, and determined their own wages for the services they provided. These individuals, who worked with their hands, had expertise in the making of barrels, binding books, or producing a gun or a plow. Advancements in technology meant that any unskilled worker could do the same jobs that had previously required years of training and extensive knowledge. From 1820 to 1860, the number of factory or unskilled workers increased from 350,000 to 2 million. A working class could now be found in most urban areas. The poor workers, who earned barely half of what was regarded as necessary to sustain a family of four, tended to live with other members of the working class in a neighborhood where everyone was an unskilled worker.

In stark contrast to the working class in America, there were already 60 millionaires in America by 1840. Twenty years later, the richest 10% in America controlled over 70% of the nation's wealth. In between the rising entrepreneurs who made up the top level of American society and unskilled laborers were another group of Americans. The term "middle-class" was used to describe those Americans who were not laborers but who were also not the owners of a factory or a plantation.

Middle-class Americans could be found in every city. Merchants, bankers, and lawyers were the main middle-class professions for males. Members of the middle-class in America showed their fellow Americans that they had earned a modicum of success by dressing in the latest European fashion styles. A middle-class family would even vacation in Europe. "Ours is a country where men start from a humble origin, and from small beginnings rise gradually in the world, as the reward of merit and industry," Calvin Colton announced in 1844. "One has as good a chance as another, according to his talents, prudence, and exertions." Thus was born the idea that one could pull him or herself up and become successful in America through hard work.

Separate Spheres

"As a moral and intellectual being, woman is entitled to exercise the same rights and enjoy the same privileges as man," William Lloyd Garrison announced in 1838. The rest of America, however, was not as advanced as Garrison. American society had clearly defined roles for men and women. Thus, **separate spheres** had been established for males and females. While males in urban areas left the household everyday so as to provide a home and food for their families, middle-class women became responsible for the moral upbringing of their children. Women ruled over the private sphere of the household while men ruled the public sphere. In the private sphere, women nurtured their children and strove to make their homes a loving and tranquil environment. The public sphere was where males showed their masculinity in the unforgiving world of business and politics. The loving and compassionate women were expected to stay away from these sordid affairs.

In the middle-class family of pre-Civil War America that embraced separate spheres, children were the centerpiece. The American family became child-centered. Middle-class Americans no longer sent their children to work in factories such as a textile mill. Working-class Americans would still be forced to do this for many years. Therefore, these children did not receive an education. Middle-class families could obtain an education for their children. Therefore, for urban middle-class Americans, the family had one objective:

raising children that would be prepared to contribute in American society. Educating children became important because one's status could no longer be passed down. This helped to break down the idea of a male-dominated family. Husbands and wives were coequals in maintaining a family. After 1820, several states passed laws giving women control over their own property and income. Some states even allowed for women to enter into legal contracts.

Women also began to get involved in politics even though no state allowed them to vote. Political leaders believed that women could influence the votes of their husbands. Women, it appeared, adored three-time presidential loser Henry Clay. "If the Ladies—Heaven bless them! could vote, the election of Henry Clay would be carried by acclamation!," one Whig announced in 1844. Women could be found at rallies for the nativist political organizations that appeared from time to time. These political groups sought to exclude immigrants from America. Some women championed this political movement because immigrants competed with them for jobs but also because these groups, as a result of their rowdy and revolutionary past, were seen as a threat to the morality of the United States. Although both parties welcomed women at their political events, neither the Whigs nor the Democrats made women's suffrage a major issue.

Education

Reformers saw knowledge as the means to make society better. In New England, churches would have a "Sunday School" to educate children. Although presidents John Adams, Thomas Jefferson, James Monroe, and John Quincy Adams had all earned college degrees, some of their successors like Andrew Jackson, Martin Van Buren, William Henry Harrison, Zachary Taylor, Millard Fillmore, and Abraham Lincoln did not. Obtaining even a simple education was very difficult for Americans living in frontier or western areas.

Many young children obtained key components of their education from textbooks. Perhaps the most successful of these textbooks were William Holmes McGuffey's, *First Eclectic Reader*. Originally published in 1836, it underwent numerous editions before the Civil War. McGuffey's texts included numerous stories that had a moral lesson. They also included nursery rhymes such as "Twinkle, Twinkle, Little Star" and tales like "The Boy Who Cried Wolf!" Lastly, the McGuffey readers contained historical speeches and documents from such luminaries as George Washington, Patrick Henry, Daniel Webster, and Henry Clay. More than 120 million copies were sold.

The best means for public education in the early nineteenth century became the lyceum. Lyceums were

Horace Mann

schools controlled by local officials and supported by local funds. The lyceum system began in 1826 in Massachusetts and quickly expanded to over 3,000 schools in 15 states by 1834. At these lyceums, students were instructed on literature, the arts, music, philosophy, science, and history. One of Abraham Lincoln's earliest addresses took place at the Young Man's Lyceum of Springfield in 1838. In this address, Lincoln warned about mob violence and sectional discord. "All the armies of Europe, Asia, and Africa combined . . . could not by force, take a drink from the Ohio, or make a track on the Blue Ridge, in a trial of a thousand years," Lincoln declared. "If destruction be our lot, we must ourselves be its author and finisher. As a nation of freemen, we must live through all time, or die by suicide."

In the early nineteenth century, American reformers began to argue all children, regardless of their social standing, should receive an education at the expense of the public. Although the struggle was bitter, the United States became the first nation in the world to create a tax-supported system of public schools that would be compulsory. Lyman Beecher, no doubt speaking for many who wanted public schools in America, proclaimed: "We must educate, we must educate, or we must perish by our own prosperity. If we do not, short from the cradle to the grave will be our lot." The most forceful proponent of the public school movement was Horace Mann of Massachusetts. A Unitarian who had been trained as a lawyer, Mann abandoned the legal profession after he realized his true calling in life was the education of children. "Men are cast iron, children are wax," Mann said. As one of the leaders of the Massachusetts Board of Education, Mann advocated for an extended school year, giving students grades based on their performance, and creating a college to train teachers. It could be argued that the idea of tax supported public education, which was deemed to be radical by many in the nineteenth century, remains the greatest contribution of America's pre-Civil War reformers. However, few lyceums or public schools appeared in the South. One did not need an education to pick cotton. This contributed to the isolation that many southerners felt in the march to the Civil War.

For those Americans who wanted to increase their knowledge but did not have access to a lyceum or the funds for an education, the best way to learn was through reading books in a library. The first libraries in America were voluntary. This meant that in order to obtain books from these libraries one had to be a member and to be a member one had to pay. Before 1848, public libraries were scarce in America. This changed in 1848 when the Boston Public Library was created. What had worked in Boston immediately spread to other parts of the country. By 1860, there were 10,000 public libraries in America.

Entertainments

When the federal government began conducting business in 1789, there were only two cities that had a population of 25,000. By 1860, over 40 cities had a population of 25,000 or more. As more Americans began living in cities, the need for forms of entertainment emerged. An American theater system began to take root. By the end of the 1850s New York City alone had 10 theaters. Other major cities such as Boston and Philadelphia had multiple theaters as well. Smaller cities and boom towns also constructed a theater to demonstrate that this area had arrived. Some of the theaters could hold audiences of around 4,000 spectators. Touring companies would travel from city to city performing wide varieties of shows.

Americans, then just as much as now, had a variety of tastes and interests. Some preferred dramas while others wanted a comedy. Some theater managers would stage two performances in the same evening—the first performance would be a serious drama while the second act would be a farce. The American theater scene also reflected the emergence of classes in America. The wealthy enjoyed refined performances and operas. Middle and working-class Americans favored farces and comedies. Theater managers, who were entrepreneurs, staged an opera and then followed it with a comedy.

Between 1800 and 1860, over seven hundred plays were written by American writers. Some of these plays were designed to comment on an issue in American society. Temperance advocates penned plays to discuss the problems of strong drink. Henry Smith's *The Drunkard, or The Fallen Saved* became very popular. The play that had the biggest impact on American society became adaptations of *Uncle Tom's Cabin*. This performance brought a visual representation of the horrors of slavery into the minds of northerners. The play became so popular at its height that it was performed 18 times in a single week in some cities. It was rumored that the actors had to consume their meals in costume during their brief lulls in between shows.

Reactions to Industrialization

As the market revolution ushered in a change from a barter style economy to a capital driven one, workers began to feel as if they were not receiving enough of the fruits of their labor. Before 1835, few strikes occurred in America. The statute books in most states contained laws that regarded labor organizations as dangerous. Most urban workers tended to support Andrew Jackson and members of the Democratic Party. The Democrats rewarded workers by easing voting restrictions in most states. Armed with a vote, workers voted for candidates who pledged to work for a 10-hour work day and better wages and conditions for workers. In 1840, President Martin Van Buren issued an order imposing a maximum of 10 hours for workers laboring on federal projects. Seven other states then passed legislation enacting a 10-hour work day.

In New England and other areas of the northeast that had developed factories, females began entering the workforce. Almost all of these female workers were unmarried young girls. Oftentimes female workers worked longer and tougher hours than their male counterparts and for less money. The best example of this was the New England "mill girl" who left the boredom of farm life for the excitement of factory work. Matrons hovered over the "mill girls" and ensured that they avoided any romantic activities. These matrons also watched over the young girls in company-owned boarding houses and accompanied them to church every Sunday. The females who worked in the mills only planned to work temporarily. They hoped to make some money, which would make them an attractive mate for a middle-class male. Once a female took a man's hand in marriage she would stop working in a factory.

Female workers, like their male counterparts, also faced stiff competition from foreign laborers. Immigrants competed with women for the lowest paying jobs in America. With an abundant supply of cheap labor available, female workers lost whatever advantages they had.

Nativism

In the late 1830s and 1840s, dozens of strikes occurred in American cities. The factory owners won more of these clashes between capital and labor than they lost. Employers could turn to law-enforcement officials to break a strike or use new laborers to end the strike. American manufacturers often turned to immigrants as a source of labor. These destitute individuals could do the manual labor of Americans and would do it at a cheaper wage.

Bishop John Hughes

After the American Revolution, 10,000 immigrants arrived each year in America. But in the nineteenth century that number increased every year. Turmoil in Europe had prompted immigrants to come to the United States in large numbers. Between 1845 and 1854, close to three million immigrants reached America. Irish and Germans represented the bulk of these immigrants. German immigrants pushed into the interior of the country and farmed. The Irish, however, had grown weary of agriculture due to the potato blight of the 1840s in Ireland. Irish families clustered into urban areas and performed manual labor jobs. The Irish tended to reside in urban areas because they would travel as far as their money would take them. Many Irish stopped in New York or Boston while some pushed into the interior urban areas of Rochester, Buffalo, Cleveland, Detroit, and Chicago. Irish immigrants worked in the emerging factories, dug canals, laid pipe to transport water to urban areas, and built railroads.

While the Irish and Germans improved the infrastructure of America, some groups did not appreciate their contributions. The Americans who sought to exclude foreign immigrants either from coming to America or from becoming citizens were known as **nativists**. These nativists wanted only native-born Americans to hold office and to vote in elections. Nativists wanted to change the naturalization laws in order to make it more difficult for foreigners to become citizens. Nativists also charged that immigrants engaged in voter fraud during elections.

Nativists focused most of their attacks on the Irish because of their Catholic faith. As early as 1835, Samuel F. B. Morse warned about the dangers of the Catholics in America. Catholics took their orders from the Pope in Rome and were therefore a threat to democracy, Morse argued. The Bishop of New York City, John Hughes, confirmed the fears of Morse and other nativists when he announced that Catholics sought to convert all Americans to their faith. Fearful that they were about to lose control of their country, nativists struck back beginning in 1844. A series of riots swept northern cities. In Philadelphia, three Catholic churches were put to the torch and 13 were killed and over 50 were wounded in religious clashes between Catholics and Protestants. Nativists next turned their attention to New York City, which had the largest number of foreign immigrants. But John Hughes, cooled the Protestant anger when he warned, "if a single Catholic Church were burned in New York, the city would become a second Moscow." This ensured peace in New York City but it did not guarantee acceptance of the Irish.

The Democratic Party became more accepting of these immigrants than the Whigs. Whigs soon began charging that immigrants engaged in voter fraud. Irish pipe layers, supposedly voted numerous times in elections. Several Whigs argued that fraudulent votes cast by Irish immigrants had cost the Whigs the presidency in 1844. "We feel here that the whole result has been changed by the foreign votes," one Whig wailed, "and unless some change is made in our Naturalization Laws, that it will soon be too late to prevent an entire foreign control of our government." Another Whig put it more bluntly: "Ireland has reconquered what England lost." Most nativists found their way into the Whig Party. Some nativists even created third parties that ran on a single issue: excluding immigrants from America. Whigs always feared that these small third parties would steal enough Whig votes to allow Democrats to win an election.

In the wake of the crushing defeats of 1844 and as a result of the belief that many Whigs blamed Irish voters for their defeat, the nativist movement gained momentum. A series of failed revolutions across Europe in 1848 brought more immigrants to American ports. The nativists' arguments now became more potent. More and more Americans came to see a threat, whether real or imagined, in America from foreigners. By the mid-1850s, nativists would become a potent force in American politics when the Know Nothing Party entered American politics.

American Literature

American literature underwent a renaissance in the early nineteenth century. American writers, architects, and painters embraced an ideology known as Romanticism. The Romantics were an optimistic and forward-looking group. They held lofty expectations for themselves and society. Proponents of romanticism stressed human emotions and individuality. Many romantics suggested that Americans should be guided by their feelings and heart rather than their mind.

Against this background romantic writers put pen to paper. Noah Webster helped to streamline the English language in America by creating a dictionary. Webster labored over the dictionary for 20 years before publishing it in 1828. One of the earliest romantic writers was James Fennimore Cooper. He had been raised in New York State and his novels used central New York as a setting. His most successful novels, *The Leatherstocking Tales*, described the interactions of white and Native Americans and the experience of the frontier. Walt Whitman's writings, eventually collected in the *Leaves of Grass*, cheered America's democratic heritage and the individualism of American society. Another writer

Herman Melville

from this era was Herman Melville. His greatest work, *Moby Dick*, published in 1851 but ignored at first, surveyed the obsessive nature of Captain Ahab, a whaling ship captain. In the end, Captain Ahab's pursuit of the great white whale leads to the destruction of his ship, almost all of his crew, and his own death. Another key member of the group of writers who made their mark during the Romantic Period of American literature was Edgar Allen Poe. Poe was one of the few writers who came from the South. His stories and poems dealt with the macabre and darker subject matter. Those individuals who rose above the confines of society endured horror in Poe's stories. Poe's life paralleled his works because he died at the age of 40 years under mysterious circumstances.

The most common form of literature from 1830 until 1870 was poetry. These artists, almost all of whom became absorbed in romantic ideas, believed that poetry could serve a purpose for the public. Through verse, a sonnet, or a couplet, a poet could bring the wayward American back from despair. Poets therefore stressed nature, America's exceptional place in the world, democracy, and individualism. William Cullen Bryant, a strong supporter of the Democratic Party and then a supporter of the Republicans, became a prolific poet. Bryant wrote and published poems from 1821 to 1876. However, Henry Wadsworth Longfellow became America's most well-known poet. Schoolchildren committed some of his poems to memory, and many Americans even celebrated his birthday as a holiday. Longfellow's genius revolved around his ability to make the mundane or trivial important. In Longfellow's poems, ordinary household items and everyday experiences had new meanings. Every American could relate to Longfellow's words.

Romantic ideals could also be found in some of the history books that appeared in the nineteenth century. George Bancroft, a Jacksonian Democrat from Boston who became one of the first Americans to complete a doctorate in Germany, labored over a multivolume history of the United States. In Bancroft's *History of the United States*, he reverted back to the Puritan idea of a "city upon a hill." Acts of Divine Providence had allowed for the growth and success of the United States. Bancroft depicted the British as villains. Bancroft's heroic (and in many ways erroneous) depiction of the United States remained in effect until the rise of professional historians at the end of the nineteenth century.

The best expression of American romanticism came from a group of writers in New England who became known as the **transcendentalists**. Borrowing from eighteenth century German philosophers Immanuel Kant and Georg Hegel, the transcendentalists advocated "plain living and high learning." By emphasizing reason and intuition, transcendentalists hoped to overcome the barriers of the mind. They sought to divorce themselves from the static nature and conformity of the elites that they observed in Boston society to have a more personal relationship with nature. Ralph Waldo Emerson perhaps sounded the clarion call for the transcendentalists in his 1836 work, *Nature.* "In the woods, we return to reason and faith. There I feel that nothing can befall me in life . . . Standing on the bare ground, my head bathed by the blithe air, and uplifted into infinite space, all mean egotism vanishes. I become a transparent eyeball; I am nothing; I see all; the currents of the Universal Being circulate through me; I am part and parcel of God."

A colleague of Emerson's who became a leading transcendentalist was Henry David Thoreau. A nonconformist, Thoreau lived for two years in a cabin in the woods along Walden Pond. He chronicled his experience in the 1854 work, *Walden.* Thoreau's rejection of the expectations of society can be seen in his opposition to the Mexican-American War. Massachusetts law required all males to pay a poll tax. Thoreau chose to go to jail instead of paying the tax because he regarded the Mexican-American war as an aggressive war begun by the United States. When Emerson visited him in jail and asked him what he was doing in a jail cell, Thoreau, according to legend, asked Emerson: "what are you doing out there?" Thoreau used his experience in jail as a basis for *Resistance to Civil Government.* This work outlined the philosophy of civil disobedience, which would be used by Mohandas Gandhi and Dr. Martin Luther King Jr. in the twentieth century.

Ralph Waldo Emerson

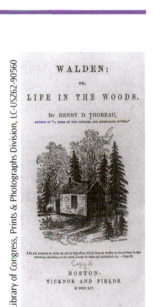

Walden; or, Life in the Woods.

Utopianism

One way in which Americans tried to perfect their country came through the creation of utopian communities. These communities, where the residents would voluntarily agree to live and pool their resources together, would serve as a model for the rest of the country. The communal aspect of these societies offered an alternative to the individualism and competitiveness that had been brought on by the market revolution. Nearly 100 of these appeared between 1825 and 1860. Karl Marx referred to these as an exercise in "utopian socialism," and the term has stuck. However, the advocates of these utopias never recommended violence or a revolution.

Robert Owen, an English textile manufacturer, created a utopian experiment in New Harmony, Indiana in 1825. Property would be held by all, religion would not be allowed, children would be raised not by their parents but by the entire community, and all marriage vows would consist of a single sentence. Although established with the best of intentions, **New Harmony** failed as a utopian community. It folded in 1828.

John Humphrey Noyes established a perfectionist community in Oneida, New York, in 1847. A perfect world, Noyes believed, would allow for the return of Christ. Like New Harmony, Humphrey instructed his **Oneida Community** followers to share all property and allow all members of the community to aid in the raising of children. What made Oneida different from other utopian communities was its adoption of complex marriage. Everyone in the community would be married to every other member of the community who was not the same sex. Another component of complex marriage became the sexual practices of the members. Liaisons were arranged ahead of time, but male members were expected to practice the art of continence as a form of birth control and also to ensure that sexual acts did not become lustful. The Oneida community survived longer than most of its counterparts.

Just outside of Boston, another utopian community developed. This community was created in 1841 through the efforts of George Ripley. Believing that they were creating "Heaven on Earth," intellectual New Englanders gravitated toward **Brook Farm**. Its most famous member became Nathaniel Hawthorne, who based his novel, *The Blithedale Romance*, on his observations at Brook Farm. This community collapsed in 1846. It had invested a large amount of its resources into the construction of a new communal building and then fire destroyed the building. The **Shakers** represented another attempt at finding utopia. Transplanted in America from England before the Revolution, the Shakers counted over 5,000 Americans as members by 1840. Shakers advocated a simple lifestyle. They dressed plainly. A shaker home had no ornate furnishings or paintings. The Shakers wanted to replicate the lifestyle of the original Christians. What made the Shakers distinctive were their dancing and sexual practices. They believed that religious feeling should be expressed through shouting, singing, dancing, groaning, and laughing. All Shakers practiced abstinence and refrained from sexual intercourse. The survival of a Shaker community depended on replenishing its membership through admitting new adult members who wanted to live the Shaker lifestyle. Not surprisingly, their numbers have diminished over the years.

Social Experiments

As reformers tried to perfect American society, they tried a series of social experiments. Maybe the most engaging became the temperance movement. Advocates of temperance believed that society's ills could be traced back to the love of alcohol. Since fatal diseases like cholera could be spread through water, and because refrigeration had not been invented, Americans could not keep milk cold. Thus, alcohol could be drunk at room temperature, and the distilling process ensured that it would not contain a disease. After 1820, the average American drank over five gallons of pure alcohol each year. Farmers realized that whiskey generated a greater profit than corn and also was easier to transport, so they turned their crop into alcohol and used canals and railroads to get their product to markets. Politicians rewarded voters with drinks after they voted. Many employers gave their workers a break at periods of the day so they could drink.

In the 1820s and throughout the 1830s, temperance advocates began a campaign to make the United States dry. Temperance supporters held conventions, distributed pamphlets, published stories describing the effects that alcohol had on a family, and also sent petitions to Congress and state capitals. By 1840, the average consumption of alcohol had dropped to less than three gallons. Starting in the 1850s, temperance advocates now fought against "demon rum" through the political system. As the second party system collapsed in the 1850s, some former Whigs joined temperance political parties. By 1855, 13 states had a law prohibiting alcohol on their statue books.

"The Fruits of Temperance"

Along with temperance, reformers believed that a better diet would improve the lives of the American people. Dietary reformers maintained that foods such as meat, white bread, and certain fruits and vegetable corrupted the body and the mind. Many young men had put off marriage until they had succeeded in their careers and were sexually active. A better diet, some claimed, could end this practice. Sylvester Graham became America's leading dietary reformer. The youngest of

"The Drunkard Progress"

17 children, Graham dedicated his life to restraining the libido of young males. He spoke out on the taboo topic of sex and how foods encouraged males to act in a promiscuous manner. The solution to this problem that plagued society was a coarse dark brown bread. Few Americans followed his advice, but his name has become forever associated with his Graham Crackers.

Institutional Reform

Influenced by the Second Great Awakening, antebellum Americans sought to reform America's institutions. Reformers believed that social problems could be solved and that human behavior could be shaped and changed. The market revolution of the early 1800s had brought the problem of poverty into focus in America. In the colonial and revolutionary periods, Americans who fell on hard times were expected to be cared for by their family. Some localities even auctioned off indigent residents to low bidders who would provide food and shelter in return for that person's labor. Children could be separated from their parents and forced into an apprenticeship where they would learn a skill or craft. Most Americans maintained that poverty was a vice caused by bad behavior. Several states constructed poorhouses to offer assistance. These houses sought to remove poor Americans from the streets and get them back on their feet. The poorhouse experiment failed to succeed. Few states wanted to appropriate the necessary funds, and most poorhouses became a residence for elderly and disabled Americans.

Dorothea Dix

While reformers had failed with the experiment in poorhouses, they enjoyed more success in changing the treatment of prisoners. In the colonial period, few prisons existed. Criminals were whipped, branded, or hung. These punishments all took place in public. In the nineteenth century, the idea of a prison or "reformatory" took root. The time in confinement would force the prisoner to reflect on the errors of his or her ways and refrain from making the same mistakes when released. Prisoners endured rough conditions inside of these early penitentiaries. Most prisons did not allow for any communication between inmates. These prisons failed to live up to the creators expectations. Escapes, riots, and assaults on guards led to sterner measures from prison officials. By the Civil War, the idea of rehabilitation had been abandoned and prisons now focused mostly on punishing inmates.

One area where reformers had more success was in their attempts to limit executions. Before the Revolution, some states allowed for capital punishment for over 100 offenses. Most prosecutors used the death penalty rarely, however. In the nineteenth century, many states limited the number of crimes that could receive the death penalty. Most states only allowed for the death penalty in cases of first degree murder. While many states did not abolish the death penalty, all abandoned public executions.

Another success story for reformers related to the treatment of those who were mentally ill, blind, or deaf. Whereas Americans from the colonial era saw these as incurable maladies, reformers established asylums to house and treat these afflicted individuals. Dorothea Dix, after observing the horrible living conditions of mentally ill women in a Massachusetts prison, dedicated her life to improving conditions for the insane. Dix proposed a system of state-sponsored asylums for the insane. More than a dozen states responded to her call. In 1854, Congress passed legislation that proposed to set aside federal funds for the construction of hospitals for the mentally ill. However, President Franklin Pierce vetoed the bill. Pierce, it appears from his veto message, did not want to set a precedent where the federal government would become the custodians for the nation's poor and afflicted.

A vice that reformers addressed was prostitution. In most American cities, between 5 and 10% of the young females engaged in prostitution. Females had oftentimes turned to prostitution because it provided them with an income. Women engaged in this profession could make more money than they could working in a factory. In the 1820s and 1830s prostitution attracted the attention of reformers. Young men and married men could be seduced by the charms of prostitutes or "painted women." Lydia Finney, wife of Charles G. Finney, established the New York Reform Society in 1834. At first, Finney and other opponents of prostitution visited houses of ill repute and prayed for the female prostitutes that worked inside and their clients. They urged state legislatures to make laws that would punish not just the female but also the male who had solicited her services. The New York Reform Society then hit on an ingenious idea: they began publishing the names of males who frequented brothels in their newspaper. If prayer and laws would not work then shame would. The movement to end prostitution brought many middle-class women into contact with many poor and working-class women. Numerous charitable organizations can trace their origins back to the encounters between middle-class reformers and prostitutes.

Abolitionism and Recolonization

Most reform movements became interconnected. Women's rights advocates, temperance supporters, and opponents of capital punishment almost always supported the biggest reform movement in America: the abolition of slavery. After the constitution went into effect, a series of abolitionist societies emerged throughout America. Led mostly by Quakers in Pennsylvania, these early abolitionists contended that slavery violated God's law and the principles of the Declaration of Independence. These abolitionists sent petitions to Congress urging members to abolish slavery. Congress ignored these petitions. Following the War of 1812, a number of antislavery societies appeared in the South. These groups were located mostly in the mountains of east Tennessee and western North Carolina—areas that had few slaves. Benjamin Lundy, a Quaker abolitionist, published the first antislavery newspaper in Tennessee for a brief period of time.

Many Americans who disliked slavery became supporters of the Colonization Movement. Supporters of colonization sought to send freed slaves back to Africa based on the belief that African-Americans and whites could not live together. In 1816, the **American Colonization Society** was established. Its members included Thomas Jefferson, James Madison, Henry Clay, James Monroe, and John Marshall. After 15 years, the society had helped to transport over 1,000 people to Africa. Support for colonization was tepid at best among African-Americans. They argued that they were as American as anyone else. Although politicians, including Abraham Lincoln, still suggested colonization as late as the Civil War, the concept failed to influence most.

Abolitionism started to become more militant near the end of the 1820s and the beginning of the 1830s. In 1829, David Walker's *Appeal to the Colored Citizens of the World* recommended African-Americans to rise up against their oppressors and use violence to obtain their freedom. Sadly, Walker, a free African-American, would die in 1830 in Boston.

Then on January 1, 1831, William Lloyd Garrison published the first edition of a newspaper called ***The Liberator***. This was an antislavery newspaper that called for the immediate and uncompensated emancipation of all African-Americans in slavery. In his very first editorial Garrison revealed his defiant streak. He wrote, "I will not equivocate—I will not excuse—I will not retreat a single inch—AND I WILL BE HEARD." Within a few months of its original publication the state of Georgia placed a $5,000 bounty on Garrison's head. He brought the horrors of slavery into the homes of many Americans.

Garrison advocated nonviolence and urged his fellow abolitionists to work outside of the political system. Slavery could be abolished, Garrison believed, through moral appeals. By speaking to the conscience of slaveholders, Garrison hoped that they would see the errors of their ways and would free their slaves. In order to accomplish this goal, Garrison and likeminded abolitionists formed antislavery societies. These groups held public conventions, gave speeches, drafted petitions, and published newspapers. By 1838 there were already at least 100,000 abolitionists in antislavery societies. In 1844, William H. Seward no doubt spoke for many northerners when he wrote, "Slavery is now henceforth and forever among the elements of political action in the Republic."

While Garrison advocated a nonviolent approach, Nat Turner, a slave on a plantation just outside of Richmond, Virginia, adopted a different approach. When Turned observed a solar eclipse in 1831, he took it as a sign from God to begin a slave insurrection. After midnight on August 22, Turner assembled a group of slaves, and they began the "work of death" in Southampton County, Virginia. Turner and his followers attacked and killed slave-masters, their wives, and children. They made no discrepancy between kind and cruel masters. The rebellion lasted less than 48 hours. When it ended, over 60 whites had been killed. Turner and his men dispersed and in the upcoming weeks and months were arrested by Virginia authorities. All told, 17 slaves, including Turner himself, were executed. White southerners were terrified over this event. If it could happen in Virginia, it could happen anywhere. Why had Turner, a literate African-American who had been baptized as a Christian, decided to attack and murder so many whites? To many southerners, the main culprits were the abolitionists in the North.

As the antislavery movement gained converts throughout the North, it was met with growing opposition. Abolitionists began sending antislavery literature to southern cities in 1835. When these antislavery tracts arrived in Charleston, South Carolina, people broke into the federal post office and destroyed the literature. In New York State in 1835, a mob led by Congressmen Samuel Beardsley, attacked the office of an abolitionist editor in Oneida. Also, in 1835, a Boston mob tried to lynch Garrison. For his safety, Garrison was confined to a prison cell. Two years later in 1837 in Alton Illinois, an abolitionist editor named Elijah Lovejoy was killed by a group of armed men trying to defend his printing press. Lovejoy became the first martyr in the cause of abolitionism. For abolitionists, it looked as if these attacks were designed to silence them. They needed no further proof that their first amendment rights were under attack when Congress enacted the "gag rule." This law said all petitions relating to the abolition of slavery would be tabled and would not be read in Congress. The gag rule remained in force until 1844.

Under the belief that their society and way of life was under siege by northern fanatics, southern states refused to allow any discussion of abolition. As the northern assault against slavery intensified, southerners became more resistant to attacks on their "peculiar institution." Southerners developed elaborate defenses for slavery. They based their arguments on the Bible, new scientific theories, the importance of cotton to the American economy, and that the constitution sanctioned slavery. After the Mexican-American War, slavery and its extension became the main issue in American politics.

Divisions in the Antislavery Movement

In 1833, Garrison helped to create an organization known as the American Antislavery Society. In addition to Garrison, the organization counted among its members other leading abolitionists including Arthur Tappan, Lewis Tappan, Theodore Dwight Weld, Wendell Phillips, and James Birney. It also included numerous women including Abby Kelly, Lucretia Mott, Elizabeth Cady Stanton, and the Grimké sisters—Sarah and Angelina. The American Antislavery Society called for the immediate end to slavery in America. Once every slave had been emancipated, Garrison believed that they should receive equal treatment in America. Garrison also believed that women were entitled to equal rights, as well. This made him unique for his time.

Other members grew tired of Garrison's dominance and his belief that abolitionists should not vote in elections. In spite of Garrison's domineering personality, the American Antislavery Society had grown to over 250,000 members by 1839. When the society convened in New York City for its annual meeting in 1839, disagreements that had been bubbling under the surface exploded. Garrison's opponents hoped to wrestle control of the organization away from him and turn into a political organization that excluded females. Foes of female participation argued, correctly, that women were excluded from the ballot box in every state. On a crucial vote, Garrison prevailed and women remained a part of the American Antislavery Society.

The opponents of Garrison now bolted from the convention and formed their own organization: the American and Foreign Anti-Slavery Society. "When in obedience to the principles of the society, I go to the polls, and there call on my neighbors to unite with me in electing to Congress, men who are in favor of Human Rights, I am met by a No-Government abolitionist inculcating the doctrine, that Congress have no rightful authority to act at all in the premises," Birney announced on behalf of Garrison's opponents. Garrison and members of his organization then sailed for London to participate in a worldwide antislavery convention. However, the females, most notably Stanton and Mott, who travelled with Garrison to London, were not allowed to participate. In a show of solidarity, Garrison sat with the excluded females in a balcony and did not participate in this antislavery meeting.

The Liberty Party

Although Garrison and his followers refused to participate in politics or even vote, other abolitionists sought to end slavery by working through the political system. By the late 1830s, they began to feel that both the Democrats and Whigs would not embrace abolition. Even though a northern Democrat, Martin Van Buren, occupied the White House, he was regarded as a "northern man with southern principles." The leading Whig, Henry Clay, delivered a Senate speech in 1839 where he criticized the abolitionists as being dangerous to the Union. When some of his friends said that this speech would injure him in the North, Clay snapped, "I had rather be right than be president." Convinced that neither of the political parties would address the issue of slavery, abolitionists began forming their own political organizations. The "Burned Over District" of western New York became the area with a high concentration of abolitionists who wanted to attack slavery using the political process.

James Birney

Library of Congress, Prints & Photographs Division, LC-USZC2-2675

In November 1839, over 500 abolitionists met in Warsaw, New York. There they established the **Liberty Party**. This became an antislavery party committed to putting abolitionists into office where they could legislate against slavery. In the presidential election of 1840, the Liberty Party's nominee, James Birney, received less than 7,000 votes. In 1844, however, Birney received over 60,000 votes including 15,000 in New York State. More than likely Birney's votes would have gone to the Whig candidate Clay had Birney not been on the ballot. If Clay had gotten most of Birney's votes he would have won New York's electoral votes and with those votes he would have won the presidency. Ironically, the Liberty Party, a political party opposed to slavery, actually helped to put a slaveholder, James K. Polk, into the White House in 1844.

Seneca Falls

The unwillingness of male-dominated society to accept women as equals had been shown by abolitionists both at home and abroad. The patriarchal mindset of American males prompted reformers to focus their attention on the plight of women. Most states held that a woman had no legal identity outside of her husband or father. Women could not vote, serve in office, or attend most colleges. Reformers wanted to change this.

After being humiliated in London in 1840 at the World's Anti-Slavery Convention, Lucretia Mott and Elizabeth Cady Stanton journeyed back to America together. During the long trek back across the Atlantic Ocean, the two abolitionists became friends and began discussing the idea of holding a convention that would address the status of women in America. With little help coming from elected leaders in Washington D.C., Mott and Stanton put their idea into operation. They issued a call for a convention to be held in Seneca Falls, New York in 1848 on the issue of new rights for women.

Over 300 women and men attended the convention. After two days of spirited debates, the attendees drafted a **Declaration of Sentiments**. Modeled after the Declaration of Independence, the Declaration of Sentiments announced that "all men and women are created equal." It then listed 15 grievances that women had against men. Among these were: women had to submit to laws even though they had had no voice in framing them, women could not earn the same wages as men, women could not get an education, and women could not participate in most churches. The delegates to the Seneca Falls Women's Rights Convention also adopted a series of resolutions. These resolutions were passed unanimously except for one. "Resolved, that it is the duty of the women of this country to secure to themselves their sacred right to the elective franchise" was the only resolution not approved by all of the delegates. This shows that the right to vote had not yet become a major issue for women's rights advocates. Only after the ratification of the 14th and 15th amendments would women's rights advocates urge that women be given the franchise. All told, 66 women and 34 men signed the Declaration of Sentiments. Only one of the signers, Charlotte Woodward Pierce, lived to see the ratification of the nineteenth amendment.

Technological Advances

The 1830s and 1840s saw a variety of technological advancements in America. As states and private corporations poured millions of dollars into canals in an attempt to replicate tthe success that New York State had enjoyed with the Erie Canal, they overextended themselves. In their attempts to cut into the Empire State's profits, states channeled money into an already antiquated form of technology. By 1840, Americans had constructed over 3,000 miles of canals at a total cost of $125 million. As the canal boom began in the 1830s, steamships on American rivers lessened the need for canals.

Samuel F. B. Morse

Library of Congress, Prints & Photographs Division, LC-USZ62-2188

The power of steam on an American waterway had first been demonstrated by Robert Fulton in 1807. After the War of 1812, Americans began harnessing the power of steam for transportation. By the 1840s, steamships could found on most rivers, lakes, and oceans. A good steamer could obtain a speed of about 20 miles an hour. Steamships made their biggest mark on western rivers. By 1855, over 700 steamships operated along western rivers. By placing the wheel in the back of the steamship, this allowed western steamships to operate in low levels of water. There was an element of truth when western steamboat captains said that all that they needed to operate their ships was a heavy dew. Steamers also cemented the class structure in American society. Some steamers were regarded as "floating palaces" which catered to the wealthy in America. Most steamers welcomed all paying customers but these vessels included ornate cabins for the rich. The lesser elements were prohibited from going to certain parts of the ship, which were reserved for the upper elements of American society. As steamboat lines competed for customers, they pushed their ships to the limits. This resulted in a series of explosions that claimed countless lives. In 1852, Congress passed the Steamboat Act of 1852, which began to regulate the steamboat industry. Steamboats could now be inspected to ensure that they were not acting in a dangerous manner.

Steamboats, in spite of numerous improvements, were cursed by geography. They could only go where a river flowed. Some steamboats had to cease operations in winter or in periods of drought. Railroads, however, were not confined by geography and operated year round. The first railroads were drawn by horses and mules. By 1840, there were only 3,300 miles of track. By 1850, that number increased to 8,800 miles. The real growth occurred in the 1850s. During that decade over 20,000 miles of track had been laid. Once the Civil War began in 1861, the railroad had emerged as the dominant form of transportation.

Changes in transportation allowed news to travel quicker across the country. Yet, it could still take more than a week for news to get from New York to New Orleans. This changed with Samuel F. B. Morse's invention of the telegraph. Originally a highly regarded painter, Morse secured funding from Congress for an experimental telegraph line from Washington D.C. to Baltimore. On May 24, 1844, Morse sent the first telegraphic message to a friend in Baltimore. Morse asked Annie Ellsworth, daughter of U.S. Patent Commissioner Henry Ellsworth, what the first message should be. She replied, "What Hath God Wrought." No longer did one need a speedy rider, steamship, or railroad to carry information. Now, news and information could be sent and received immediately. The telegraph remained a work in progress, but by 1850 there were already 10,000 miles of lines in operation. "Doubt can no longer exist" newspaper editor James Gordon Bennett announced, "steam and electricity, with the natural impulses of a free people, have made, and are making, this country the greatest, the most original, the most wonderful the sun ever shone upon. Those who do not become part of this movement, will be crushed."

Conclusion

The changes brought on by the market revolution, were more pronounced in the North and West than in the South. The North and West now became more linked during the 1830s, 1840s, and 1850s. With changes occurring at a slower pace in the South compared to the North and West, this contributed to a growing sense of isolation amongst southerners. Already on the defensive because of slavery, they seemed to be out of step with the rest of the country in terms of reforms, education, literature, transportation, and manufacturing. The approaching Civil War sapped most of the energy out of the reform movements in America. Sadly, in the years after the Civil War, Americans would stop offering a helping hand to their fellow men that had fallen on hard times. Influenced by the ideal of Social Darwinism, Americans increasingly believed that every man was an island.

CHAPTER EIGHT

Slavery

Chapter 8: Key Concepts

O In your view, was secession by the southern states inevitable and explain your reasoning for why or why not.

O Could there have been a national compromise on slavery? Explain your view.

O What was the most decisive event of this period and explain your reasoning behind the choice.

Slavery was the defining issue of America before the Civil War. It could not be limited to those who had slaves and those who were opposed to its existence. On both sides, those numbers were few when compared to the all of the masses of Americans. Most people did not own other human beings and were mostly indifferent to the practice, itself. Thus, the politics of slavery must be understood as a very unique phenomenon that tended to absorb other, seemingly unrelated issues into it. Almost nothing went untouched or unaffected by slavery. The existence of the "peculiar institution" was a threat to make any innocuous political debate turn into a very serious or violent one.

Origins of Sectionalism

The beginning of slavery as a political problem, to some, is a topic that can be debated. At the Constitutional Convention of 1787, delegates understood the problems of creating a country that was both free and un-free. Those "founding fathers" mostly tried to ignore slavery until it came to the necessity of creating a system of legislative representation for the states. If slaves were to be counted in southern populations, power would shift a bit toward states south of the Mason–Dixon Line. If people were not free, many northern delegates argued, how could they be considered in the total number of citizens? The famed Three/Fifths Compromise settled the issue as a compromise between North and South. Yet, the odd situation remained where a large group of human beings within America were considered both people and property at the same time. The Three/Fifth Compromise, like those to come, only delayed conflict and did not end the inevitably of it.

One must also consider when the concepts of "North" and "South" actually began. The Mason–Dixon Line forms the southern border of Pennsylvania. It also came to represent a symbolic divide between states that perpetuated slavery below it and those that gradually ended it above like Pennsylvania. So, in one sense the terms northern and southern represent geographical places in America. Yet, it is difficult to always demark each place in one of those two categories. In the nineteenth century, places in the Upper South, like Kentucky or Maryland, were places where slavery was not as entrenched as in the Deep South. Some counties or regions in the South were opposed to slavery, altogether. In the North, some states held more of a commitment to slavery than others and retained the institution much longer-like New York. Therefore, geography alone cannot dictate how the southern/northern divide fueled the politics of slavery.

History has left a record of those, early on, who commented on the differences between North and South. In 1785, in a letter, Thomas Jefferson described what he saw as several distinct differences between northerners and southerners. Still, he maintained that variances occurred from the norm. In Jefferson's words, northerners were "cool," "sober," "laborious," and "persevering," while their counterparts were "fiery," "voluptuary," "indolent," and "unsteady." Jefferson wrote that "these characteristics grow weaker and weaker by gradation from North to South and South to North, insomuch that an observing traveler, without the aid of the quadrant may always know his latitude by the character of the people among whom he finds himself." Furthermore, in the middle of the country "northern" and "southern" characteristics seemed to come together, according to Jefferson. Thus, "it is in Pennsylvania that the two characters seem to meet and blend, and form a people free from the extremes both of vice and virtue." Jefferson's observations do not have to be taken at face value. In other words, he may not have been right. Still, his words help to indicate that people had some understanding of the differences in character and lifestyle that existed between the two regions.

Differences between regions of the country were both real and perceived. That is to say, historians can trace and prove ways in which the North and South have not been the same. Sometimes, however, a perception about a region becomes so widely disseminated that it becomes a fact in the minds of most—regardless of the truth of that particular claim. Then, people sometimes take on that perception as part of their identity and act it out in their daily lives. Therefore, a belief in a difference in character that existed between North and South could actually make that difference come true. Both regions took on traits others perceived about them, magnified them, made these things apart of their identities, and thus furthered the division of the "southern" vs. "northern" character. Like the Mason–Dixon Line, once drawn, these partly artificial differences led to the hardening of bad feelings between the sections.

To understand North vs. South in both reality and perception, one must review the specifics which caused one part of America to see another as fundamentally unique from themselves. Frenchman Alexis de Tocqueville traveled America during the 1830s and wrote

Everett Historical/Shutterstock.com

Alexis de Tocqueville (1805–1859)
French author of the classic
"Democracy in America" (1835–1840)

a famed book entitled, *Democracy in America.* Tocqueville lauded and helped define the American character. He described Americans as industrious, inquisitive, hard-working, energetic, and prosperous, among other things. Clearly, Tocqueville prized American democracy, but he made it clear that "I speak here of the Americans inhabiting those States where slavery does not exist; they alone can be said to present a complete picture of democratic society." He was less sure about the South and had much less to say about it. From reading his work, one gets the impression that the free states defined America and the South represented something strange, unique, old, and perhaps even odd.

Historians have noted how the South retained a different culture and way of life from the northern states. Southerners seemed both more hospitable and violent than Americans elsewhere. Capitalism was present in the South but not as much as in busy, northern commercial centers. Generally, the South seemed behind in almost every category including education. Class issues seemed more pronounced in the South, where wealthy, slave-owning planters controlled so much of the land, banks, and important positions in government. Family ancestry seemed more important in the South, as well. In short, the South seemed more traditional and older like pre-capitalist Europe. These sometimes hard-to-detect peculiarities were made all the more visible as the South was frequently compared with the bustling North. So, as northern states increasingly grew more modern, the South's traditions became all the more obvious and apparent.

One thing that might have distinguished the South was the idea of honor. Southern honor is a broad concept that includes many things. Basically, honor is similar to an individual's reputation. In traditional societies, people have very little more important than what others think of them. Maintaining respect in the public realm was the key to advancing in one's trade. Also, one's public standing (males, here especially) was key to finding someone to marry and start a family. In other words, no father would allow his daughter to marry a known coward, liar, or thief. So, honor is displayed every day, but for young males, this meant one needed to confirm to the public his bravery, strength, and general fighting ability. According to de Tocqueville, martial honor of this kind was not alive in the North. Instead, the Frenchman commented that northerners displayed honor by conquering new endeavors in business or creating a new invention, and so on. He might have been wrong about northerners, but there is no doubt that masculine honor, to some degree, was alive during the Old South.

In the South, upholding one's honor often meant fighting and killing. Men of the upper class sometimes participated in duels. This was a ritual borrowed from Europe that was very characteristic of a traditional, pre-modern society. Generally, a duel did not end in death; the idea was that each participant had the courage to show up, and then both went home alive. Most southerners were poor and did not duel, but they did fight or compete in different ways. Horse-racing and shooting contestants were somewhat common in the South. None of these things were exclusive to the southern states, but they seemed more popular and important there. Protecting honor also applied, not only to the individual, but to a community and region. Thus, southerners sometimes reacted to political intrigue as if their region, "the South," itself was being impugned. Generally, southerners were very critical of language or actions they deemed as disrespectful of themselves as individuals or as those who represented a vast region.

So, one must answer the question of why the South was more traditional than the North, and the answer would be: slavery. Well, there can be multiple answers to the question, but one is by far the most obvious and important. More than anything, what marked states as southern was the existence of the institution of slavery. This had something to do with climate, of course. The weather of the Deep South was the most conducive to plantation slavery and those areas were more politically committed to it. By the time of the Civil War, slavery was growing stronger, not weaker. Southerners increasingly became more hardened to protect slavery and keep anyone from criticizing it. This meant that non-slave-owners were heavily involved in the protection of slavery. The institution of human ownership that existed in southern states came to define those places and people who lived there. Slavery slowed the building of cities, factories, and infrastructure like roads and canals. Slavery cannot be separated from a class system in the South that, for American standards, was quite rigid. In other words, it was not supposed to matter in America what one's last name was or what his or her father did or did not do. In the South, it often did matter.

Slavery

The institution of slavery was not predestined to dominate the southern landscape. The fact that it did resulted largely from the profitability of cotton. This staple crop, as it spread through what was known originally as the Southwest, brought slavery with it to largely unsettled places like Mississippi, Louisiana, and Texas. Though plantations were few, their scope and size made them much more powerful than their numbers, alone. Very few people could afford to own slaves in the South. Slaves were expensive. Those who managed to own 20 or more slaves, commonly known as planters, held a kind of authority that went beyond their actual monetary holdings. Planters were rich in land and human possessions more than money. Their sons were among the few who could afford a good, formal education. Thus, planters and their offspring became the people who literally controlled the politics of southern states. Thus, they perpetuated their own interests (the continuance and spread of slavery) despite of the needs of the masses.

Historians debate whether plantations operated like modern businesses or feudal estates. They had elements of both. Some slaves worked in the master's house as cooks, laundrywomen, maids, and servants. Though considered a more favored position, female house slaves often were the ones who faced sexual abuse from their owners. Most slaves worked in the fields under the supervision of a white overseer, or sometimes, a trusted black male who held a position almost like a foreman. Those who worked the fields had a toilsome life of forced labor. Overseers typically did not come from the upper class and were often disliked even by some of the planters. Plantation life was seasonal, based on the planting and harvesting of staple crops.

Am I not a man and a brother? Society for the Abolition of Slavery in England in the 1780s. This woodcut accompanied John Greenleaf Whittier's anti slavery poem, "Our Countrymen in Chains" of 1837

Everett Historical/Shutterstock.com

Not everything about the life of a slave was exploitative. People who live in an oppressed state usually find ways to create some kind of control over their own lives. Though not recognized by law, slaves got married and had families. Owners usually encouraged such unions as beneficial to the maintenance of the institution. Slaves created their own gardens, for the use of their families, hunted for food or sport, fished, and had some possessions. Many became skilled in a trade and even worked for other people. Some slaves were trusted to go on trips with the master's family or even on their own.

None of this detracts from the reality that slavery was based on the coercion of people to perform labor backed by threats and actual incidents of violence. Slavery could not have lasted hundreds of years if not for white southerners using various forms of violence against enslaved people. Most planters preferred not to use harsh measures against slaves. After all, slaves were an investment, and it did not benefit the master class for their property to be damaged. Yet, slaves thought to be disobedient were sometimes subjected to whippings, mutilations, or death. Some were sold from their families as punishment. Sexual abuse of female slaves certainly occurred, as well.

The domination of the slave-owner toward his or her property could never be 100%, however. Planters very often complained of the opposite: that slaves could not be made to perform up to their expectations. Plantation journals are filled with befuddled masters trying to understand how to make work more profitable and efficient. Most preferred not to take drastic action and risk upsetting other slaves. Planters tried to walk a fine line between being too strict and overly forgiving. It is also true that some slave-owners were known to be unusually harsh, brutish, and torturous. There were as many different kinds of slave-owners as there are kinds of people in the world. Thus, it might make sense there was not only one typical plantation experience. Each was unique based on time, place, and characteristics of the master.

Starting roughly during the Antebellum Era (about 1830–1861), slave-owners did create a commonly held view toward the practice of owning other people known as paternalism. This broad idea was a justification for slavery which allowed owners to rationalize their actions as humane, just, and needed. Planters began to see themselves as father figures of huge, extended families that included slaves. The plantation thus became a family setting with the male patriarch acting, in the minds of many, in the best interest of his human property. A whipping of a slave then becomes a father disciplining his child. In this way, paternalism dulled the harsher realities of slavery while also providing justifications for it. The idea was prevalent that black people, no matter how old, were much like children who needed to be looked after and controlled. If released, proslavery southerners argued, blacks would commit crimes, become destitute, and regress into a more uncivilized state. Ultimately, following this logic, blacks needed slavery in order to be given a chance to prosper. Paternalism was a powerful mental construct that is fundamental to understanding the Old South mentality.

Slaves were aware of the assumptions and desires of owners and used them to make their own lives better. Slaves often played the part assigned to them as inferior human beings in order to avoid punishment or work. Already thought of as unintelligent, some slaves "played dumb" when talking to white southerners. They also had coded language, often expressed in song, to talk to other slaves without white detection.

Slaves certainly resisted their condition, but it was usually done in a manner that did not include open rebellion. It was best for slaves to be secretive and careful when negotiating their lives as the property of the master class. Planters frequently accused slaves of theft—a charge that further supported the paternalist position. Slaves did take from owners, usually in the form of food, but it was often in response to something perceived as mistreatment. For example, a planter might reduce food rations for his slaves or change them to something less desirable. In response, slaves might take more than the allotted portion thinking they were owed something better. Also, slaves might feign sickness or "accidentally" break tools to escape work. Again, resistance usually came after something, like violence, that slaves considered beyond the terms of their agreement with owners. Even if masters were not aware of any agreement with their property, it existed in the minds of those who were enslaved. It was a survival mechanism and a means to carve out a better kind of existence.

Open slave rebellions did infrequently occur. The low number of these is due to several factors. For one, reprisal against any such occurrence was swift and extreme. Most white southerners, not just planters, treated even a rumor of a planned revolt very seriously. Some slaves were punished based only on the accusation of a rebellion. Also, there were few places for slaves to go to even if they made it out of the master's residence. Their skin color made them conspicuous anywhere in the South, as most assumed a black person was also a slave. In order to make it to freedom, slaves needed a connection to the "Underground Railroad" of white and free black sympathizers who opposed the institution. Not actually a railroad, this was a system of meeting places and safe-houses that could get an escaped slave to a free state. It was highly dangerous and secretive, and most slaves would not risk it.

The largest slave uprising during the Antebellum Era took place in Southampton County, Virginia in 1831. Nat Turner was a respected slave known to be both educated and religious. He saw himself as a spiritual leader with a special destiny. Visions appeared to him, and fellow slaves looked up to Turner as someone unique. On August 31, Turner and six other slaves killed his master's family, including women and children. Turner's rebels then moved from plantation to plantation in Virginia killing at least 55 people over a matter of days. As they did, other slaves joined the ranks until Turner's band was several dozen strong. The governor of Virginia quickly mustered a large militia to hunt down Turner. The group disbanded, but most were captured or killed. Turner himself managed to avoid the authorities for about two months before being found and executed. Nat Turner's rebellion made white southerners much more paranoid than ever before. Throughout the South, slaves were killed or beaten afterward for a perceived connection to Turner's men. This was exactly the nightmare scenario that the South would work to prevent by any means.

Yeoman Farmers

The average, non-slaveholding white southerner was affected by the institution of slavery and things like actual or imagined slave revolts. Though most whites did not benefit directly from slavery, the vast majority supported it. Supporting slavery at first seems illogical given that it only cemented the power of the planter class thus denying most whites badly-needed reforms. Yet, race was a very powerful thing in the South. As long as slavery existed, yeoman farmers knew they would never occupy the lowest class in the South. Their white skin guaranteed a certain status simply due to the fact of not being black. In addition, small farmers feared that slavery's end would mean competing with freedmen for work. The propaganda of slavery convinced most white southerners that the institution actually made their region superior to all others. Slavery was defended as the best kind of civilization, and most white southerners fell in line with the rhetoric.

The lives of yeoman farmers defied the traditional image of the plantation South. These men and women had something in common with most people in America, no matter the location. Most in the nineteenth century worked as farmers in some capacity and struggled just to survive. Life was difficult. Southerners, for the most part, did not have servants of any kind to do their work. Most did not live on plantations with columned-houses. Their lives were not romantic, and most of all, yeoman thought of the crop and if it would come in on time and in what amount. These were first, second, or third generation immigrants born with little or no advantages.

Many yeomen who were more successful also supported slavery because it offered an opportunity, at least the chance, to become a powerful planter. The ambitions of middling men of some means are largely what drove the spread of cotton/slavery west as far as Texas. Before it was a state, Texas was a part of Mexico. American settlers flocked to the area, and by 1835, Texas was fast becoming a slavery kingdom built on the pattern of the Deep South. The Mexican government feared the foreign influence on their territory and rightly predicted that American settlers would try to take it for themselves. The Texas War of Independence was not an official conflict of the United States. Yet, many well-known Americans fought it in like Davy Crockett and Sam Houston. In addition, the "last stand" at the Alamo became a part of American legend. The result was that Texas declared its independence.

The Mexican War, Slavery, and Public Opinion

Mexico did not recognize an independent Texas, but that did not stop America from annexing it. In 1846, a war resulted called the Mexican-American War, and Texas was the chief prize at stake. America provoked the war by sending an army to protect Texans, but Mexican president Antonio Lopez de Santa Anna saw this as simple provocation into a place still considered part of his territory. Winfield Scott and Zachary Taylor were the two primary American generals. The war was not long, ending in 1848, and the Americans won a decisive victory. Winfield Scott's army occupied Mexico City and forced authorities to sign the Treaty of Guadalupe Hidalgo that gave the United States Texas and the lands that became the future states of California, Utah, New Mexico, and Nevada. The Mexican War was a huge victory for the Democratic Party and President James Polk. Democrats tended to support expansion but not all Americans agreed. Many Whigs opposed the war for pure political reasons and others accused Polk of conspiring with southerners to perpetuate slavery into new places. These critics called this collusion of government and southern planters the "Slave Power;" a clandestine group of individuals and interests committed to expanding slavery no matter the cost.

Slavery could not be left out of the equation as new territorial gains brought it to the forefront in political discussions. In the wake of the Mexican Cession (a term for lands America acquired due to the war), Pennsylvanian Senator David Wilmot proposed a solution to the fears that slavery would be allowed in new lands. The Wilmot Proviso suggested that slavery would not be allowed in lands of the Mexican Cession. The bill passed the House of Representatives but had no chance of succeeding in the Senate, where representation was equal. The bill divided people in America. Southerners were shocked that so many northerners supported the idea of barring slavery in the territories. The mere suggestion of it seemed dangerous and counter to their interests. The Wilmot Proviso was a simple attempt to fix a very complicated and explosive problem. Unfortunately for the nation, there were no easy solutions to the growing problem of defining slavery's role in new, western lands.

The American government dealt with issues concerning slavery and expansion by trying to create compromises. In 1820, Henry Clay helped to steer the Missouri Compromise through Congress. The bill allowed Missouri to become a slave state but said that no others, above the 36'30 parallel, would become so in the states that would be carved out of the Louisiana territory. After the Mexican War, the government faced a similar situation when it came to western territories. California was already heavily populated and was ready to become a state. Congress debated the issue and finally came up with a solution that appeased but did not please both northerners and southerners. In all these debates, the primary problem was trying to keep a balance of free and slave states. Neither northern nor southern congressmen wanted the other side to have the upper hand. Per the Compromise, California would become a free state, the slave trade would be abolished in Washington D.C., and a stronger fugitive slave law would become national law. Southern slave-owners had long complained that northerners were either aiding escaped slaves or doing nothing to return them to their masters. Under the new law, any black person accused of being a fugitive would appear before a special board of commissioners who would decide his or her fate. This meant that more people and resources would be committed to returning runaway slaves. It also made it likely that thousands of people, who had been free for years, whether or not they had ever even been slaves, would be shipped south for a life in bondage. Northerners were outraged. The fugitive slave law made northerners think that slavery could never be controlled or suppressed.

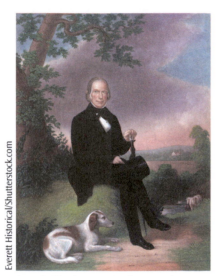

Henry Clay (1777–1852) was active in U.S. politics for first half of the nineteenth century

The vast majority of northerners were not abolitionists and did not concern themselves with slavery on a day-to-day basis. In other words, slavery was not present in the everyday concerns of people preoccupied with their own work and families. However, the fugitive slave law made it harder for northerners to ignore slavery. If they now had to monitor the human property of southerners, then slavery was now extending its reach and impacting their lives. Some had no problem with slavery as long as it stayed isolated in the South. However, more northerners were taking a moral stand against slavery. The Second Great Awakening helped to spur a religious-based opposition to the suffering of others. Yet, religious-based appeals that criticized slavery were still in the minority.

Harriet Beecher Stowe, likely more than anyone else, raised awareness about the evils that resulted from slavery. Stowe was a northern abolitionist from a famous and devoutly religious family. She began to write antislavery stories that were compiled and published as *Uncle Tom's Cabin* in 1852. It was a smashing success, and basically everyone had either read it or heard something about the details of the novel during the 1850s. The main character, Tom, was both a slave and a perfect example of a self-sacrificing Christian. Tom is finally beaten and killed at the demand of a cruel master after refusing to change his religious beliefs or stop ministering the Christian faith to others. In the story, all the white characters are not depicted in a negative way. Instead, Stowe sought to show how slavery corrupts people and makes them turn away from compassion and love. Also, Stowe humanized slaves for a northern audience and showed them capable of being just as Christian as anyone else. Furthermore, *Uncle Tom's Cabin*

Harriet Beecher Stowe (1811–1896), author of "Uncle Tom's Cabin"

drove home a point that northerners did not miss: slavery cruelly separates family members from each other. This idea crossed all racial barriers. The book allowed northerners to sympathize with the plight of people they viewed as quite different if not inferior.

Southerners sought to counter the success of Stowe's book and offer a counter narrative to the growing call of abolition. In the 1850s, a whole new genre of anti-*Uncle Tom's Cabin* literature emerged inspired by proslavery activists. Southerners correctly said that Stowe had never seen slavery for herself before writing the book. They claimed that Stowe exaggerated or lied about the South and the institution of slavery. The proslavery side of the debate made arguments that many found valid. Those who argued for slavery did not just make the claim that it was profitable and did not actually hurt those who were owned. They went further to say that slavery made the best kind of society and it was actually the North that exploited and caused harm to people. The industrial North, many southerners argued, without protections, with a bottom-line profit motive, created unsafe conditions for workers. Cities were dirty and unhealthy, and families were not taken care of by an uncaring factory system. Slaves were cared for from birth to death without any possibility of losing a job and being thrown out on the street, proslavery advocates claimed.

Dred Scott and Bleeding Kansas

For most of the 1850s, it seemed as if the proslavery faction was winning. Dred Scott was a slave who worked for a military owner, John Emerson. Scott and his wife followed his owner around the country as Emerson served in different places. Scott lived many years in free states such as Wisconsin and Minnesota. Scott, with the help of abolitionists, sued several times for his freedom. Eventually, after being sold to someone else, the case made it all the way to the Supreme Court. Dred Scott v. Sanford was one of the most important decisions the Court ever made. Chief Justice Roger Taney offered the Court's opinion that Scott was not free and must remain a slave. More than this, Taney said that no black person, either free or slave, had the right to take a case before a federal court. The decision was clear: slaves will always be as such, black people are not citizens, living in free territory for any length of time does not change one's status, and the Court has no right to decide issues about slavery in the territories. This last part perhaps stung northerners the most. From their perspective, the Court was saying that slavery always superseded freedom. Likewise, it seemed as if slavery could not be kept from entering any place. The evidence seemed obvious that slavery was growing more powerful.

Dred Scott (ca. 1795–1858)

The Dred Scott decision, it must be understood, appeared to silence all debate on slavery's relationship to states formed from new territories. Even those who had no problem with southern slavery tended to see new lands as places that rightfully should be kept for free people. For decades, the debate what to decide on this question raged with at least four options for discussion. One view, expressed by many including Illinois Senator Stephen Douglas, offered that new states would decide by voting whether it would slave or free. This was called popular sovereignty. The Wilmot Proviso type of view simply wished to ban slavery in new places where it did not already exist. Proslavery southerners voiced the opinion that slavery could never be excluded from any place in the United States because it was protected by the Constitution—and this included the territories in the West. A few popularized the idea to simply extend the 36'30 Missouri Compromise line west all the way to the Pacific. With this plan, everything north of the line would be free and everything south slave. None of these options were satisfying to Americans, but they did allow for a debate to take place. The Dred Scott case indicated that slavery simply could not be stopped, anywhere.

Northerners would also not be pleased with the results of Stephen Douglas's attempt to organize Nebraska into new states. Nebraska was a vast territory first thought to be barren and mostly useless to white settlers. Time proved this not to be the case, however. A new transcontinental railroad was in production, and it would run through the Nebraska territory all the way to California. This meant that Nebraska must be settled and organized into a state. The sly and shrewd Douglas took this opportunity to make a name for himself while aiding the interests of his home state, Illinois. Several Senators were competing for the railroad, because it would bring vast jobs and money to any city or state. Douglas successfully lobbied for the railroad to have a major hub in Chicago, but that was not the controversial part. Douglas conceded to break Nebraska into two states. In addition, both would use the popular sovereignty method to vote on the issue of slavery. This was despite the fact that Nebraska was north of the Missouri Compromise line that had for decades distinguished free from slave territory. Douglas hoped he had taken the issue off the table and calmed the volatile debate. Yet, he did the opposite and ignited a wave of discontent. It seemed more likely than before, to northerners, that the American government was little more than a tool of the Slave Power.

Douglas hoped to run for president but faced increased opposition due to the Kansas Nebraska Act. Political allegiances were complicated and ever-evolving during the 1850s. By then, the Whig Party was mostly dead and a new one, the Know-Nothings, had earned a small following. The Know-Nothings were the popular name of the American Party that stressed nativism and tried to limit immigration into the country. The new Republican Party emerged in the wake of the Kansas-Nebraska calamity. Republicans were antislavery and consisted of former members of the short-lived Free Soil Party along with both ex-Democrats and Whigs. The Democratic Party was still hoping to maintain a national unity without being split by the issue of slavery. For Douglas, popular sovereignty was a good position to take, as it basically allowed him not to choose a side on the slavery/territorial argument. Increasingly, though, the debate was becoming either/or in the sense that one was either for or against slavery.

The debate turned wildly violent in Kansas. In fact, war would be a better word to describe what became known as the era of "Bleeding Kansas." The stakes in Kansas were high, as everyone knew that this would become the battleground for pro and antislavery forces. The prize to be won would be a new state that would be added to the totals of either the slave or free faction. People poured into Kansas by the thousands. The "Border Ruffians" from proslavery Missouri came to Kansas ready to wage battle. Prominent minister Henry Ward Beecher sent over a thousand antislavery New Englanders to Kansas armed with rifles. Many more came from all over the country with the clear intent of influencing the vote in Kansas through legal or extralegal means.

For a while, it seemed as if the proslavery forces would win. The first legislatures that were elected were dominated by proslavery representatives. It seemed apparent that fraud of some kind had taken place and the first legislature was disbanded, but the next one in 1855 was likewise filled mostly with proslavery sympathizers. Congress intervened and tried to restore order while having a legitimate vote take place. Despite this, two different governments functioned in Kansas each representing one side of the fight. The proslavery body passed laws while the antislavery delegation negated them.

Kansas erupted into a full-fledged guerilla war. Lawrence, Kansas was known as a haven for the antislavery interest in the state. In May 1856, a proslavery force invaded the town in what became known as "The Sack of Lawrence." Homes were burned and looted and one person died as a result. The antislavery contingent would have revenge, however, in the form of the militant abolitionist, John Brown. During May 24–25, 1856, Brown, his sons, and a company of allies committed five murders of proslavery activists near Pottawatomie Creek, Kansas. Brown's party went to three different houses of people known to aid, in some way, the cause of slavery. The killings were committed largely by using swords to hack and stab the victims until they were dead. Brown's actions were due to revenge for the Lawrence raid and his deeply-committed mission to defeat the forces of slavery. Brown, a

John Brown. Portrait May 1859

New Englander, was largely motivated by a religious zeal that told him slavery was wrong. More revenge killings followed in the coming months on both sides of the struggle. The violence of Bleeding Kansas would soon dissipate, but it was a sign of things to come.

The blood-letting even spilled over to the halls of the U.S. Congress. A few days before the Pottawatomie Massacre, Massachusetts Senator Charles Sumner made an impassioned speech damning the Kansas–Nebraska Act and haranguing the South for its commitment to slavery. He also criticized South Carolinian Senator Andrew Butler, one of the authors of the Kansas–Nebraska Act, and questioned his character. The speech was bold, angry, and a bit too personal. Preston Brooks was Butler's cousin and was a representative in Congress. To Brooks, Sumner's speech was an insult to the honor of his cousin and to that of the South as a whole. In this case, a duel was not warranted because only two gentlemen of equal standing took this route—and Brooks did not consider Sumner to be anything more than a scoundrel. Therefore, Brooks approached Sumner as he sat in his desk in the Senate. Brooks told Sumner he had offended Butler and the South, and then he raised his walking cane and began beating the shocked senator on the head. Brooks continued until Sumner was knocked to the floor with blood gushing from his wounds. Sumner was never the same again, as he suffered from head trauma for the rest of his long life. The South applauded Brooks as a hero, while northerners were aghast by the actions of Brooks. A common northern reaction was to blame slavery for brutalizing the character of white southerners. Only a savage kind of person, from a brutish society, could undertake such an act, northerners commonly repeated.

Bleeding Kansas and the Sumner/Brooks affair actually strengthened the resolve of the small but growing Republican Party. The Republicans believed in a vision of America that did not include slavery. They emphasized the value of the common man's labor along with business and improving transportation and infrastructure. Violence over the issue of slavery further convinced many Americans that it was time for change. People who joined the Republican Party were antislavery but not necessarily abolitionists. The latter group wanted to immediately end slavery. Republicans believed that future western states should not be burdened with the outdated institution of slavery.

Lincoln/Douglas Debates and John Brown

In 1858, a national audience learned more about Republican views due to a series of debates between Stephen Douglas and Abraham Lincoln. The challenger, Lincoln, was vying for a seat in the Senate from Illinois, while Douglas was the incumbent candidate. Douglas was one of the most skillful politicians and best orators to be found in the whole country. The unknown Lincoln towered over the much shorter opponent, but Douglas had by far the better reputation and higher profile. In other words, the debates should have been a mismatch. Instead, Lincoln impressed audiences and matched Douglas on every point. For the most part, the topic was always the future of slavery. Douglas made it clear he neither was an abolitionist nor a promoter of slavery. Lincoln was not an abolitionist either, but he took a strong stance against slavery in the territories. The press followed the debates and they propelled Lincoln to some degree of popularity. Lincoln lost this election, but the debates allowed him to win a higher office in the immediate future.

Abraham Lincoln speaking during one of the Lincoln–Douglas debates

Southerners cared little about what Lincoln had to say. By the 1850s, the South was increasingly isolated due to the institution of slavery. Most of the world had moved past it and abolished slavery. The Industrial Revolution had swept through Western Europe and also influenced America. Western Civilization was advancing toward building the modern world of factories and wage labor. Republicans appealed to people of various types who wished to be respected for doing honest, free work. Southerners felt besieged and surrounded by enemies. The need to construct an argument of slavery as the best form of civilization forced southerners into a position almost always on the defensive. It came to the point where southerners could not accept any political position that did not guarantee the extension of slavery into the territories. Any politician who did not acknowledge the essential rightness of slavery could not be trusted. The Republicans were not even on the radar for the average southerner.

Northerners were not united against slavery, but they had grown tired of it. There never was a majority of abolitionists in America or anything close to that. Things like Bleeding Kansas and the Dred Scott decision angered people and helped move them to feel that slavery was an evil for the future of the country. Still, most northerners were not egalitarians and plenty of them were racist. It was not that one event or idea convinced everyone that the South needed to rid itself of slavery. Neither were most northerners particularly concerned with the fate of slaves, themselves. Northerners also had a certain pride about not being a slave society and disliked the South's rhetoric that usually labeled them as a greedy, heartless, and "soft" civilization.

No one in the North was angrier or more committed to ending slavery than John Brown. Throughout his life, Brown tried to help former slaves with a zeal that made him very unique.

Without question, Brown was a determined abolitionist. Brown created an audacious scheme meant to end slavery, and ever since, the debate has been waged whether he was mentally disturbed or simply misguided and naïve. Gathering a small force of men that included his sons, Brown planned to capture a federal arsenal at Harper's Ferry, Virginia. Using these arms, Brown believed he could attack plantations in Virginia, gather slave allies, build an increasingly larger army, and continue to make his way throughout the South doing the same. Brown hoped to terrorize southerners and force an end to slavery, but he never made it out of Harper's Ferry. None came to aid Brown's small band. Local militia first surrounded the group and then the U.S. Army came to end the raid. Brown was forced to surrender to a contingent of troops led by Colonel Robert E. Lee on October 18, 1859. Thirteen people were killed on both sides of the struggle, and Brown himself was wounded but taken alive.

The raid on Harper's Ferry alarmed, shocked, and terrified Americans in both the North and South. Brown was put on trial, found guilty, and executed. It would have probably been better for southerners had he died during the fight. As Brown never backed down nor said anything apologetic, he appeared to some northerners as a martyred hero. One of the last things Brown wrote was a prophecy about slavery and the future of America. He believed, "I John Brown am now quite certain that the crimes of this guilty, land: will never be purged away; but with Blood." Therefore, Brown continued to preach to the masses about the evils of slavery while awaiting his own death. The poet Henry David Thoreau wrote a strong defense of the intentions of Brown and his men. The song "John Brown's Body" became a popular tune for Union soldiers during the Civil War and continued to be adapted and repeated after it. Northerners, though, were divided on whether to make Brown a hero or not. Some called him a madman and condemned Harper's Ferry. Others pointed out the folly of the plan but said his intentions were noble. In the South, there was agreement that Brown was nothing more than a murderous criminal. In fact, southerners could not believe that even one northerner could express anything positive about a man like Brown.

For any war to take place, northerners and southerners had to feel like the interests of the other section conflicted with their own. This is exactly the situation that developed. Northerners heard the claims of the superiority of the slave society and understood that southerners would never align themselves with an emerging modern world. Southerners were appalled that John Brown was treated by some as a martyr, and felt like everyone in the North was turning against them. Even though the vast majority in the North were not abolitionists, the work of a few made it seem like they were everywhere. Likewise, though Brown was unlike the average northerner, his actions made it seem like others like him were waiting in the wings to invade and kill slave-owners. To most southerners, the North simply was not acting in an honorable way.

The Growing Sectional Divide

By 1860, southern talk of secession had become commonplace in America. Northerners might have felt like southerners were "crying wolf" and had no real intention of leaving the Union. Some indeed did understand the seriousness of the situation and took southerners at their word. Whatever the case, many southerners believed they had a sound argument that secession was constitutional. The radicals, those in the South who talked the most and loudest about secession, were called fire-eaters. A few of the most prominent southern radicals were Edmund Ruffin (Virginia), Robert Barnwell Rhett (South Carolina), and William Lowndes Yancey (Alabama). These and other very powerful leaders could play a part to sway public opinion. Still, most southerners looked at resigning from their own country as extreme and not something to be taken lightly.

Southerners were not all of the same opinion about what to do. Some remained loyal and even fought in Union armies during the Civil War. A select few went on record to say that secession would be a dangerous mistake. South Carolinian James Petigru was a lawyer and firm opponent of following the path that the fire-eaters prescribed. He famously said that "South Carolina is too small to be a republic, and too large to be an insane asylum." In other words, Petigru warned that secession would not work, and those who believed it would were not of a sound mind. Texas governor Sam Houston refused to cooperate with secession and warned his fellow southerners about what was to come. Houston said "The North is determined to preserve this Union. They are not a fiery, impulsive people as you are. . . but when they begin to move in a given direction. . . they move with the steady momentum and perseverance of a mighty avalanche."

Southern secessionists often talked about states' rights as a reason for leaving the country. States' rights doctrine was a mainstream philosophy before the Civil War and could be traced back to founding fathers such as Thomas Jefferson. Many southerners framed their objections to limiting slavery in terms of the federal government infringing on the power of the states. In fact, the two, states' rights and the defense of slavery, cannot be separated when it comes to the Civil War. There is no doubt that the wish to guarantee a future that included slavery was the primary cause of the Civil War.

Slavery was on the minds of southern fire-eaters who convened at the Democratic Convention of 1860. The Democratic Party was one of the last national organizations powerful enough to possibly form a compromise between northerners and southerners. Many were optimistic that some agreement could take place. The frontrunner and likely candidate for president was Stephen Douglas. He was well known for the Kansas–Nebraska Act and hoped that would win him the favor of southern delegates. He was wrong. The most radical members of the Party demanded that slavery not be only tolerated, but explicitly protected. Northern members refused to make a proslavery statement in the official Democratic platform. Northern representatives also refused to endorse the Dred Scott decision that was hugely unpopular. The fire-eaters denounced Douglas as a potential candidate and walked out of the convention. The remaining Democrats nominated Douglas to run for president in the 1860 election. The Southern Democrats met at a different location in the same city of Baltimore, Maryland. Now a separate wing of the Party, this convention elected John Breckinridge of Kentucky as their presidential nominee.

The Republicans certainly benefitted from the Democratic split. Among the frontrunners for the nomination were William Steward and Salmon Chase. Seward especially was considered a good bet to win, but many Republicans thought he was too radical. Lincoln

Stephen A. Douglas (1813–1861)

was a long shot for the nomination but benefited from not being an easterner and having a reputation as a moderate. His debates raised his national profile, as well. The Republicans knew they had to win the favor of westerners and would not gain much ground in the South. Though he had much less experience than the other choices, the delegates elected Lincoln as the Republican candidate for president. In their platform, the Republicans made it clear they were opposed to slavery in the territories. In addition, the Republicans stressed the construction of railroads as well as other internal improvements.

The presidential election of 1860 was not a common one and was one of the most important political contests in American History. The mood of the country was confrontational, paranoid, and fearful. The major candidates were Douglas, Lincoln, Breckinridge, and John Bell of the Constitutional Union Party. The latter was a new party based on keeping the country together at all costs while ignoring the issues of slavery. By this time, it was too late for compromise. Americans entered the presidential election mostly resolved to vote either in favor or in opposition to slavery. Lincoln won all the northern states. Bell won a handful of border states. These were classified as Upper South states where slavery still existed such as Kentucky and Virginia. Breckenridge won a clear victory in all Deep South states. Douglas finished last and did not even carry his home state of Illinois.

Abe Lincoln painting

The final results gave Lincoln the White House, marking the first Republican president in History. The election spoke volumes about the present and future of the nation. Americans simply were no longer interested in someone, like Douglas, who appeared to waffle on the issue of slavery. He was one of the most talented and well-known politicians of his generation, and he failed miserably in this presidential bid. It is also very noteworthy that Lincoln won easily over his competitors. The reality was that his margin in the Electoral College would have given him the presidency even without the break-up of a national Democratic Party. The growing population in the free North meant this section was beginning to dominate southerners in presidential elections. In the South, Lincoln was not even a consideration for voters.

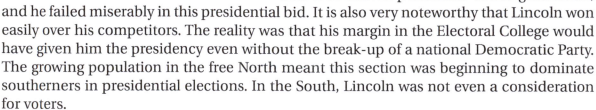

To Secede or Not to Secede

Diehard secessionists took Lincoln's election as the last straw and began campaigns to bring about an end to the Union. Fire-eaters argued that southerners had become a marginalized community whose interests were no longer represented by the U.S. government. It seemed likely to most southerners that Republicans could control the White House indefinitely no matter how they voted below the Mason-Dixon Line. It seemed just as probable, to the South, that Republicans would begin a campaign to end slavery. It did not matter that Lincoln was a moderate, nor did most listen to anything he said to the contrary. Still, radicals in the South had to convince more conservative southerners that secession was the only thing left for them without any other recourse.

Factions existed in every slave state who tried to delay or stop the momentum of secession. Not everyone committed to slavery thought that leaving the country was the best way to protect the institution. Even many planters feared that a potential war would disrupt and threaten slavery even more than the Lincoln administration. Moderates (sometimes called cooperationists) preached a cautious approach in order to see exactly what the Republicans had planned. Still, two factors limited the overall success of southern moderates: the twin commitment to secession as constitutional right and to white superiority as the only option for the South. It was a given that most white southerners believed that secession was a viable, and longstanding right for people to express a major grievance with the government. To prove their case, southern leaders referenced things like the Enlightenment-inspired social contract theory or Thomas Jefferson and James Madison's Virginia and Kentucky Resolutions. Secondly, the all-powerful belief that the end of slavery would bring about the total collapse of the racial hierarchy in the South cannot be overestimated. Simply put, white southerners could not fathom a world where slaves would become free in a multiracial, functioning civilization. Thus, all those who did not own slaves felt a great incentive to do whatever it took to preserve the bedrock institution of the South.

In the Deep South, most were convinced that immediate action was the best approach to keep their fears from coming true. In December of 1860, South Carolina called a convention of representatives who unanimously decided in favor of secession. In the weeks that followed seven more states followed the lead of South Carolina, including Mississippi, Florida, Alabama, Georgia, and Texas. Unlike radical South Carolina, there was significant opposition to disunion in these other southern states. The first seven Deep South states to separate from the rest of the country represent what historians call the "first wave" of secession. Still, in early 1861, it was not clear what these states intended to do to defend their self-proclaimed new status. Also, no one knew for sure how many, if any, other states would join them.

On February 4, delegates from the seven states (though Texas was not involved from the start) met in Montgomery to create a new government and country. The governing principles and structure of the newly formed Confederacy was heavily based on the American Constitution. However, the president was to serve only one six-year term, and clear laws were put in place that protected slavery while forbidding protective tariffs. There was significant debate as to who would become the first president of the Confederacy, and among the candidates were Robert Toombs and Jefferson Davis. However, Davis was easily the most popular choice and was elected to the office. Davis had been a military hero and was previously the Secretary of War under Franklin Pierce. In addition, Davis served multiple terms as a senator representing Mississippi. Davis was a conservative who was not a fire-eater, although he did defend the right of a state to secede. He was probably the most qualified man to become president. In electing Davis, the Montgomery convention was sending the message that they were neither rash nor radical.

In his inaugural address, Lincoln hoped to calm the fears of southerners. Lincoln took the oath of office on March 4, 1861. The tone of his speech relayed his resolve that the Union was permanent and no states held the right to leave it. At the same time, Lincoln spoke directly to southerners in an attempt to make clear he would not interfere with slavery where it existed. The new president emphasized that the property of all Americans would be protected, including slaves. Lincoln hoped that other slave states would not join the Confederacy. He also wished that the Deep South states would change their minds without any kind of violent confrontation. Yet, Lincoln was clear that he saw all the states as one entity and would not validate any act of leaving the Union. In what would become Lincoln's signature style, he said "We must not be enemies. . . The mystic chords of memory, stretching from every battlefield and patriot grave to every living heart and hearthstone all over this broad land, will yet swell the chorus of the Union, when again touched, as surely they will be, by the better angels of our nature."

Conclusion

America had come to a crisis point that could not be resolved by the actions or rhetoric of politicians. The politics of slavery had run its course with no resolution. To a previous generation, it was unimaginable that Americans could be driven to take up arms and shoot at one another. There was only one issue that could inspire Americans to do so: slavery. Arguments about the goodness or evil of the institution ultimately forced people to harden their positions to the point where compromise was not possible. Two societies, the North and the South, were defined either by the existence or lack of slavery. The South, not seeing any way that it could be ended, sought to perpetuate slavery through any means. The North, viewing it as incompatible with their society, wanted to keep slavery at arm's length. The institution also came to define how each section viewed the free, white members of the other. Northerners looked at the South and saw a decadent, despotic class of planters and a degraded, uncivilized class of yeoman farmers. Southerners characterized northern society as one based on the exploitation of labor and the pursuit of money. Both sections thought the other did not represent the best future for America. The American road was coming to a dead end. Finally, theories and accusations would be put to the test on the battlefield.

CHAPTER NINE

Civil War

Chapter 9: Key Concepts

- What is the most interesting military aspect of the Civil War period in your view and what is your reasoning for this choice?

- Who is the most vital Confederate figure during the conflict and why do you feel this way?

- Do you think Lincoln did a good job as commander in chief of the Union during the Civil War and explain your answer.

The country could not know what to expect in early 1861. Secession did not guarantee a war, but it did make one probable. Still, no one was sure what kind of war could result. After all, Americans from North and South had mostly cooperated in the brief history of America. People traveled from one section to another. Southerners and northerners married each other and had families with ties to both sections. People often did business in both North and South. For most, it seemed most probable that any conflict would be brief and everyone would then come to their senses. A few observers, however, feared the worse. Southerners appeared extremely committed to defending their honor and the institution of slavery at all costs. The Republican government gave all indications that secession was rebellion—and this was something that had to be suppressed. Both North and South had enough young men of fighting age to prolong the war much longer that most thought was possible.

President James Buchanan has received much criticism for his handling of the initial wave of secession. Basically, Buchanan did very little while finishing his last few months before the inauguration of Lincoln. Perhaps it is true he could have done more. Yet, like most Americans, it was thought that a few radicals were to blame in Deep South states. These few could not rouse the mass of southerners for a long war, it was commonly perceived. When Lincoln took office, he immediately faced a problem unlike any president in the American past. Southern states that had declared allegiance to the Confederacy were also claiming federal property as now belonging to the newly-formed country. This also meant that federal troops, long-stationed in these southern states, were now hostile ones in a foreign land. Lincoln was determined to not allow

James Buchanan (1791–1868), American President (1857–1861)

any state simply to declare it had left the Union. He saw the country as permanent and secession as an empty argument. Very soon, his ideas would be put to the test.

Lincoln's Dilemma

Lincoln's first crisis as president was the spark that ignited the Civil War. In Charleston, South Carolina, the Confederacy was pushing U.S. forces to leave a fort and surrender it to the state. Fort Sumter was occupied by Union soldiers under Major Robert Anderson of the U.S. Army. Confederate General Pierre Gustave Toutant Beauregard commanded a force with the mission to take the fort for the Confederacy. From the point of view of South Carolina, Fort Sumter now fell under the jurisdiction of another country other than the United States. Lincoln was in a difficult position. He could not be weak and simply allow South Carolina to do whatever it wanted. This would encourage other southern states to follow suit. After all, he firmly believed that the Union must be defended at all costs. Yet, the last thing he wanted was to start a war. Somehow, the president wanted to keep all the states

The firing on Fort Sumter in Charleston, South Carolina in response to a Confederate attack

a part of America while avoiding bloodshed. The Confederacy besieged the fort while trying to keep Anderson's men from being resupplied. Desperate, Lincoln authorized a ship to make its way into Fort Sumter's harbor in an effort to relieve the suffering Union troops. In response, on April 12, Confederates fired on Union troops in the first official engagement of the Civil War. Anderson surrendered and South Carolina reclaimed Fort Sumter.

There was still no guarantee that all-out war would follow the minor scuffle at Fort Sumter. Lincoln won a public opinion victory in the North, due to what occurred in South Carolina. The president promised that he was only sending a noncombatant resupply ship to feed Anderson's men. He likely knew that Confederate forces would not see any difference and attack the ship. In this way, Lincoln forced the Confederacy to fire the first shot of the Civil War thus making the South the aggressor. Southerners certainly did not see it this way, but the president had to contend with some in the North who had sympathies with the seceded states. Every move had to be careful and calculated.

It was also key that Lincoln never recognized the Confederacy as a separate country. He considered this a rebellion and an act of treason. Thus, on April 15, Lincoln issued a call for 75,000 volunteer militia to be furnished from each state not in rebellion. The militia would be called for service for only three months. In this way, Lincoln believed he was following a precedent set by George Washington when he summoned men to come together to end the Whiskey Rebellion in 1795. Lincoln wanted to make it clear that he was not forming an army to subdue the entire South or start a war. It was important that he used language that indicated the new force was only to put down a rebellion and that this was not an overreach of presidential power.

Lincoln was playing a game of chess, then and throughout the war, which he knew he must win. The call for volunteers outraged many southerners who were previously lukewarm on the idea of leaving the Union. At stake were those slave states that had not joined the Confederacy. Among these were large or strategically important places like Maryland, Kentucky, and Virginia. To lose all the slave states would make the coming fight much more even. Kentucky was the state Lincoln most feared losing. It had many navigable waterways that provided the link between North and South. Whoever controlled Kentucky would have an advantage of invading the interior of the enemy. In fact, Lincoln famously remarked, "to lose Kentucky is nearly the same as losing the whole game."

Each slave state now had a very difficult decision to make. These tended to be states with strong ties to the Union, in part, because of location. Each was internally divided even more so than the first seven Confederate states. Arkansas, Tennessee, and North Carolina all declared for the Confederacy after Lincoln's move to put down the southern rebellion. Slavery was less entrenched in these semi-mountainous states, but the institution was strong enough that all three strongly identified with southern interests. Lincoln and most in the North knew this would be the likely result, but looked to Maryland, Missouri, Kentucky, and Virginia as the major players in the game. The outcome of their decisions could go as far as to determine the result of the war.

The Second Wave of Secession

Virginia quickly decided to secede after Lincoln announced he would end the revolt in the Deep South. Only a few months before Fort Sumter, one would have likely predicted that the state would never break ties with America. Virginia had a proud place in the short history of the country. It was the birthplace of American heroes like George Washington, Thomas Jefferson, and Patrick Henry. Virginians loudly proclaimed their place in the creation of the country and boldly wore their identity as Americans. The commitment to the Union, despite slavery, was strong enough to make secession unlikely. However, the election of Lincoln, Fort Sumter, and the call for militia all helped to turn moderates into pro-secessionists. Or, at least, these events helped convince enough people previously on the fence to endorse secession that Virginia ultimately joined the Confederacy. In the end, it was the idea of aiding Lincoln's government in attacking and killing other southerners that appalled Virginians. After all, Virginians were asked to form regiments that would be used against fellow slave states. Pro-secessionists also argued that Virginia would be vital to the war and federal troops would necessarily march through it in order to get to the lower South. Thus, Virginians used appeals to southern honor—arguing that proud people would not be occupied (as that would be what it seemed like) by troops sent by the hated Lincoln. After all, most southerners considered Lincoln and all antislavery advocates as scoundrels, not worthy of respect. Virginians did not trust that Lincoln would keep any promise nor refrain from harming themselves or their property.

Virginia was vitally important to the Confederacy. The Confederate government was well aware of this fact and encouraged secession in the state. It was the most populous slave state. Also, it produced a large amount of food, in part, due to the fruitful Shenandoah Valley. Richmond's Tredegar Iron Works was by far the largest of its kind in the slave states. It could be argued that, without Tredegar, the Confederacy could not have produced enough materials for weapons, railroads, and other things to survive very long in the Civil War.

Maryland was key due to its location. The northern capitol of Washington D.C. would obviously be in jeopardy should Maryland join ranks with Confederate states. The harbor in Baltimore was also very important to any nation that controlled it. Violence broke out in Maryland between pro and anti-secessionist factions. Those who sympathized with the Confederacy seemed more aggressive and effective. Furthermore, Maryland appeared poised to leave the Union before Lincoln took drastic action. The president understood that any border state that fell could spark a domino effect that gave pro-Confederates in other states the momentum for victory. Thus, losing Maryland could mean the loss of another. To keep Maryland in the fold, Lincoln suspended the writ of habeas corpus in the state. This meant that authorities arrested secessionists and kept them off the streets without the usual evidence or trial. Lincoln has often been criticized for his actions. However, they were successful in keeping Maryland out of the Confederacy.

Kentucky was a large state with many advantages for either side. It was a pathway to the heartland of the Confederacy. Any Union Army would likely have to pass through it to reach the lower South. Likewise, Confederates would probably traverse through Kentucky to reach the valuable agricultural centers of the Midwest. Lincoln and his advisers also knew that Kentucky would be important for the Union Navy. Its many waterways would be central to controlling the vital Mississippi river. Beginning in Kentucky, the Union could begin to chip away at the small number of Confederate forts along the pathway, down the Mississippi, reaching New Orleans. The Confederacy's largest city, it was also by far the most important port for the newly established nation. For many reasons, it seemed likely that Kentucky would be a key battleground state. As it occurred, Kentucky was even more solidly pro-Union than Maryland. The state declared its neutrality, but this was another win for Lincoln. As it turned out, Kentuckians fought for both sides in the war. Though, it seemed it leaned more to the North than the South.

Missouri never left the Union. It was a place with sharply-divided, contrasting loyalties. Due to location, it was as much western as either northern or southern. Here, old grudges remained from the days of Bleeding Kansas and the Border Ruffians. One could say Missouri had its own internal civil war. Bands of nonofficial soldiers fought each other in the name of either the Union or Confederacy. War atrocities took place. Revenge killings, more than traditional warfare, characterized fighting in Missouri.

Comparing North and South/Strategies

At the beginning, neither side was prepared for war. The U.S. Army was very small. Yet, most officers, at the start, would have to come from the few ranks of experienced soldiers. The army was spread out all over the West at isolated outposts, and they did little except when they fought Indians. The major thing that soldiers fought was boredom. In addition, America's last experience with war was The Mexican War. This was short and rather easily won with relatively few casualties. At the same time, a small national army would have to furnish the beginnings of two separate forces. In time, both Confederate and Union forces would dwarf the numbers of the old Army. The new recruits would have to come mostly from raw volunteers. These men were brave but inexperienced.

Common men enthusiastically went off to war expecting it to be short. Neither side believed the other would fight for long. Soldiers tended to have a romanticized view of war that was unrealistic. It was hard to forecast that this would be the deadliest war in American History. For many, war was a chance to prove one's self among friends, relatives, and back home to people in their communities. Women were often the catalyst for men to enlist on both sides. There was even more of a stigma, in the nineteenth century, for men to shirk their responsibility to serve during wartime. Failing to do so could result in a lifetime of a shame upon individuals and families. This was especially true of southerners. These were men where a sense of honor, in a violent or martial sense, still carried more weight than in other regions. Southern men probably exuded more enthusiasm to fight than any others.

Yet, southerners faced key disadvantages in the coming contest. To win, one side of any war needs more than valor. Civil War armies occasionally reached as numerous as 100,000. This was not the norm, but armies here were by far the largest the American continent had ever seen. Soldiers, who marched more than they actually engaged the enemy, needed food, clothing, and obviously, guns and ammunition. The Confederacy had trouble producing enough of any of these. Factories were more numerous in the northern states. So much so, that 97% of all guns produced before the war came from northern states. Furthermore, travel was more difficult in the new Confederate states than in those further north. Railroads had long begun to replace all other modes of transportation as the quickest way to travel. Railroad lines, however, were being built mostly in places not in the Confederacy. One also found more dams and bridges in northern waterways than in the South. Transportation would be an important aspect of moving thousands of men place-to-place.

These issues were not as apparent in 1861 as later, and to many it seemed the Confederacy held the key advantages. Most assumed that the Union would have to conquer the entire Confederacy in order to win. This would come only after a long time and an incredible loss of life, most understood. At the same time, many around the country thought that the Union resolve to fight would not hold up, and sooner than later northerners would demand an end to the Civil War. Observers also believed that the Confederacy had the best generals. Many of these came from Virginia, trained at West Point, and were among the most experienced in the old army. Cotton could have been an advantage, as well. Knowing the European demand for cotton, perhaps England or France would intervene on behalf of the Confederate cause.

Realizing the part to be played by cotton was partially a reason for the Union's grand strategy called the "Anaconda Plan." Devised by then Secretary of War Winfield Scott, it was a general means to defeat the Confederacy without the kind of long, endless conflict that seemed almost inevitable. The federal navy would use its superiority over its Confederate counterpart to blockade southern ports. Hopefully, this would keep the Confederacy isolated and without ability to profit from its cotton. The combined efforts of both the navy and army would then try to control the Mississippi River. Hopefully, it was thought this would divide the Confederacy east of the Mississippi from the western portion. It would also deprive their government and military from using the best and fastest way to travel in the southern states. Also, according to the Anaconda Plan, the northern military would attack and capture the Confederate capitol of Richmond. (It was moved to Richmond partly due to Virginia deciding to join the seceded southern states.) This way, Lincoln's armies could squeeze the Confederacy until it could no longer offer resistance.

Bull Run (First Manassas)

The first major battle of the Civil War occurred in northern Virginia as part of the Union want to seize Richmond. The battle would become known as Bull Run, named for a small creek nearby. Lincoln urged General Irwin McDowell to engage Confederates and get to Richmond, and the Union tried a surprise attack on the Confederate flank. At first, Federals were advancing and winning the contest. At a crucial moment in the fighting, General Barnard Bee remarked to Confederate Colonel Thomas Jackson that the Union looked like it would prevail. At this Jackson supposedly replied "well, we will give them the bayonet." Bee looked at Jackson and rallied his men behind the slogan: "look at Jackson there standing like a stone wall." This would make the young colonel forever known as Stonewall Jackson.

Thomas J. "Stonewall" Jackson (1824–1863), Confederate general during the Civil War

The soon-to-be General Jackson was a peculiar man. Soldiers and civilians alike described him as strange and not befitting the appearance of a general. He had a Presbyterian zeal much like a Puritan. Some imagined the pious Jackson like an Oliver Cromwell during the English Civil War. On the march, Jackson was known to suck on lemons. He had an injured hand that caused him to ride with it pointing upward in the air. Yet, he was fearsome and a very good general. Jackson would go on to win fame for his accomplishments.

Bull Run did more than jump start Jackson's career. The Unionists fled the battle as Confederates pushed them back north toward Washington. The retreat was hasty and disorganized. Lincoln was dismayed that his army would be routed—especially as the battle was only a few miles from Washington D.C. Southerners began to say that the enemy capitol could be taken in a matter of days. The victory gave the Confederacy a sense of over-confidence. Perhaps the northerners will not fight. Maybe the war will be over soon, was the refrain. Civilians also did not understand that this was just the opening scene of the coming conflict. Many spread their blankets and picnicked while watching the battle. Soon, all would learn that the Civil War was not entertainment for the masses.

Shiloh

In the western theater of war, Ulysses S. Grant would prove the Confederate confidence misplaced. Grant was tasked with moving down along the Cumberland and Tennessee Rivers toward the ultimate goal of the Mississippi. Confederate resistance was little match for Grant's combined land and sea forces. At Fort Henry and Fort Donelson, Grant gave the

Union some of its earliest and most decisive victories. Before a year had passed, the Union had a stronghold on Kentucky and looked poised to do the same in Tennessee. It was during this campaign that U.S. Grant earned the nickname of Unconditional Surrender. As a result of his ruthless resolve, Grant was promoted from Brigadier to Major General.

The next target for Grant's Army of Ohio was Corinth—a town in extreme northwest Mississippi. Corinth was important as a railroad hub where many different lines of track merged together. Both sides understood that controlling Corinth was central to commanding North Mississippi, Tennessee, and possibly beyond. Davis appointed Albert Sidney Johnston's Army of Mississippi with the mission of stopping Grant's advance on Corinth. Johnston, Davis' favorite general, devised a plan to attack Grant's forces before they could

Ulysses S. Grant (1822–1885)

get to Corinth. On the morning of April 6, 1862, Confederates came pouring out of the woods near Shiloh, a small community in Tennessee only miles north of Corinth. On this day, luck was on the side of the soldiers in gray. The surprised and unprepared Union troops were pushed back as the Confederates advanced. Johnston's perogative was to either force Grant's men into the nearby Tennessee River or utterly destroy them. As Johnston surveyed the battlefield, watching his strategy succeed, a bullet caught him while on horseback. Johnston died only a few minutes later.

An overly optimistic Beauregard took over from his senior general, Johnston. In fact, by the end of the day, he telegrammed Davis that a total triumph had been achieved. However, Grant and his subordinate General William Tecumseh Sherman had not yet given up the fight. Actually, it was probably a heroic stand by Sherman's troops on the first day of action that prevented a total calamity. On the morning April 7, the tide turned as Grant counterattacked the stunned Confederates, driving them from the ground gained on the first day. Even though some northerners criticized Grant for not being ready to fight and losing ground initially, Lincoln's faith in both Grant and Sherman was growing with every new victory. It seemed Grant, an unknown before the war, was becoming Lincoln's man to prosecute this war.

Shiloh was the bloodiest battle to that time in the Civil War. This time, there were no onlookers with picnic baskets. The results of Shiloh had several consequences. It further established Union dominance within the interior of the Confederacy. It meant that Grant would most likely take Corinth, though Confederates would desperately try to defend it. Shiloh deprived the Confederacy of a general that many believed would be its greatest in Johnston. Perhaps most of all, Shiloh signaled that the Civil War would be unlike any Americans had seen. The 20,000 men lost shocked people of both sections. Parts of the battlefield were so violently contested, and so strewn with dead bodies, they were given names like the "Sunken Road" and the "Hornet's Nest." Yet, not much ground seemed to be gained. Most understood both sides would simply regroup and fight again.

Lee Takes Command

In the first half of 1862, things were not going much better for the Confederacy in Virginia. Here, General George McClellan led his Army of the Potomac in operations to threaten and eventually take Richmond. McClellan was a favorite of the newspapers and many others in the army. A man well-schooled in the military arts, he was considered the most likely to be the savior of the cause of the Union. His Army of the Potomac was likely the best supplied and organized of any other of the Civil War. His men adored their general, because he rarely risked a fight without overwhelming numerical superiority. During March through July 1862, McClellan launched a massive movement from south of Richmond known as the Peninsula Campaign. His counterpart, Joseph Johnston, was usually as cautious as McClellan and preferred retreat to engaging a force of superior numbers. At first, it appeared that Richmond might be taken rather easily.

Johnston was wounded at the Battle of Seven Pines, and an emergency change in leadership altered the course of the Peninsula Campaign and the entire war. General Robert E. Lee took over command of the Army of Northern Virginia from Johnston. Lee had been involved in some relatively unimportant action as a commander, but immediately before Seven Pines, he was an adviser to Davis. Lee was trusted, and thought capable, but most southerners did not think of him as the man to ensure Confederate victory. Lee was quite different from his predecessor. He soon showed more aggression and willingness to attack McClellan's men even when outnumbered. The Army of Northern Virginia found success from June 25 to July 1, in a series of engagements known as the Seven Days' Battles. Both combatants suffered roughly the same number of casualties. However, the Confederates were able to force McClellan away from Virginia in what seemed to most as a loss for the North. It cannot be overestimated this effect on those loyal to the Confederacy, and especially the citizens of Richmond. From the brink of disaster, Lee had saved the day.

The result of the Seven Days was disappointment in McClellan's leadership, among some, and a growing faith in Lee's decision making. After the failure to subdue the rebel capitol, Lincoln called McClellan to a meeting to discuss it. The president's will to win was only growing more pronounced. He was heard to say "I expect to maintain this contest until successful, or till I die, or am conquered." One of McClellan's undeniable faults was a contempt of Lincoln and most others deemed less talented than him.

Robert E. Lee (1807–1870), celebrated Confederate General in the U.S. Civil War, ca. 1860s

Everett Historical/Shutterstock.com

Lincoln, as he demonstrated time and again, was a pragmatic type willing to work with others despite any personal enmity. The president urged his stubborn commander to fight more battles instead of waiting for the ideal time to attack. With such a fine army one should use it, Lincoln believed. The unmoved general clearly did not listen nor have much respect for the commander in chief. This relationship would only further deteriorate while chances of Union success in the eastern theater decreased.

Antietam

In late 1862, it was more than confusion in the northern command structure that bolstered the confidence of Davis and Lee. The Davis government, at least in Virginia, had ever-soaring hopes of success mostly due to the Army of Northern Virginia—and successful generals like Lee, Jackson, and cavalry leader Jeb Stuart. After another triumph near Bull Run (also called Second Manassas), the southern leadership was thinking of an even bolder move: a foray into northern territory. This could only mean that Davis and others felt strong enough to attempt more than a defense of their own capitol. The leader of the Army of Northern Virginia felt the time was right to threaten a northern city. Hopefully, Lee surmised, his troops could strike fear in the heart of the average American citizen. As well, if Lee could provide Davis with a victory, especially near a major urban, northern center, perhaps Europe would intervene. This had been the hope of many southerners from the beginning of the Civil War.

The Davis administration had reason to think a major power from overseas would become an ally. The Mason/Slidell or "Trent" Affair was a disaster for Lincoln's government. James Mason and John Slidell were Confederate diplomats on a trip to Paris and London, respectively to gain recognition for the Confederacy. This would have been a major step toward the Confederacy's final goal. In November 1861, the U.S Navy stopped the diplomats aboard the British ship "Trent." The United States then seized Mason and Slidell as prisoners. England and France viewed this as a breach of etiquette and international law, and there were some rumblings of a rift between the United States and the two most powerful nations of Europe. Lincoln apologized. Though, some across Europe continued to express interest and support for the fledging Confederacy. Davis, Lee, and others had a reason and a precedent to think that Europe might come to their aid. Perhaps proof of their ability to launch a counter-offensive was enough incentive to make this happen.

In late 1862, Davis and Lee devised their most extensive and far-reaching series of campaigns of the entire war. It was decided that Lee would invade Maryland. It was hoped that Lee's troops would temporarily relieve Virginia of fighting thereby allowing southern soldiers to live off of northern food. Confederate leadership thought the move would frighten northerners, cause panic, hopefully convince them to pressure Lincoln for peace, while rallying pro-Confederate Marylanders. At the same time, Confederate General Braxton Bragg would invade Kentucky while convincing enough people there to make their state a part of those that had seceded. Thirdly, Confederate Generals Earl Van Dorn and Sterling Price would move against Grant in Mississippi, hopefully dislodging him from the vital fort at Vicksburg. Despite many strategic goals, all of these were aimed at showing Europe that the southern states in the Civil War could defeat Lincoln's Union.

Once again Lee's Army of Northern Virginia faced McClellan's Army of the Potomac in one of the most important battles of the Civil War. Lee was counting on McClellan to move slowly as usual, and overestimate Confederate strength. He was mostly right. McClellan believed Lee's army was about 120,000 strong but was about 40,000, instead. While searching an abandoned Confederate camp, a Union soldier found, wrapped in a cigar, Lee's entire battle plan. Union leadership now knew where the Confederates were going and when they would be there. In response, McClellan reportedly said: "here is a paper with which if I cannot whip Bobbie Lee, I will go home." Lee decided to concentrate his forces around Sharpsburg, Maryland, waiting on McClellan to arrive. On Sept 17, 1862 the Battle of Antietam began with the Union army enjoying both the tactical as well as a two to one numerical advantage. However, Union mistakes as well as Lee's ability to shift his troops to meet every advance prevented a decisive victory by the Army of the Potomac. The soldiers in gray were forced to retreat, but the fighting did not identify a clear winner. As for Davis' plans for better results in Kentucky and Mississippi, both were overwhelming southern failures and northern gains.

The results of Confederate aggression led to many important outcomes for the war. Lincoln was certainly glad about turning back Lee, though searing mad at McClellan, but Antietam came at a high price. Antietam was the bloodiest single day of the Civil War. Casualties were four times the American losses at Normandy, and twice the number of dead than in the War of 1812, Mexican War, and Spanish-American war combined. Though the Union was mostly pleased to repel Confederate advances in the western theater, Lincoln's attention was still on the lack of progress in the East while fearing the enemy's capability to threaten Washington D.C. Sensing that McClellan could not win a decisive decision here, he finally removed McClellan for good from the command of the Army of the Potomac after Antietam. As for the opposing side, Antietam hurt but did not end Confederate chances for success in the East. Never again would the southern states be as close to convincing Europe to enter the Civil War. After all, the grand plan of Davis, after failing, indicated that his armies could only fight on the defensive. It stymied the momentum of the Army of Northern Virginia. It forced them back south and thwarted Lee's plan for a long stay in the North.

The Emancipation Proclamation

Most importantly, Antietam gave Lincoln the opportunity to act on doing something to end slavery. The more radical Republicans had been pressuring Lincoln to try to put an end, or at least confront, an institution that most northerners felt gave the Confederates an advantage. After all, one could reckon that a population of about 2 million forced laborers could allow more white southerners to fight on the battlefield. Northern generals also faced tough decisions when it came to what to do about slaves while also prosecuting a war. Thousands of slaves flocked to Union armies as they marched through the South. At first, the American president had them returned to their southern owners. To the army, this seemed both like a waste of energy and time as well as basically giving back a source of labor and wealth to the enemy. Later, slaves were labeled as contraband of war, much like guns or horses, and could be confiscated without return. This too was not ideal. Antietam gave Lincoln a position of strength to issue his Emancipation Proclamation in September. It officially went into effect on January 1, 1863. It did not end slavery but freed all those in bondage in southern states who had seceded then under Union control. Basically, this was a huge step toward the destruction of slavery but did not guarantee that much. Even in the North, it was controversial.

Commemorative print of Abraham Lincoln with the text of the Emancipation Proclamation of January 1, 1863

Lincoln's decision to strike a major blow against slavery came after much deliberation. Union generals understood slavery proved a great asset to the Confederate war effort. Approved by Congress in 1862, the Confiscation Act legalized the contraband policy, but did not say whether or not slaves would become free. Radical Republicans pushed for immediate emancipation and included men like Frederick Douglass and Charles Sumner. Douglass believed Lincoln was "allowing himself to be the miserable tool of traitors and rebels" by not acting against slavery. There was also strong anti-Emancipation sentiment, especially among immigrants and the poor who did not want to be put on an equal footing with blacks. In August 1862, Horace Greeley, editor of the *New York Tribune* and a strong supporter of Emancipation, wrote the editorial called "The Prayer of 20 Millions." Greeley hoped to publicly call out Lincoln and embarrass him into taking action against slavery. Lincoln responded that "my paramount object in the struggle is to save the Union, and is not either to save or destroy slavery. If I could save the Union without freeing any slave I would do it, and if I could save it by freeing all the slaves I would do it; and if I could save it by freeing some and leaving others alone, I would also do that." Eventually, Lincoln did feel emancipation was the right move, but he tried to make sure everyone knew this was only a means to try to win the war.

The Proclamation opened the door for black men to join Union ranks and fight in the Civil War. Approximately, 180,000 black Americans participated in the Civil War as soldiers. They were earnest to do so even before Lincoln issued his Proclamation. Black soldiers fought for most of the same reasons as anyone else, but of course their circumstances made them unique. Entry into the U.S. Army brought pride and status, especially if one was a former slave. The most renowned of all black regiments was the 54th Massachusetts. In July 1863, the 54th, led by Colonel Robert Gould Shaw, stormed the Confederate-held Fort Wagner in South Carolina. Their bravery charging into heavy fire inspired other blacks to enlist and generally impressed Lincoln's government and the northern masses. Within the military, Union officers remarked that black soldiers were as good as any others.

Though, black men in the military still faced some discrimination and scorn from their white counterparts.

In addition to adding numbers to the Union army, the Emancipation Proclamation also changed the stakes and purpose of the Civil War. Before it, there was no guarantee that slavery would not continue even with a northern victory. Now it was clear that Confederates were fighting for the continued existence of slavery, and to some degree, northern troops were battling to destroy it. The Proclamation would only have effect in relation to the success of Union armies. Yet it also freed Union commanders from any complications from deciding what to do with southern slaves. It might be said that slaves themselves forced the hand of Lincoln to introduce the Proclamation. It was clear that these men, women, and children were mostly not content to remain in their current condition and sought escape to a life of freedom. Their pressure on the armies of the North ultimately was the catalyst for the landmark act from the president. Lincoln, a conservative Republican, previously hoped not to make the war about slavery. After all, he had to also win the support of northern civilians who were not that keen on sending their sons to risk their lives on the behalf of black slaves.

Confederacy and the Western Theater

Davis also faced many hurdles as Confederate president. Most campaigns in the western theater did not succeed in part due to a confused command structure. The president appointed Joseph Johnston as overall commander of the western theater. Yet, what Johnston really wanted was to return to his post at the head of the Army of Northern Virginia. Davis and Johnston did not work well together in a manner similar to Lincoln and McClellan. In fact, there were few other than Lee who had the full trust of Davis. The headstrong Davis also had a strained relationship with the flamboyant Beauregard—and it so happened that both were two of his most important generals in the West. Unfortunately for the Davis administration, both were also fairly popular with the masses of southerners. They were two of the highest ranking generals when the war began and thought to be two of those who would lead Confederates to victory. Davis' suspicions of Johnston and Beauregard were mostly right as neither seemed capable of meeting the generalship demands of the Civil War. In the western theater, Davis never found his general(s) who could successfully prosecute Confederate goals.

In the West, Confederates acheived its most consistent success in places like Tennessee, Alabama, Mississippi, and Georgia due to small bands of mounted raiders. Generals Nathan Bedford Forrest and John Hunt Morgan harassed the Union endlessly and then disappeared. They slowed down much larger Union Armies, forcing them to stop or sometimes change direction. For the most part, Confederate guerillas attacked Union supply lines. In a war, these describe the support groups of men who connect an army back to its base of supplies like food and clothing. The farther any force moves from its supply base, the more vulnerable the line becomes. Sherman was known to describe "that devil Forrest" in regards to the only man of the war to be promoted from private to general. In 1863,

Morgan went further north than any other Confederate reaching as far as Ohio. With only about 1,000 men Morgan's raiders captured thousands of Union prisoners and supplies. Ultimately though, most of Morgan's troops were caught and imprisoned. Despite the successes of these small bands, what still mattered most were the movements and engagements of the major armies.

Fredericksburg and Chancellorsville

By far, the most successful Confederate effort was Lee's in Virginia. Lee and Grant are most often considered the best generals of the Civil War. Lee's greatest victories depended on timing, great leadership, and knowledge of the enemy. The Army of Northern Virginia had the greatest cavalry of any other during the Civil War. The cavalry, led by men like the dashing and audacious Jeb Stuart, acted mostly as the "eyes and ears" of the main force. In other words, they were charged with locating the enemy to determine which way it was going and when it might get there. Lee also had great subordinate generals like Jackson and James Longstreet. Jackson acted as the fierce and unrelenting, bold executioner of Lee's flanking movements. Some even consider Jackson greater than Lee, but it was the latter who was more in keeping with the chivalrous idea of the southern gentleman. To those who knew him, Lee became an exemplar of the Old South planter class.

Lee's greatest successes came in late 1862 through the early months of 1863. At Fredericksburg, Virginia, Union General Ambrose Burnside commanded about 110, 000 troops against Lee's roughly 75,000. Pushed by Lincoln not to be like McClellan, Burnside wanted to make a more aggressive move against Lee in order to take Richmond. He designed a feinting movement to make the Confederates think he was attacking in one place, but really aimed at Fredericksburg, Virginia, and to do so he had to cross the Rappahannock River. In war, it is always dangerous to cross a major body of water unless the other side is not aware of it. Burnside felt that he had plenty of time to do so before detected. Unfortunately for the Union, Jackson's wing of the Army of Northern Virginia had already arrived just outside the city.

Fully armed Confederate African-American pickets as seen through a Union officer's field-glass, while on outpost duty at Fredericksburg

Lee took a very strong position along a hill, fortified by a long stone wall, called "Marye's Heights" near Fredericksburg, Virginia in December 1862. Lee then patiently waited for a Union attack that probably should have never been ordered. The men in blue bravely, but with great loss of life, emerged out of the town only to encounter firmly entrenched

Confederates who occupied an ideal high ground. Union soldiers had to cross a half-mile open field in order to get to the Confederates' strong position. Burnside foolishly refused to call off the advance, and ordered charges over and over into the teeth of Lee's men. Fredericksburg was a victory for the Confederacy and one of the most lopsided of the war. The Union lost about 13,000 men to about 5,000 Confederates. It was here that Lee uttered his famous words: "It is well that war is so terrible—we should grow too fond of it." The sights were horrifying, as the Fredericksburg battlefield was strewn with piles of dead and dying soldiers. One Union soldier described the scene: "One without a head, there one without legs, yonder a head and legs without a trunk . . . with fragments of shell sticking in oozing brain."

Burnside was disgraced as a commander because of Fredericksburg, and Lincoln replaced him with "Fighting" Joe Hooker. He was known as being combative and a braggart. Again, Lincoln was looking for his anti-McClellan. When Hooker took command his idea was to force Lee into a fight in open terrain. Supposedly Hooker said, "May God have mercy on General Lee because I will have none." Hooker took a defensive position around the wooded area of Chancellorsville, Virginia only miles from Fredericksburg. Hooker believed his numbers would force Lee to retreat or make him attack in the open, and either way, he thought the Union would gain the advantage. Despite being outnumbered almost 2 to 1, Lee decided to take the offensive. Stuart and his cavalry notified Lee that Hooker's right flank was open (vulnerable to attack). In a bold move, Lee split the army in two while already facing a superior force. This broke one of the first rules of warfare. If everything did not go right, Lee's and Jackson's forces could be separately crushed.

On May 1, 1863, Lee and Jackson met to discuss what to do, and they decided on the riskiest gamble up to that point, and maybe of the entire war. Lee sent Jackson and 30,000 men through the woods on a 12-mile track to attack Hooker's flank. Lee only had about 15,000 men left only miles in front of the bulk of Hooker's huge army. Jackson and his men, moving close to Union lines through the woods, had to be almost completely quiet. Jackson arrived on May 2 and found the Union completely surprised and unprepared, and the Confederacy began to roll over Hooker's fleeing soldiers. Chancellorsville was a total rout of the Union.

Fredericksburg and Chancellorsville were Lee's greatest victories but also represented much of the futility of fighting in the East. Jackson's flanking march has become legendary. Both battles were brilliantly conceived and carried out. Yet, not much changed in terms of one side gaining a firm tactical advantage. Most battles between the Army of Northern Virginia and the Army of the Potomac occurred within a hundred miles between Washington D.C. and Richmond. Lee often remarked privately about his frustration that he could not provide the ultimate checkmate—that stroke which would annihilate his opponent. This was very hard to do during the Civil War.

At Chancellorsville, Lee also suffered a kind of loss that could not be recouped. After the day's battle, Jackson and some of his officers rode ahead to see the practicability of pursuing the fleeing Yankees. It was Jackson's way to want to always seek to pursue and kill more soldiers in blue. Returning at nightfall, Confederates mistaked him and his party for Federals and fired on them. Jackson was shot in the arm and had it amputated. Lee remarked that "Jackson has lost his left arm, but I have lost my right." A few days later, Jackson died from his wounds.

Gettysburg

Even with Jackson's death, Lee was emboldened and decided once again to invade the North during the summer of 1863. On June 9, the Union crossed the Rappahannock River in Virginia to see what Lee was doing where they confronted Stuart's Confederate cavalry. The southern cavalry was defeated at the Battle of Brandy Wine, one of the few times Stuart was bested, bruising the proud Virginian's ego. Stuart's cavalry then embarked on a long and mostly pointless ride around Union forces. Lee lost contact with him and his men for a week, depriving the Confederate officers of their usual reconnaissance concerning their opponent's location and intentions. Yet, Hooker was moving slow and seemed unsure of himself after Chancellorsville, prompting Lincoln to replace him with General George Meade. As it turned out, Meade would be wiser and more able than his predecessors, Burnside and Hooker. Still, neither the Union nor Confederates were very sure of the location of the other. It turned out that Lee's fabled army was in Pennsylvania waiting for someone to fight.

The Battle of Gettysburg, the charge of the Confederates on Cemetery Ridge, July 2, 1863, from Leslie's Weekly

On July 1–3 the Battle of Gettysburg would go a long way toward deciding the winners of the Civil War. On July 1, Confederate forces entered the town of Gettysburg, Pennsylvania looking for shoes and other supplies. The town was insignificant and Confederates had no plans to engage the Union at this place and time. Without Stuart, though, Confederates did not know that nearby was a small group of federal soldiers. The accidental battle began as a small skirmish, but once Lee realized a fight was under way he ordered his troops to attack and take the offensive. Lee understood that the Union would be reinforced at some point, so the Confederates would have an advantage if they fought them early rather than late. Confederates drove the Yankees back and it seemed to be, on the first day, an easy southern victory. Although July 1 was a success for the South, the Union still occupied the high ground around Gettysburg, and the entire Army of the Potomac would soon join the fight.

A huge battle was brewing on the hills and fields near this little Pennsylvania town. Union General Winfield Hancock arrived and positioned his forces along the high ground of Cemetery Hill, Cemetery Ridge, and Little Round Top. On July 2, the Confederacy now faced a very formidable task: ousting a superior Union force from a very good defensive position. Lee could have left the battlefield and chose to fight at another time, as Gettysburg held no strategic importance. Lee's top general Longstreet urged Lee to do so, believing there was no reason to fight here. To do so would to commit a similar mistake as did Burnside at Fredericksburg. Lee believed that this battlefield was as good as any, saying to Longstreet: "the enemy is there, and I am going to attack him there." Next would come the deadliest combat the American continent had ever witnessed. The fields surrounding Gettysburg would be soaked with blood at places like "The Peach Orchard," "The Devil's Den," and "The Wheat Field." The Army of Northern Virginia threatened to break through Union lines several times, but Meade did what Lee accomplished at Antietam—shifting his troops back and forth to ensure they did not break.

Perhaps the most desperate fighting took place at Little Round Top. This is where the pivotal action of the second day occurred when Union troops held this small, yet strategically important hill. Union troops led by Joshua Chamberlin were under a furious rebel attack. The fighting was ferocious, and it seemed as if the hill would be captured by the Confederates. The bluecoats atop Little Round Top were dying and running out of ammunition, and after the rebels surged up the hill, Chamberlin ordered a bayonet charge as a last desperate attempt to keep their position. It worked, and the surprised soldiers in gray were forced back down the hill. Chamberlin became one of the Union's premier Civil War heroes, and Little Round Top remained in the possession of the Federals.

Despite that the enemy held the key defensive heights, Lee believed complete victory was in his sight. The now legendary Lee believed in the Napoleonic strategy of fighting a big battle and completely destroying the enemy thus eliminating its ability to continue. He had a taste of victory before but something always happened to deny him a total one. The plan involved attacking Meade's army from the rear, the right flank, and finally with a frontal assault. Lee's reasoning was the Union had to be weakened from the previous two days believing Meade would remove men from his center to counter his rear and flank, thus the center would be vulnerable and ready to be destroyed. The final and pivotal part of Lee's strategy would forever become known as Pickett's Charge. Led by General George Pickett, it was something Longstreet warned against. Later, Longstreet noted that, "I could see the desperate and hopeless nature of the charge and the hopeless slaughter it would cause . . . That day at Gettysburg was one of the saddest of my life." On July 3, Pickett led 15,000 men across a near mile-long field, over a fence line, into a heavily fortified Union position believed to have been weakened. The slow-moving rebels were easy targets, and the Unionists tuned loose their rifles as well as their cannons, slaughtering the Confederates. Only about half of Pickett's men returned. After three days of warfare, the battle was a loss for the southern side.

Gettysburg was a huge boost for Lincoln, the deadliest battle of the Civil War, and a monumental disaster for the Confederacy. Lee took the blame for Pickett's Charge which was his worst decision as commander of the Army of Northern Virginia. Never again would the rank and file feel invincible nor be as strong in numbers. Overall, 28,000 Confederates were dead wounded or missing—about a third of his army. Lincoln again was upset that Lee was allowed to retreat back to Virginia. Yet, he and the northern populace understood that a historic and tide-turning conflict had taken place in Pennsylvania. So much so, Lincoln traveled to the battlefield on November 19, 1863, to dedicate a veteran's cemetery. His short thoughts on what happened there, known later as "The Gettysburg Address," became as notable as any speech in American History. His last word on the matter summed up his take on the importance of Gettysburg and the cause of finishing and winning the war. Lincoln declared, ". . . that from these honored dead we take increased devotion to that cause for which they gave the last full measure of devotion—that we here highly resolved that these dead shall not have died in vain—that this nation, under God, shall have a new birth of freedom—and that government of the people, by the people, for the people, shall not perish from the earth."

Lincoln's words would mean less if Grant continued to fail to capture Vicksburg. While Gettysburg was not an important town, Vicksburg was the opposite. Many felt the war would turn in either direction based on this heavily fortified city in Mississippi. Davis heavily invested in the city, thinking it could not be taken. Lincoln did the same, appointing his best general with its downfall, and believed in him after many failures. From December 1862 to July 1863, Grant's army fought many battles and was repulsed time and again. It seemed like Davis could be right.

Vicksburg

Grant finally devised a different way to capture Vicksburg in a campaign that began in April, 1863. His Army of the Tennessee would march down the west bank of the Mississippi. Meanwhile, naval gunboats would have to run the gauntlet past heavy guns to get south of the fortified city. Next, the Army of the Tennessee could be ferried to the east bank of the river to attack from the South. The plan was very complicated and included feinting movements in Mississippi to distract the primary Confederate army charged with defending it—commanded by General John Pemberton. This campaign was dangerous. The terrain around the Mississippi was muddy and difficult to navigate. If the Union navy failed, and were destroyed, Grant could be trapped and defeated.

Everything worked the way that Grant had planned. Pemberton, who was not known as a great military strategist, never caught on to the plan until it was too late. Vicksburg's guns failed to stop Union ships. Sherman and his troops kept any other potential

The First Mississippi Negro Cavalry bringing Confederate prisoners into Vicksburg, 1864.

reinforcements at bay, isolating Pemberton against a much larger force. After a series of defeats, Pemberton and the Confederates retreated into Vicksburg itself. As a result, the Federals dug in for a siege—encircling the city and denying people inside supplies. For three months, civilians suffered and were starving. Union ships bombarded the city. Desperate, people in Vicksburg lived in caves for shelter. After three months, Pemberton surrendered Vicksburg to the Union on July 4. Two consecutive days, July 3 and 4, changed the war decidedly in favor of the North.

Union Momentum

Grant's astounding successes made it very difficult for the Confederacy to defend itself in the western theater. Outnumbered, Davis tried to transfer troops here and there to meet every demand. A continued lack of structure and cooperation made it almost impossible. Johnston often simply ignored the orders of Davis. General Braxton Bragg's tenure as commander of the Army of Tennessee was simply a fiasco. Though experienced and qualified, Bragg alienated almost every one of subordinate officers. Neither did he fare much better on the battlefield. This was especially true of his disastrous campaigns to save Chattanooga in 1863. Forrest even threatened to kill him.

Though winning the war, Lincoln, Grant, and Sherman understood that the Confederacy had a resolve to keep fighting for years. Women on the homefront were urging men to keep fighting. They were also doing much of the labor on plantations and on small farms. It was southern women, after all, who were sometimes in the line of fire as Union armies increasingly were marching unfettered throughout the South. Lincoln and his favorite generals realized that the Union must make war against the South as a society. In other words, southerners' morale must be shattered. Their ability to make food for their men in the field must be reduced. This meant destroying private property and terrorizing the southern populace. As Sherman famously said, "war is cruelty and you cannot refine it. . ."

Sherman seemed best equipped to grasp this concept of "total war." He appeared hardened by the war. Early on, Sherman understood that only a total war against the South could bring the Civil War to an end. Grant agreed, and in March 1864, he was put in charge of the entire war effort second only to Lincoln. Sherman would take over in the West, going against Joe Johnston's Army of Tennessee in a drive toward Atlanta, and in the East Grant would personally command in Virginia. In the Shenandoah Valley of Virginia, General Phillip Sheridan was assigned with making sure it could no longer be of use to the Confederacy. The Valley was a great source of food for Confederate armies. The Confederacy had also used it as a sort of highway to advance toward Washington D.C. It was in the Shenandoah that Jackson, in 1862, with lightning speed won several impressive victories, threatened Washington D.C., and diverted Union attention away from the primary contest against Lee's main force. Still, the term total war would become more synonymous with Sherman than any other general of the Civil War.

Sherman's strategy to capture Atlanta was to continuously flank Johnston, destroy railroads, cut off supply lines, and try to take the city with a minimum of fighting. Johnston preferred retreating instead of facing Sherman who commanded many more soldiers than the Confederates. In July 1864, Davis finally removed Johnston from command and replaced him with an eager but inexperienced John Bell Hood. Known as a skilled and brave corp commander, Hood attempted several unsuccessful assaults to push Sherman out of Georgia as the Union general was approaching Atlanta. Simply put, Hood was a reckless soldier who was not qualified for his position. On September 1, 1864, Hood's men evacuated the city burning any military supplies or anything of use to the Union. The city was Sherman's, and Atlanta virtually burned to the ground.

Lee vs. Grant

In Virginia, Lee was trying to make sure Richmond did not suffer the same fate as Atlanta. Over the last year of the war Lee and Grant faced off in what may have been the worst, most grotesque, and merciless fighting of the entire war. The Overland Campaign was Grant's idea to destroy the Army of Northern Virginia and capture Richmond. In fact, the former was more important. As long as Lee's army survived, so did the Confederacy. Lee knew that he faced a different kind of opponent after the Battle of the Wilderness fought May 5–7 near the old Chancellorsville battlefield. Technically, a Confederate victory, it did not matter that much to Grant. The battle derived its name from the fact soldiers squared off in an area of thick, heavy underbrush and trees. Much of the battlefield caught on fire, and the sounds of soldiers burning alive, wounded and unable to move, filled the air. This time, instead of regrouping and waiting to fight another day, the Army of the Potomac continued to pursue Lee's Army of Northern Virginia. This was different than other generals in the eastern theater. At this point, a minor win did not make that much difference. In addition, Grant could much easier replace those who died more so than could Lee.

The results of the Overland Campaign were inconclusive, and it took a terrible toll in life for both sides. Battles such as Spotsylvania Courthouse and Cold Harbor became infamous for futile charges and senseless slaughter. Lee began with about 65,000 troops to Grant's 120,000. Grant lost more men, but the disparity in numbers was only growing stronger. Both armies settled in around Petersburg, Virginia from June 1864 to March 1865. It was a stone's throw from Richmond, and each army began to construct a series of trenches around the city. As it was called, The Siege of Petersburg really was a series of battles that foreshadowed the trench warfare of World War I. Grant often gambled and lost, while Lee skillfully met most Union advances in his attempt to save Petersburg and thus the Confederate capitol. Every day, the Army of Northern Virginia was shrinking.

There was now little hope for the Confederacy. Sherman's capture of Atlanta all but assured the reelection of Lincoln in 1865. "Copperheads," Democrats who opposed the Civil War, had significant support. A vote against Lincoln was one in protest of the war. It was possible that a different president, like Democratic nominee George McClellan, could initiate talks of peace with the Confederacy. Lincoln's defeat in the election was the best hope for the Confederacy to have any chance at not losing. Lincoln, as he made it clear, would not cease the war effort until the Union was saved and the government of Davis dismantled. To further crush southern resistance, Sherman conducted his infamous "March through Georgia" after the fall of Atlanta. From November to December 1864, Sherman's troopers ravaged the Georgia countryside before arriving at Savannah. The idea was to take or burn anything useful to the Confederates while living off the land. Civilian property was destroyed. Southerners would never forget or forgive what they would call "Sherman's Bummers."

In practical terms, the Army of Northern Virginia was the last thing keeping the Confederacy afloat. On April 7, 1865, remnants of Lee's tattered troops were awaiting a resupply train at Appomattox Courthouse, Virginia. Most of all, they needed food. However, after a series of small battles in the area, they found the supplies destroyed. On April 8, Grant petitioned Lee for his surrender. After some discussion and a few more skirmishes, Lee agreed to Grant's terms, meeting him at the home of Wilmer McLean. The terms were generous. Confederate soldiers could go home immediately with their rifles and horses. No revenge was taken here. Onlookers noted that Grant and Lee treated one another with utmost respect. In appearance, the two could not have been different. Grant looked straight from the field with his muddy boots and unkept uniform, whereas witnesses remarked that Lee appeared in formal attire wearing his dress sword by his side. In any case, most understood that the capitulation of Lee guaranteed the end of the Civil War.

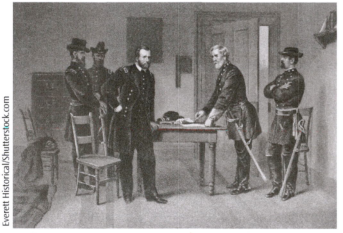

Everett Historical/Shutterstock.com

Confederate General Robert E, Lee surrenders to Union General Ulysses S, Grant at Appomattox Court House, Virginia, April 9, 1865, from The New York Times.

The Civil War was over on April 9, 1865, though not everyone agreed. There was still minor fighting out west, and Joseph Johnston still commanded a small band of soldiers. It was not long until Johnston and the remnants of the Army of Tennessee also surrendered. Not all immediately agreed to stop fighting, including Jefferson Davis. After leaving Richmond, Davis hoped to make it west of the Mississippi and somehow reestablish the Confederate government. There was talk that guerilla bands could prolong the Civil War, but most southerners were not willing to go this route. Union armies, massive in size, could go and come basically wherever they wanted.

Conclusion

Some historians have called it the first modern war, but the Civil War was a mix of the old and the new—with terrible consequences that resulted. Most Americans identified warfare with the type seen during the American Revolution. Here, men lined up in rows and columns and fired on the command of an officer. This was also the case during the Civil War. Discipline and training was the key. It was thought only the bravest could stand firm in the face of oncoming fire, keep their positions, load, and then march forward. However, new rifling technology meant that guns fired more accurately and at a longer distance. This helps explain why so many lines of men were cut down so fast, leading to unthinkable numbers of killed and wounded. Civil-War bullets tended to burrow and lodge into the bodies of men, and doctors knew little else to do than amputate arms and legs. Thus, there were an unprecedented number of veterans who were amputees. The brave charges, those that young men had read and dreamed about in books, now were almost useless against accurate, long-range weapons. The Civil War thus was not quite the romantic test of manhood that most forecasted. Instead, it became more of a nightmare of gore amid the screams of slow-dying soldiers. It was said at Fredericksburg, Union men, still alive, became trapped under the weight of the heaps of their dead comrades unable to escape, until they too eventually drew their last breath. America was lucky to survive.

The Civil War tested a young nation to its limit. At several moments, had luck or decision-making been different, so could have been the outcome. The war tended to identify talent. Lincoln, the seemingly unqualified country lawyer from Illinois, proved the shrewdest of wartime leaders—probably, the greatest in American History. Few would have anointed Grant and Sherman as the great duo to prosecute the war and save the Union. Lee and Jackson, likewise, were an unlikely pair to, almost, win the war in the Eastern Theater. Certainly, the war was about more than famous names. Both Union and Confederate soldiers were equally as brave and committed to winning. Most often, soldiers only knew the fight directly in front of them and did not and could not see the big picture. Everyone suffered. Women lost sons, husbands, nephews, and so on. Some people went insane during the Civil War. People had to wonder if this American road was the one that the founders envisioned. Most must have pondered what was next and if there could be a nation again like the one before the great tragedy of the nineteenth century.

CHAPTER TEN

Reconstruction

Chapter 10: Key Concepts

- How would you evaluate the performance of the Federal government during Reconstruction?

- What do you think is the most positive legacy that can be taken from Reconstruction and what is your reasoning behind this choice?

- What do you think is the most negative legacy that can be taken from Reconstruction and what is your reasoning behind this choice?

Edmund Ruffin is credited with firing the first shot of the Civil War at Fort Sumter. By 1861, he was in his sixties. Ruffin was a well-known planter and political activist in Virginia. He was very accomplished. Ruffin studied the soil and was probably the leading Old South advocate of agricultural reform. Despite his advanced age, Ruffin enthusiastically greeted secession and fought in the Civil War. He despised Lincoln, abolitionists, and northerners in general. The surrender of the Army of Northern Virginia caused Ruffin to become despondent. On June 18, Ruffin took his rifle up to his room. Among his last written words was his commitment to never live under "Yankee rule." Ruffin put the rifle in his mouth, pulled the trigger, and he fell dead.

For most of the white South, Reconstruction was an unthinkable scenario to dread and ultimately seek to end through any means, and for others it was a time of uncertainty and experimentation. From 1865–1877, Americans were not sure what road the nation would take. It is wise to consider how most must have felt in the wake of the Civil War. For one, it seemed possible if not probable that at least a few southerners would not stop fighting until the last man. It was even more likely that another war would erupt at some point in the future. Though this did not happen, it is easy to see why many northerners desired harsh measures toward the South. As for southerners, they would not be happy with any form of Reconstruction. Some became violent, and others resisted Reconstruction in other ways. In the middle were those black southerners who too often were forgotten and then abandoned when Reconstruction was over. For those people who were once slaves, Reconstruction promised much, delivered some, but ultimately failed. Reconstruction was a wish left unfulfilled and a contested idea that, in many ways, was just a continuation of the Civil War.

Civil War Aftermath

On April 4, 1865, Abraham Lincoln entered Richmond after it had been abandoned by the Confederacy. At this point, the southern leadership understood no army could keep it from falling to the Union. He rode in accompanied only by a few aids. This was not the arrival of a conquering Caesar, as Lincoln slowly made his way through the ruins of Richmond. Slaves understood at once who this man was and what it meant for him to be there. It is said that slaves flocked to Lincoln, even bowing in gratitude, while wanting to touch his coat or shake his hand. When he arrived at the house of Jefferson Davis, no one was there. Legend has it that Lincoln even sat in the chair of Davis. He knew that surely the war was all but over.

Lincoln must have breathed a sigh of relief at the news of Lee's surrender on the 9th of April. His nightmare, the dissolution of the Union, had finally ended in what most saw as the end of the Civil War. The victorious president sat in the balcony of Ford's theater on April 14. As he and his wife, Mary Todd, watched *Our American Cousin,* a disgruntled actor named John Wilkes Booth waited for his opportunity. Booth, a Confederate sympathizer, could not abide Lincoln's plan for the nation that included what he perceived as racial equality. Making his way to Lincoln's box seat, the assassin lifted his pistol and fired one

The assassination of President Lincoln by John Wilkes Booth at Ford's Theater, Washington, D. C., April 14, 1865

shot into the back of Lincoln's head. As the first lady cried out, Booth jumped a considerable distance to the stage and shouted, in Latin, "death to tyrants." It looked grim. The doctors did what they could, but in a few hours the president, at the moment of his long-awaited victory, passed away. Northerners collectively cried out in anguish.

When word came of his counterpart's death, Confederate President Jefferson Davis was already on the run. Davis abandoned Richmond after Lee advised he could not protect the capitol. Unlike most of the country, however, Davis did not believe that Lee's defeat meant the war was over. Davis and his entourage made it to the outskirts of Danville, Georgia, before Union troops caught up with them. On the morning of May 9, Davis was awakened by his aide, Burton Harrison. There were riders fast approaching, and Harrison, along with Davis' wife Varina, urged the president to flee. Davis was not at first convinced that the riders were Union men, but upon closer inspection, Davis realized that they were. Intending to make it to a nearby swamp and continue west, Davis quickly slipped on his boots and exited his tent. Fearing for her husband's health, Varina threw a shawl over her husband's shoulders as Union cavalrymen

Jefferson Davis (1808–1889), President of the Southern Confederacy

entered the camp. Davis did not make it far. The Union officer likely did not know who it was at first, but when Davis dropped his shawl and overcoat, the officer recognized him. What happened next is not clear, although it was reported in the North that Davis reached for his gun. Whatever the case, the officer pulled his pistol, aimed it at Davis, and ordered him to stop. Varina pleaded for him not to shoot and for her husband not to resist. Davis would be jailed for two years before released.

The murder of Lincoln and the capture of Davis foreshadowed the difficulties of Reconstruction. It is indeed remarkable that so few Confederates faced reprisal, prison, or worse for the rebellion. If this was a civil war then it was reasonable to assume those who joined the Confederacy were treasonous. Only Henry Wirz, the commandant of a northern prisoner of war camp (Andersonville, Georgia), was executed for his actions during the war. Yet, wounds were clearly not healed. Southern diehards saw their mission to end Reconstruction. For them, the Civil War was never over. Most did not commit suicide like Ruffin, or carry out murder like Booth, but in the coming years they would try to restore their region to something approaching the Old South.

The Stakes of Reconstruction

Certainly, former slaves were hopeful to finally leave the Old South behind. The 13th Amendment ended slavery (at least formally) in America after Union victory in 1865. Without Union armies, and the actions of free and enslaved black people during wartime, the Amendment could not have been passed. Some masters hoped to keep knowledge about emancipation from their slaves. However, word spread to most slaves. Many sought out family members that had long-been sold away from them. An untold number simply packed their belongings and went north—thinking that life up there must be better. Others stayed on their plantations, or nearby, and continued to work for the same white family. After all, so many did not know any other place, where to go, or how to get there. In any case, freedmen now had some ability to negotiate their livelihoods.

From this reality of black agency came some of the primary questions of Reconstruction. Black southerners were no longer slaves, this much was not debatable. However, it was not clear exactly what rights former slaves would have and what role they would play in the future of the nation. It was not just southerners who questioned the ability of freedmen to be good, productive citizens of the country. Plenty of northerners doubted that a group of people, deemed inferior by most, could simply become free and then be anything more than a burden on the rest of Americans. Racist attitudes were more common than not. The issue was what rights freedmen would have after the Civil War. Those who expressed the desire for full black citizenship did not always do so for egalitarian reasons. The fear was that the South would revert back to the kind of paternalist, race-based class system that most northerners believed caused the Civil War. Many Republicans understood that black voting would create a great southern bloc of those who would support their candidates. Some northerners supported full equality, and some did not.

Right after the Civil War, southerners realized the stakes and tried to implement measures that would subvert any attempts to disrupt their racially stratified traditions. The Black Codes are the name given to a wide range of measurements aimed at freed blacks shortly after the Civil War. They varied from state-to-state but were more alike than different. The Black Codes were reactionary from a fear of black mobility. They included laws preventing black southerners from owning weapons and meeting together in large groups. Most states had a version of the notorious vagrancy laws. In sum, southern states desired to be able to arrest freedmen as vagrants if they violated the customs or desires of the local power structure. Basically, vagrancy covered everything. In practice, these laws meant that former slaves could be jailed for not laboring for local white landowners. For a former slave, going into business for one's self was not acceptable. Thus, the Black Codes tried to ensure that black labor would continue to serve the interest of white landowners while trying to deny the ability of freedmen to work for themselves.

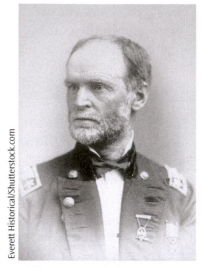

William Tecumseh Sherman (1880–1891)

The denial of former slaves land was high on the list of southern priorities. Part of the reasoning behind the Black Codes was to ensure that former slaves were kept in some state of dependency—relying on the prerogatives of white landowners. Black landownership would be the gateway for ex-slaves to reach an independent status while securing some means of equality, as everyone understood. William Sherman issued Field Order 15 in January 1865. In limited areas around South Carolina, the general set aside lands for former slaves that were divided into 40-acre tracts. They were also to be given work animals that the army no longer needed, like mules. Ever since, the idea of "40 acres and a mule" has represented the unfulfilled possibility of the government distributing land to former slaves. In modern times, the term has been used to promote anti-discrimination measures against black Americans. In any case, wide-ranging land redistribution never took place. Though, many northerners were for the idea of taking land from owners and giving it to their once-property. Without land, it was much easier for white southerners to dictate to former slaves the terms of Reconstruction.

The institution of slavery had already begun to fall apart even before Lee's surrender. The Civil War proved wrong the longstanding southern claim that slaves were happy to be in bondage. Slavery tended to divide the wartime South against itself. For the masses who did not have slaves, there was resentment toward the wealthiest planters. Many planters could buy a replacement to fight in their stead. Also, the potential of arming slaves as soldiers was an issue that had to be at least thought of, if not considered as a possibility. Some in the army, like General Patrick Cleburne, were steadfast proponents of creating slave regiments. Most realized the paradox of black, Confederate soldiers and were solidly opposed to the idea. It is likely that desperation convinced some to think otherwise. The Confederate government, urged to do so by Lee, authorized a slave regiment late in the war that never saw any action. Southerners assumed that blacks were only fit to be slaves and should not become regulars of the army. Confederate politician and General Howell Cobb summarized why this idea would be troublesome for all those who supported slavery. Cobb said "You cannot make soldiers of slaves, or slaves of soldiers. The day you make a soldier of them is the beginning of the end of the Revolution. And if slaves make good soldiers, then our whole theory of slavery is wrong." In other words, anyone fit to become a soldier certainly deserved to and was able to live as a free man.

Andrew Johnson Takes Over

The war taught Lincoln that black men could and would fight as well as any others, as he contemplated how to put the country back together in April, 1865. Perhaps things would have been different if Lincoln had lived, but that is hard to forecast. Lincoln rejected the

Wade-Davis Bill of 1864 that would have required all southerners to take an "Ironclad Oath" that they had never supported the Confederacy in order to vote. The president vetoed it. Lincoln favored a plan that only 10% of southerners make a pledge of future loyalty to the United States. Many in his own party disliked Lincoln's conciliatory stance. For Lincoln, the Civil War was over and it was time to move on with the nation's business. If he had a religion, it would be the country, itself. Maintaining and uniting America was his goal, and he did not wish to punish the South.

The radicals within the Republicans did not share this vision, and they were hopeful that the new president would be more forceful toward the defeated South. Andrew Johnson became the new commander-in-chief after Lincoln's passing. Johnson was the only southern senator from a Confederate state who remained in the U.S. Congress. He renounced secession and remained

Andrew Johnson, 17th President, ca. 1860s

loyal to the Union. Growing up poor in Tennessee, Johnson resented the privileges of the planter class he had seen all his life. It was thought that Johnson would be vengeful toward ex-Confederates, especially those who owned many slaves and had been in positions of leadership. However, Johnson soon began issuing pardons to former Confederates as long as they personally petitioned him. The country began to realize that Johnson would take a very lenient position toward ex-Confederates.

When Congress reconvened in December, the Radical wing of the Republicans had gained more power. Johnson had allowed Confederate states to hold their own elections. When Republicans saw high-ranking former Confederates, including ex-vice president Alexander Stephens, entering the congressional halls it caused an outrage. Furthermore, Johnson clearly was not concerned with the rights of freedmen. He allowed the Black Codes to take effect and seemed to endorse them. In reality, he was more anti-elitism than pro-black rights. The majority of northerners did not like Johnson nor his policies. The Radicals were gaining momentum, and soon, they would go to war with Johnson.

In 1867, Congress passed the Tenure of Office Act. This legislation stated that the president could not remove from office any official that Congress had approved. Johnson vetoed it, but Congress had the votes to override it. To a large degree, the act was aimed at keeping Edwin Stanton as Secretary of

Edwin M. Stanton

War. Stanton was a firm Radical Republican who sharply disagreed with Johnson's methods of Reconstruction. In general, the act was aimed at stripping any power Johnson would have over Reconstruction. Johnson served the rest of his term as unpopular and largely powerless.

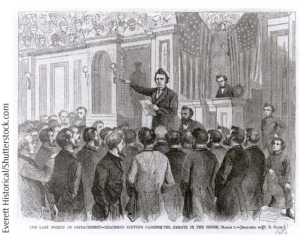

The Last speech on impeachment of President Andrew Johnson. Thaddeus Stevens closing the debate in the House, March 2, 1868

Republicans and Reconstruction

Radicals in Congress began to take over Reconstruction beginning in 1867. In 1868, Johnson was impeached. The vote was not enough to actually remove him from office, however. At that point, as for Reconstruction, it did not matter that much, anyway. Republicans led the way toward passing the 14th Amendment in 1868, but it had been discussed years before this. The Amendment guaranteed due process and equal treatment to all persons under the law. It was adopted as a measure to stop the abuses of freedmen after the Civil War. It also indicated, unlike the Dred Scott decision, that black Americans could be citizens. Southern states protested this and other civil rights legislation.

The Congressional response was to attempt to force former Confederate states into accepting the new reality. In 1867, Radical (also called Military) Reconstruction began in the South. The Military Reconstruction Act of 1867 was quite a departure from either Lincoln or Johnson's vision of the postwar country. The South was divided into five zones with each ruled by a military general. Southern governments were dissolved and new constitutions would have to be created in each state that rebelled. All black males had to be able to vote or a state would lose delegates in the House of Representatives. Those who supported the Confederacy could not vote, though most actually did in time. Congress also required states to ratify the 14th Amendment and generally

The Freedmen's Bureau was established by Congress in March 1865. The 1868 political cartoon depicts General Oliver O. Howard, head of the Bureau, mediating between belligerent groups of whites and blacks

guarantee equal rights for everyone. In sum, Radical Reconstruction put the South under the direct control of northern Republicans.

Even before Radical Reconstruction, the Freedmen's Bureau was one of the more helpful government-created institutions after the Civil War. With Oliver Howard at its head, Lincoln sanctioned and approved of the Bureau in 1865. Johnson tried to end it but without success. The Bureau mostly was an attempt to ease former slaves into a life of freedom while offering a wide range of services. Bureau officials hoped to be able to intervene between black and white labor agreements. They desired to ensure that freedmen would receive fair treatment and not be returned to slave-like conditions. In addition, the Freedman's Bureau sometimes provided food and clothing to former slaves. The most positive long-term effect of the Bureau was in education. It was responsible for creating black schools across the South that remained even after the end of Reconstruction. By 1870, there were over a thousand schools for freedmen in the South. Education was vitally important, as, under slavery, it was illegal to teach slaves to read and write. Certainly, the Bureau was far from perfect. Often, its officials were corrupt and received payoffs from white southerners not to do the intended work. Neither was the Bureau sufficient to prevent many freedmen from intimidation and violence.

The KKK and President Grant

In the early years of Reconstruction, the most notorious violence stemmed from the group called the Ku Klux Klan. The group formed in Pulaski, Tennessee right after the Civil War. The origins and original intent of the Klan is clouded in mystery. It was composed of Confederate veterans and seems to have been, at first, mostly a social group. Soon, the Klan's mission became to end Reconstruction and drive Republicans out of the South. There was little organization. Local groups emerged around the South and acted independently. Typically, the Klan would ride at night to the residence of someone somehow suspected of supporting Reconstruction. They targeted both blacks and whites. The Klan viewed white Republicans as degraded and as on the same level as freedmen—which is to say as inferior to everyone else. They maimed, murdered, and intimidated people all over the South. For the most part, the Klan was unsuccessful in its goals.

President U.S. Grant had much to do with countering the Klan. In 1868, the nation elected the military hero to the presidency. The Republicans urged Grant to run for the highest office until he finally relented. His slogan became "Let Us Have Peace," but he was committed to continuing Reconstruction while trying to rid the South of the kind of violence that was increasingly making northern newspapers. Grant initiated several anti-Klan laws, but the most important was the Force Act of 1870. This legislation forbade anyone from attempting to prevent another from voting through acts of violence or any other means. The Force Act clearly targeted the Klan and any others like them. As a result, most Klansmen were either arrested or deterred from continuing to terrorize their neighbors. By 1871, the Klan was mostly subdued, and it took decades for them to once again become a

President Grant with group of men signing the 15th amendment banning voting racial discrimination. Vignettes show African-Americans in military service, at school, on the farm, and voting. 1871

formidable force. It was also under Grant that Congress passed the 15th Amendment. This statute said that no state could deny citizens the right to vote and made clear that this included former slaves. It seemed that America was deciding that former slaves could and should be full citizens.

Despite the gains in civil rights for some, Grant was not known as an effective president. By nature, he was a soldier and not a politician. Grant never sought out public office and only ran after being urged by others. Grant's downfall was probably choosing his cabinet more on personal relationships than earned merit while remaining blindly loyal to his friends. His legacy has become the many scandals that took place during his tenure more than anything else. In 1869, Jay Gould and John Fisk, with the help of Grant's brother in law, attempted to corner the market on gold. In the end, thousands of people lost money due to the conniving of these two speculators. Exposed in 1875, the Whiskey Ring included an elaborate web of politicians, distillers, and shop owners who stole a few million dollars of federal revenue. Grant's secretary, Orville Babcock, was one of the many implicated for wrongdoing as part of the Ring. With these and other public scandals, Grant was never formally charged. It is likely that he was not part of any but was rather naïve or perhaps neglectful while president.

Successes and Failures

Not all was trending downward during Reconstruction, as black Americans advanced in many ways. Historians estimate that over a thousand black men held some sort of public office in the South during the period. Hiram Revels was elected as a senator, representing Mississippi, in 1870 but did not serve a full term. Also of Mississippi, Blanche Bruce was the first black American elected to the Senate who completed his full tenure in office. There were other success stories. Some former slaves opened thriving businesses. Despite the restraints on them, others were able to procure land and became relatively wealthy. Some of these were those who went west due to the Homestead Act. This act offered free land in the west to those willing to live on and improve it over a period of years. Many blacks were able to receive an education and start families.

Conservative, southern Democrats worked to reverse the gains made during Reconstruction while trying to rid the South of perceived enemies. Southerners called outsiders who were seen as profiting on the South's woes after the Civil War carpetbaggers. They were given this moniker because many of them carried cheap luggage of a similar description. Southerners resented any who seemed to be capitalizing on a postwar South that was reeling from four years of war. These especially included land speculators who seized the opportunity to purchase plantation estates for a low price. Though, in general, anyone who was not welcome and from some other place was at risk of being called a carpetbagger. Unfortunately, for southern diehards, the South was full of them during Reconstruction. Without a leadership class that was native born, so many offices and positions were filled by Republicans who were not from the South.

During Reconstruction, those known as scalawags were southerners who joined the Republican Party. White southerners became Republicans for many different reasons. Some had never supported the Confederacy and even fought for the North during the war. Many southerners sincerely wanted the former Confederacy to modernize and have a multiracial, cooperative society. Southern Republicans fought for more education and better infrastructure for their region. Most commonly, scalawags hoped to compromise for better terms from Republican administrations while looking after their own best interests. It must be understood, choosing to become a Republican, for a white southerner, was much more than a mere political decision. It signaled to all that one was ready to accept Civil War defeat, emancipation, and equality for blacks, while turning away from the Old South both literally and figuratively. Political affiliation had important implications to one's well-being in the South. Conservative Democrats considered a turn toward the Republicans as a betrayal of the South.

James Alcorn was one of the more notable examples of a white southerner who embraced the Republicans. Alcorn was a successful planter and representative before the Civil War. A member of the Whig Party, he opposed secession. Nonetheless, Alcorn served in the Confederate army and became a general. After the war, Alcorn became one of the leading Republicans in the South—serving as both governor and senator. The first land-grant college for blacks, Alcorn State University in Mississippi, was named in honor of him.

Southern Opposition

Southerners opposed to those like Alcorn, who hoped to end Reconstruction, were collectively known as Redeemers. Conservative Democrats, sometimes called Bourbons, worked to "redeem" the South from Republican rule. Most white southerners did not consider their state governments as legitimate as long as they were composed of carpetbaggers and scalawags. The business-oriented Redeemers sought practical solutions to getting their candidates elected while fighting against the Republicans. Certainly, Redeemers were not above corruption and threats. Yet, it was not the aggression of the Klan that turned the contest of Reconstruction in the favor of conservative, white southern Democrats. It took a more pragmatic approach to secure the goals of those who wanted to turn back the clock and recreate something approaching the Old South.

The Red Shirts was a paramilitary organization in the South known to oppose Reconstruction and Republicans. The Red Shirts began in Mississippi. They harassed black voters

African-Americans being discriminated against at the polls by members of the White League. Cartoon, 1874

and discouraged any from casting their ballots for Republican candidates. Red Shirts were most visible in South Carolina during the campaign of Wade Hampton. A former Confederate general, Hampton served as governor and senator of South Carolina as a Democrat. The Red Shirts were known to intimidate voters as they made their decisions on election day. They made themselves very easily identifiable by their red-colored shirts, and everyone knew that this gun-toting group worked on behalf of the Democratic Party. The threat of violence was enough to keep many people from supporting Republican candidates.

Another similar type group, the White League, was most prominent in Louisiana. As its name implied, the purpose of the White League was to suppress gains in black civil rights while fighting against Reconstruction. Unlike the Klan, White League members worked openly without secrecy. In New Orleans in 1874, the League used violence to try to oust the local government. For three days, thousands of people basically held hostage the government of New Orleans. White League members were much more numerous than the police and overwhelmed them in what became known as the Battle of Liberty Palace. They were upset about the Republican government and desired to turn it in favor of the Democrats. Eventually, Grant sent federal troops, and the White League was dispersed. Most members of groups like these were veterans of the Confederate army. For them, the Civil War was not yet over.

The Knights of the White Camellia were also based in Louisiana. An ex-Confederate founded the Knights in Louisiana in 1867. Other groups became affiliated with them throughout the Deep South. Like the Klan, the Knights used violence and threats to terrorize anyone deemed a friend of Reconstruction. Unlike the KKK, members tended to be from the upper class. Though not formally connected with the Klan, they shared their goals of redeeming the South from the hated carpetbaggers and scalawags.

Labor and Race

Apart from trying to end Reconstruction, white southerners also struggled with figuring out how to define the terms of labor in a slave-free society. The Civil War was fought mostly on southern soil, and the region paid a heavy price with millions lost in damaged property. White southerners also were forced to reconsider a kind of existence without slavery—long the bedrock of its society. White landowners were now in the position where black laborers could, to some degree, negotiate the terms of their work. Some freedmen now received wages. However, southerners generally did not have enough money for a wage system to persist. There had to be another way.

After the Civil War, sharecropping became the primary means of agricultural life in the South. Not every sharecropping agreement was the same. However, usually a landowner provided another with housing, tools, and land to cultivate. In exchange, the sharecropper paid with a portion of his crop. Very often, a sharecropper also was indebted to a local merchant. This would include things like food and clothing. Unfortunately, landowners and merchants sometimes conspired together to ensure that a poor sharecropper would remain forever tied to the land. In other words, the debt many times was so great that a poor farmer could never repay what he owed in order to provide for his family. Without much money, everything that a family needed was acquired on credit based on the outcome of the harvest. Sometimes, a crop was poorer than expected. The cycle of poverty, for both black and white sharecroppers, continued long after Reconstruction.

Certainly, black southerners suffered under a system where almost everything was stacked against them. Despite Constitutional guarantees, during Reconstruction a system of oppression slowly regained momentum and politicians could do little to stop the process. Congress could and did pass laws, like the Civil Rights Act of 1875, aimed at protecting black southerners and helping them to achieve something approaching equality. Yet, it seemed that the Redeemers were winning Reconstruction. Most black southerners did not own land and had little or no education. As the years progressed, northerners were growing tired of reports of violence toward freedmen or carpetbaggers. Newspapers tended to confirm the northern fear that southerners were simply recreating the Old South in another form.

The Decline of Reconstruction

During his second term, Grant was growing unpopular among many Americans. This included one of the mainstays of the Party, Charles Sumner, who was beginning to work against the Grant administration. Among the thousands of army veterans, Grant remained the idol of the nation. Yet, his scandals and inability to reconstruct the South left many questioning his leadership. The Panic (depression) of 1873 did not help the progress of Reconstruction. Many carpetbaggers were discouraged by it and returned to the North. It hurt an already reeling southern economy. The Panic damaged hopes that the South could be reformed and made to be as prosperous as the northern states. Grant's political enemies used the Panic to foment opinion against him. Historians usually consider Grant among the worst presidents in American History.

Southern redeemers were also beginning to win the war of public opinion on Reconstruction. The common southern rendition of Reconstruction said that it was a terrible mistake to unloose slaves and give them power. Southern Democrats accused Republicans, black and white, of corruption and mismanagement of governments. To some degree, they were right. Though, Democrats and Republicans both in most every southern state resorted to various unscrupulous methods during Reconstruction, including voting fraud. One might imagine that Americans during the two terms of Grant would start to see politics as fundamentally flawed and unsavory. At every turn, it seemed the current administration was mishandling Reconstruction.

Americans also had more to think about than what was occurring in the South. Railroads were beginning to connect people from distant parts of the country. Cities were growing. The Republican program was much more than a plan to reconstruct the South. Republicans wanted to expand the scope of government, build infrastructure, support business, and leave behind sectional strife. Northerners reckoned that the Civil War was caused by the selfish elitism of the southern planters. Their world of privilege and human bondage seemed like some kind of artifact of Europe better discarded and forgotten. Republicans especially believed in a vision where America would become the most modern, and the most free, civilization in the world. Thus, northerners soon had no more time to consider the South's problems. If it would not conform to the American pattern, then the South itself must be left to its own apart from the rest of the country.

Rutherford B. Hayes (1822–1893),
U.S. President 1877–1881, ca. 1880

The 1876 presidential election pitted Republican Rutherford B. Hayes versus Democrat Samuel Tilden. The election was very close with Tilden winning more of the popular vote. It was so close, in fact, the House of Representatives was forced to decide the next president. The Democrat-controlled House consented to elect the Republican if Hayes agreed to finally end Reconstruction for good. South Carolina, Florida, and Louisiana were the last southern states with federal troops. The election, also called the Compromise of 1877, is considered the end of Reconstruction. By then, Redeemers had mostly spoiled the dream that the South could be remade into something fundamentally different from the days of slavery.

The important issues of Reconstruction became lost in the "bloody shirt" politics of the nineteenth century. As the story went, Massachusetts Congressman Benjamin Butler, in 1871, offered a fiery speech in protest of Klan violence in the South. As people related then and after, Butler held aloft the blood-stained shirt of one of their victims. It does not seemed to have actually occurred, but certainly the Klan and those with the same sympathies were guilty of brutality toward thousands of black southerners and others. Waiving the bloody shirt became a metaphor for politicians who invoked the Civil War, or more generally sectional discord, in order to gain political success. Most often, southerners accused northerners of this practice. It was believed by many that bloody shirt politics was a cheap and divisive way of winning over a crowd or simply getting one's name in the paper. Ultimately, politically-charged squabbling replaced most real attempts at reforming the racial order in the South.

The Lost Cause

Much of what actually occurred during the Civil War and Reconstruction was also lost due to the southern interpretation of the era known as the Lost Cause. There is no identifiable start and end to the not-easy-to-define idea. It probably started right after the war ended with the publication of Virginia newspaperman Edward Pollard's *Lost Cause* in 1866. However, this southern version of the Civil War really was not defined until the 1880s. The Lost Cause was a set of ideas and rituals that proclaimed the greatness of the Old South, defended secession, explained why the Confederacy did not prevail, and either downplayed slavery or made it seem like something beneficial to both owners and enslaved. It so gripped the southern states that it became orthodoxy, appeared as the true History of the Civil War, and was taught to children in schools. The Lost Cause was manifested through the media, books, art, and about every medium one can imagine. It is said that the winners write the History. In the case of the Civil War and Reconstruction, this might not be accurate.

"The Union as it was. The lost cause, worse than slavery." The White League and the Ku Klux Klan united. Cartoon by Thomas Nast, 1874

Historians continue to debate what motivated southerners to create the Lost Cause. It might at first seem as simply a rationale, an excuse, for secession. After all, southerners maintained a unique position in the country for a long time after the end of Reconstruction. They were highly nationalistic and wore their American identity proudly, yet they or their fathers took up arms against the very country who they proclaimed to love. Certainly, part of the Lost Cause was white southerners attempting to justify the whole period to themselves and the world. Historians have also described this phenomenon as an attempt to regain lost pride. After all, the white South had long-boasted as being tougher, more martial and strong, than the North. Much of southern identity wrested on these claims before the war. As it happened, they learned that the North had plenty of resolve and manhood, and they ultimately bested the Confederacy. In this way, the Lost Cause becomes more of a psychological construct to defend what was lost during the era. Actually, the southern retelling of the Civil War may not be that unique in the history of the world. Defeated peoples very often reclaim their sense of identity by rearranging the facts to the fit the desired end goal. One example would be how Germans blamed their loss in World War I on perceived internal enemies, like their Jewish population. Most likely, the Lost Cause was created for many reasons and fulfilled differing sets of objectives.

The Lost Cause posited that the Confederacy was not defeated in the Civil War, but overcome by the overwhelming northern industrial-military machine. This is a subtle but important difference. Postwar southerners maintained that the Confederates, particularly the Army of Northern Virginia, could have never been defeated in an equal contest. It was northern advantages in industry and numbers that did not give the Confederates a fair fight, the story went. Many pointed to immigration to the North as an explanation for defeat. Within the Lost Cause, immigrants became something like mercenaries—not true soldiers and somehow less legitimate than native born combatants. Grant's battles with Lee were a central component with explaining the southern narrative of the war. Southerners explained that Lee was the greatest general who would have beaten Grant if not for the latter's numerical superiority. In the South, Grant was often called a "butcher" who recklessly used his men to batter the brave soldiers of the Army of Northern Virginia. In this way, the Civil War became the last stand of a traditional, agrarian society against a modern, but soulless, military machine.

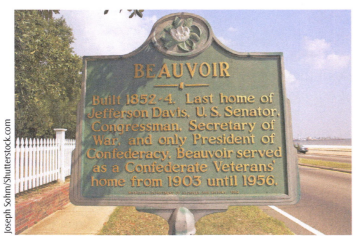

Beauvoir, last home and museum for Jefferson Davis, Biloxi Mississippi

Generally, southerners created a portrait of the Old South as an idyllic, unspoiled paradise. The Confederacy was fighting to protect a quaint, picturesque, pre-modern, courtly society, southerners frequently said. Furthermore, the Lost Cause made this a last stand, a desperate struggle to maintain a way of life unsullied by large cities, industries, greed, bureaucracy, and so on. Every southern man became a knight fit for Camelot and every southern lady was the ideal of womanhood. This is much of what the term Lost Cause meant in the first place. It was a grand cause; it should have and deserved to prevail but was doomed from the start. Here, enslaved people were happy and kind and never were mistreated. Losing the Civil War became more than a military defeat. It was the destruction of one kind of civilization that could never fully return.

Though lost, southerners could still celebrate their military heroes as emblems of virtue. Much like heroes of the American Revolution, Confederate military generals and others became symbolic of the Lost Cause. Among these were Stonewall Jackson, Jefferson Davis, Jeb Stuart, and especially, Robert E. Lee. Though Lee died in 1870, his legend only grew over the years. Part of it was that he left behind an impressive record of victories. Just as important was that Lee seemed to possess every quality that southerners told themselves was who they were as a people. Lee was considered the ideal Old South version of the chivalrous knight, and people jealously defended him from anyone who said otherwise. As a paternalist, his men were more "his boys" than mere soldiers. Symbols are always important. Within the Lost Cause, Lee offered proof why it was a shame that the Confederacy lost and Reconstruction tried to create something new in its place. Only an Old South chivalrous civilization could have produced such a man, southerners believed. Telling stories about Lee and making dedications and monuments to him was a favorite pastime after the Civil War.

Former President Davis was also an important figure within the Lost Cause but for not quite the same reasons. Davis lived longer than most other prominent Confederates, as he died in 1889. He was the favorite single individual for northerners to blame for secession and war. They often criticized him and told stories that he was captured in 1865 while disguised in women's clothes, which was untrue. For his part, Davis was defiant in the occasional public utterance, seemed to never back down from anything, and refused to apply for a pardon from the government. Lost Cause diehards made Davis into a suffering figure who nonetheless remained strong and proud of his Confederate past. His last home on the Mississippi coast, Beauvoir, became one of shrines of the Lost Cause. Four years after his death, his body was buried once again, moving from New Orleans to Hollywood Cemetery in Richmond. Along the way via railroad, thousands of southerners came out to cheer as their once and future king passed by.

Organizations led the way in keeping the memory of Davis and the Lost Cause as a whole, alive. The Southern Historical Association in Virginia was one of the first to retell Civil War stories and provide narratives that provided the core of Lost Cause History. Certainly, they defended Lee's reputation as spotless. The SHA published materials that reflected a very pro-southern point of view. Though, it is doubtful that any Lost Cause group was as influential as the United Daughters of the Confederacy. UDC chapters were all over the South. The UDC lasted longer and was more active than probably any other likeminded southern organization. They published literature and helped raise money and fund projects like statues honoring both Confederate leaders like Lee and the average foot-soldier. The UDC zealously guarded the white South's Confederate traditions.

The white South was so dedicated to the Lost Cause version of the past, that alternative and more inclusive interpretations had trouble finding acceptance. The Lost Cause allowed white southerners to not address slavery except in some superficial or misleading way. They did not have to consider if slavery had been wrong or if it had hurt the long-term economic growth of the South. Reconstruction became a horrible mistake instead of a potential fresh start with some successes. In fact, southerners would use Reconstruction as an example of outside interference that could never be allowed to occur again. Thus, the Civil Rights Movement seemed a second Reconstruction that, for many, had to be resisted. Most importantly, the Lost Cause made it easier for people to allow black southerners to be slowly stripped of most legal and customary rights. Lost Cause History was what southern children were taught for a few generations.

The Lost Cause appealed to many northerners. The romantic view of the Old South had some attraction, as most Americans increasingly lived in a modern world. As people tend to do, Americans enjoyed being transported to a simpler time via the stories of the Lost Cause. There was also a racial component. As immigrants increasingly populated northern states, many with nativist and/or racist views sympathized with the South's past. A harmonious Old South with an established racial order even seemed preferable to the modern, multicultural world, some believed. Joel Chandler Harris' *Uncle Remus* collection of folk tales was widely read across the country. The title character was a kindly old black slave, and the stories were set on or around southern plantations. A native of Georgia, Harris was an adherent of the Lost Cause view that, under slavery, everyone was mostly happy. In this kind of interpretation of the Old South, things moved slowly, people took the time to be kind, and slaves were comical and harmless.

In 1915, the film *The Birth of a Nation* premiered and was popular all over the country. It was based on a book by Thomas Dixon called *The Klansman*. The primary setting of the story was the South during the Civil War and Reconstruction. In *Birth of a Nation,* black characters are depicted as either buffoons, criminals, or both. Reconstruction was shown to be a terrible experiment when black men ran wild without constraint and attacked white women. The Ku Klux Klan were the good guys who helped to restore order. In the film, Reconstruction was a terrible disaster inflicted on white southerners, when the world was turned upside down and an inferior race was given undeserved opportunities. It was the first film screened in the White House, and President Woodrow Wilson endorsed it as an accurate account of Reconstruction. It seemed Americans in the North and South could at least agree on white superiority.

Conclusion

In the end, most of America retreated from Reconstruction and former slaves and their offspring would have to fend for themselves. It must not be construed that Reconstruction was a total failure. This was the idea of the propagandists who later justified Jim Crow based on the fact that black southerners were not capable of being good, fruitful citizens of the United States. Especially during the early twentieth century, the narrative of Reconstruction was that emancipation created a newly freed class of people who were not ready for it. Chaos was the order of the day. Freedmen were serial thieves who preyed on the poor South—and they could not help themselves. The perception was that former slaves helped create nightmarish conditions while everyone, including themselves, suffered as a result. This kind of retelling of Reconstruction was a variant on the Old South conception of paternalism. Here, freedmen were not capable of managing themselves and needed others to direct them. This later buttressed segregation and the notion that it was acceptable for black Americans to occupy a permanent subclass. In reality, black southerners made many strides, voted, and when permitted to do so, cooperated with whites in a society that could have benefitted all who belonged to it.

The story of Reconstruction is about partial success that ended with failure. It was a path almost but not quite taken. Diehard Confederate loyalists certainly were a primary reason why Americans did not yet create a true society where all men were created equal. Mostly, it was not violence but manipulation and corruption that helped redeem southern states. Neither were northerners free from blame. Just a few years earlier, most would not have signed up for a war to make black southerners free. Northern cities were far from free of racial prejudice of every kind. As it happened, Americans from all over looked the other way and let the drama of emancipation, and the struggles of newly-freed people, play out without much interference. For black southerners, their road to American freedom had not yet been completed.

INDEX